949

BLACK SEA

GEORGIA

CAUCASUS MOUNTAINS

Tiflis

Batum

Samsun

Trebizond

ARMENIA

LAKE SEVAN

Merzifon

Yerevan

40°

R K E Y

Erzerum

Mt. ARARAT △

PERSIA

I A

Sivas

Harput

LAKE VAN

Van

Sassoun (Sason)

Bitlis

Diyarbakir

KURDISTAN

Zeytun (Suleymanli)

Marash

CILICIA

Area in dispute

Mosul

Alexandretta (Iskenderun)

Aleppo

MESOPOTAMIA (British Mandate)

35°

SYRIA

(French Mandate)

SMYRNA PROVINCE

Beirut

Bagdad

Damascus

Ayvalik

Mitilini

Pergamum (Bergama)

Thyatira (Akhisar)

PALESTINE (British Mandate)

Jaffa

Jerusalem

Phocia (Foka)

Magnesia (Manisa)

Menemen

Kasaba (Turgutlu)

Smyrna (Izmir)

Nif

TRANS-JORDAN

(British Mandate)

Chesme

Alachati

Urla

0 10 20 30 mls

Aydin

35°

40°

30° N

The Smyrna Affair

The Smyrna Affair

Marjorie Housepian

HARCOURT BRACE JOVANOVICH, INC.

NEW YORK

The lines from Henry Miller, *The Colossus of Maroussi*, copyright 1941 by Henry Miller, are reprinted by permission of New Directions Publishing Corporation. The excerpts from *Certain Samaritans*, by Dr. Esther P. Lovejoy, copyright by American Women's Hospitals Service, are reprinted with the permission of American Women's Hospitals Service. The quotations from *The Blight of Asia*, by George Horton, copyright 1926 by The Bobbs-Merrill Company, Inc., renewed 1953, are reprinted by permission of the publisher. The quotations from Ernest Hemingway's *In Our Time* are used with the permission of Charles Scribner's Sons. The excerpts from Hemingway's *The Wild Years*, edited by Gene Z. Hanrahan, copyright Ernest Hemingway 1950, are quoted with the permission of Alfred Rice.

DS51
.I9 H68

To the victims

72-28877

To mention the name of Sherman to a Southerner of the
United States is to fill him with burning indignation.
Even the most ignorant yokel knows that the name Attilla
is associated with untold horrors and vandalism.
But the Smyrna affair . . . has been somehow soft-pedalled
and almost expunged from the memory of present day man.

HENRY MILLER
The Colossus of Maroussi

FOREWORD

The burning of cities is nothing new. Rome, London, and Chicago provide examples of cities reborn from cinders, while the legends of these conflagrations have themselves achieved a measure of immortality. But the fire of Smyrna, Turkey, was of a different nature and bore a different result. Smyrna died in 1922. Its character was obliterated, its name erased from the maps of the world—although, commerce dying harder, it survives in the name of a fig. In its place grew Izmir, an undistinguished, some would say second-rate, place, drawing whatever charm it has from the rubble of a distant past with which it now tries to lure the tourist trade. Privately, Izmir deplores its past and its legends do not include the fire. No one in Izmir wants to talk about that. Indeed few travelers ask, for few have heard of it.

Izmir emerged from Smyrna's ashes to the accompaniment of official applause by the great World Powers, who had a short time before witnessed the city's destruction in deafening official silence.

They welcomed Turkey into the consortium of civilized nations—as they have more recently welcomed Nigeria—congratulated its leaders for so expeditiously resolving the problem of the nation's minorities, and hailed it as a peaceful, independent state.

But fundamentally little has changed in fifty years. Elsewhere in what once comprised the vast Ottoman Empire hostilities simmer and explode. The Western Powers still hover over the scene, now shifted to the south, struggling to maintain their profits and their pre-eminence, and to preserve world peace—in that order. There and elsewhere at this writing, the slaughter of innocents goes on.

So today it is perhaps all the more essential for men of good sense to review historical cause and effect; to ponder the resolution of a minority problem in Turkey half a century ago; to contemplate the forces that distort the past and pervert the future; to recognize the forces within ourselves that will save or consume us all.

ACKNOWLEDGMENTS

My immeasurable gratitude goes to those eyewitnesses who, either as survivors or as retired members of the United States Navy, offered me their memories, however painful, and their letters, diaries, and news clippings, when these were available. Without their help this account would obviously have been impossible. I should record here, as well, my debts to those entrusted with the Naval Records Collection and the Files of the Department of State at the National Archives, and to the staff of the Historical Reference Library of the YMCA. The exigencies of space prevent my mentioning by name all those to whom I am indebted for suggestions, assistance, and encouragement. I cannot pass, however, without a special word of thanks to Miss Nancy Horton for her warm hospitality and for so generously making her father's papers available to me, to Professor Thomas Bryson of West Georgia College, Professor Ruth Kivette of Barnard College, and Dr. A. O. Sarkissian of the Library of Congress, for their diligent assistance above and beyond the call of friendship.

MARJORIE HOUSEPIAN

The Smyrna Affair

CHAPTER I

I know of no other country where the minorities were so safe and prosperous during the centuries before they had so-called equal rights.

Memoirs of Halide Edib

Some say that the Amazons founded Smyrna, endowing her with her astonishing capacity for survival. Others favor the legend that her founder was Tantalus, the mythical king from whose fearful tortures in the underworld evolved our milder "tantalize." Smyrna was the cradle of Greek legends, the ancestral home of demigods and the mortal kings of Mycenae and Lydia. She was thought to be Homer's birthplace, providing the inspiration for his *Odyssey*. Here the muses were known to deal kindly with poets: Quintus, a mere shepherd, had found that they would come to him so long as he tended his flocks near the Temple of Diana. There they dictated to him a poem of fourteen stanzas, describing the Trojan wars.

The city suffered under the Lydians and Ionians and was already in ruins when Alexander the Great arrived on the scene. Exhausted from hunting, the story goes, he stopped for the night on Mount Pagus, and while he slept under a plane tree near the temple to

3

Nemesis, that brooding goddess appeared in his dream and urged him to rebuild the city. This the Emperor did, after consulting an oracle who assured him of Apollo's blessing and predicted great prosperity for the new Smyrna.

The Smyrneans learned to accommodate themselves to their more benevolent Roman rulers. According to Tacitus, the citizens of Smyrna boasted that they were the first in all Asia to raise a temple to Rome in the days while Carthage stood and while there were still "powerful kings in Asia who as yet knew nothing of Roman valor."* For their part, the Romans perceived the value of Smyrna's unsurpassable harbor and they treated the Smyrneans kindly, "so as to preserve to themselves the finest port in Asia."

Strabo, writing in the Augustan age, described Smyrna as "the finest city in Asia. One part is built upon the mountain," he wrote, "but the greatest part stands on the plain upon the port, over against the Temple and the gymnasium of Cybele. The streets are the most beautiful that can be, running at right angles and paved with fine stones. There are large and fine porticos, and a public library, and a square portico where stands the statue of Homer, for the inhabitants of Smyrna are very fond of having Homer to have been born here and they have stamped a copper medallion which they call Homerion. The river Meles runs along the city walls. Among other conveniences there is a port which may be shut up at pleasure."

In a day when "Emperors were more feared, and consequently more honored than goddesses," Tiberius was so partial to the city that of all the great places of Asia that clamored to dedicate a temple to him, the Emperor gave his blessing to Smyrna. The goddesses may have felt slighted, for in Tiberius's day an earthquake destroyed the city. But Marcus Aurelius built it again, and soon Smyrna, with her school of philosophy, her library, and her orators, rivaled ancient Ephesus. She was known as the Crown of Ionia, the First City of the East, the Ornament of Asia.

Saint Paul brought Christianity early to Smyrna, whose stadium soon provided the spectacle of believers being torn apart by wild beasts. Saint John the Divine proclaimed the city one of the Seven of the Revelation, bestowing on her the Lord's command: "Be thou faithful unto Death and I will give thee a crown of Life." And there Polycarp, one of the first Christian bishops, followed the

---

* Bibliography and Notes are on pages 228–263.

Lord's counsel and was spectacularly ignited in the stadium, thus providing Smyrna's contribution to Byzantine saintdom.

It was under Byzantine rule that Smyrna first established her character as a commercial gateway, when those hardy Norsemen, the Varangians, prevailed on the Byzantine emperors to grant them the right to trade and to govern themselves within the eastern territories. In the eleventh and twelfth centuries the emperors gave similar concessions to the great seamen of the day: the Venetians, Amalfians, Genoese, and Pisans. For a few centuries Smyrna turned her face West, only to be struck by invading hordes from the East.

The Seljuk Turks destroyed the city in 1084, the Persians in 1130. In 1402 Tamerlaine butchered the inhabitants and razed the buildings in an orgy of cruelty that would become legendary. While the inhabitants slept, his men stealthily undermined the city's walls and propped them up with timber smeared with pitch. Then he applied the torch, the walls sank into ditches prepared to receive them, and the city lay open to the invader. Smyrna's would-be defenders, the Knights of Saint John, escaped to their ships by fighting their way through a mob of panic-stricken inhabitants. They escaped just in time, for Tamerlaine ordered a thousand prisoners beheaded and used their skulls to raise a monument in his honor. He did not linger over his victory—it was his custom to ravage and ride on. He rode on to Ephesus, where the city's children were sent out to greet and appease him with song. "What is this noise?" he roared, and ordered his horsemen to trample the children to death. Twenty-two years later Smyrna passed into the Ottoman Empire.

By then the will of Allah had conquered a formidable territory. It had been amassing converts since the seventh century, barely a generation after the Prophet Mohammed dictated his often contradictory, occasionally capricious,* and wholly immutable doctrines. The Arabs, the most intelligent and imaginative of the desert nomads, first grasped the torch and passed it from clan to clan, until pagan tribes from Persia to India and even westward along the North African coast had been inflamed by Mohammed's more aggressive precepts. "When ye encounter infidels strike off

---

* As an example of caprice, it was Mohammed's suspicions about his fourteen-year-old wife A'isha that brought about the seclusion of Moslem women for over a millennium.

their heads until ye have made a great slaughter among them and bind them with bonds," said the Prophet. "For whosoever fighteth for the religion of Allah, whether he be slain or victorious we shall surely give him a great reward."

The Ottomans took their name from their first great leader, Othman. They had been a small clan, essentially mercenaries who hired themselves out to larger tribes, such as the Seljuks, or to one or another of the Christian rivals during the years when rivalries were shredding Byzantium. Othman had been acting as fief of the Seljuk state when he declared himself an independent sovereign in 1295 and began acquiring territory on his own, absorbing numerous Byzantine Christians in the process. Abandoned by their leaders, many of these Greeks and Slavs readily converted to Islam. They joined the ruling class of the growing Ottoman state, whose members called themselves *Osmanlis* and came to use the word *Turk* as a term of derision toward the lowly. Successive sultans took over country after country until the Empire encroached on the very heart of Western Europe.

During these years numbers of Byzantine Greeks fled westward from Anatolia to avoid forcible conversion and because the trade routes eastward were blocked off. But as Ottoman rulers continued to expand their territories, virtually all Greeks became subjects of the Empire.

Like the Greeks, the Armenian minority had been established in the Empire at least fifteen hundred years before the Islamic invasions. Mount Ararat was the symbol of their homeland, for according to legend their nation had been founded after the flood by one of Noah's sons. Their unique language, although unrelated to any other European group, was derived from the Indo-European root (it is considered the closest survivor of that extinct form), leading scholars to deduce that they had migrated eastward from Europe approximately six centuries before Christ, absorbed the indigenous Urartu, and settled in the region from Lake Van northeastward into the Caucasus. They were a mountain people and shunned the seacoasts, a fact that contributed to their undoing in one of the most persistently besieged areas on earth. A relatively small, peaceable group, they accommodated themselves to subjugation with one notable reservation: after their king, Tirdat, proclaimed Armenia the first Christian nation in A.D. 301, they clung tenaciously to Christianity. Their kings had become vassals to the Persian and Roman rulers, but when the Persians attempted

6

forcibly to convert them to the Zoroastrian faith in A.D. 451, the vastly outnumbered Armenians battled so fiercely that the Persian king acknowledged that they might worship as they pleased. Thereafter, the Armenian church remained independent of both the Roman Catholic and the Greek Orthodox churches, and it preserved the national identity when the land was successively stormed by Saracens, Seljuks, Mongols, Tartars, and, lastly, the Ottoman Turks.

During these invasions many Armenians fled south to Cilicia, where they enjoyed a few hundred years of autonomy in a small kingdom known as Lesser Armenia. There they welcomed and supported the Crusaders, but when the last of these returned West, the kingdom was swiftly conquered by the Mamelukes of Egypt, who had heretofore left the Armenians alone.

Sephardic Jews constituted a third sizable minority group in the Empire, having arrived there after their exodus from Spain during the Inquisition. The Moslems made them welcome and allowed them cultural and religious autonomy at a time when many Christian nations were notoriously inhospitable. They had settled in the larger towns and cities, where they dealt in trade and continued to speak their fourteenth-century Spanish dialect interspersed with some Hebrew and Turkish words.

Traditionally the Ottoman Christians and Jews had been the farmers, merchants, and professional men of Turkey, while the Moslems had constituted the warrior, civil service, and governing classes. Under this arrangement non-Moslems were left alone to work, worship, and govern themselves as they pleased, so long as they paid the taxes demanded of them and submitted to Islamic law in their relationship with Moslems. The system worked well enough while fresh territory lay ready to be conquered or while there existed a measure of enlightenment among the Moslem rulers. Unhappily, for all practical purposes the Ottoman Empire ran out of both by the middle of the sixteenth century.

Before then the great Ottoman leaders had wisely recognized that it was in their interest to preserve the Christian communities, since the commerce of the vast regions they controlled depended on the natives. Thus Mohammed, the conqueror of Constantinople —after culminating three days and nights of orgy with a banquet where the heads of the fallen Byzantine commander and his family were displayed as centerpieces on his table; after riding his horse to the altar of Saint Sophia and proclaiming the edifice a

7

mosque; after exterminating the Frankish lords and Greek notables and handing their lands to his own veterans to be held as reward for life (ultimately all territory belonged to the Sultan)—pacified the Christian populace and prevented their mass migration by declaring himself protector of the Greek church and conferring on the Greek and Armenian patriarchs full autonomy in the internal affairs of their communities.

But the conduct of the minorities toward Moslems, and vice versa, was traditionally circumscribed by "contract" between the Moslem ruler and the "people of the book," as Christians and Jews were known. These tolerated infidels were referred to as *rayahs,* "sheep," or, more often, as *giaours,* "infidel dogs," and the regulations controlling their behavior were calculated to demonstrate their inferiority. Until the mid-nineteenth century, when some of the outward marks of their status were removed, they could not ride horses or use saddles. Their houses could not be tall, airy, or decorated, or located on higher ground than those of Moslems. Their clothes had to be of a plain, dark material, "so that they may not be confused with true believers." *Giaours* could build no new churches. They had to pay special taxes. If some of these rules were relaxed in the European portions of the Empire, there Christian Serbs, Bosnians, Hungarians, and Bulgars had for centuries to pay a form of blood tribute by giving up their ablest sons to the service of the Sultan. Every few years, men "more skilled in judging boys than trained horse-dealers are in judging colts" selected the strongest and most intelligent boys between the ages of ten and twelve and took them away to Constantinople, where they were converted to Islam and subjected to the discipline of the Janizary Corps, the Sultan's personal army. They would become the elite of the Empire, but they were lost to their families and would be taught to "beat down the Cross and elevate the Crescent." If payment of a military tax relieved other infidels from military service, an injunction against possessing arms forbade them the means of self-defense against a Moslem. If they could worship freely as a condition of maintaining their segregated status, they held no rights under Moslem law, for their testimony was not acceptable in a Moslem court. In short, their condition was totally dependent on the pleasure of their conquerors and it was tolerable only so long as there was a modicum of statesmanship and control within the Ottoman administration.

Suleiman the Magnificent (1520–66) was the last in a line of able Ottoman administrators and legislators. During his reign the Moslem element was well employed, since the Empire was almost continuously under arms. He was a liberal patron of the arts and sciences, and he reformed the land laws by offering tenure to the *rayahs*. But Suleiman also set the stage for the subsequent degeneration of the Empire. He stopped attending meetings of the Divan (the Council of State), preferring to keep an eye on the proceedings through a window he had built into the wall of an adjoining chamber. His successors left the Council to itself. It was Suleiman who initiated the custom of appointing inexperienced men to high office when he promoted to the post of Grand Vizier his favorite slave, Ibrahim. Ibrahim happened to be an able man, but later sultans were less discriminating and their appointments were often dictated by whim, or by conspiracies hatched among the population of viziers, would-be viziers, eunuchs, slaves, wives, concubines, and hangers-on that constituted the Seraglio. The harem bubbled with intrigue as its inhabitants schemed to dispose of one another's protégés and offspring in order to enhance the candidacy of their own.

The great and able Suleiman had shortsightedly ordered the murder of his more promising sons and so was succeeded by the surviving halfwit, who came aptly to be called "Selim the sot." From Selim's day it became a common practice to immure the principal heir to the Ottoman throne in a sumptuous prison on the palace grounds known as the "cage," whence—if he survived the plots of the harem and the life of extravagant debauchery to which he was restricted—he emerged to rule over his far-flung territories without the faintest knowledge of any world beyond his cushioned enclosure.

Meanwhile corruption seeped down through the administrative ranks as viziers sold civil and military appointments to the highest bidders and each officer recovered his outlay by demanding still more exorbitant sums from his own appointees. From provincial governors and judges down to the communal tax collectors, this system unleashed a chain of bribery that inevitably extorted its way down to the most productive but most helpless element of the population.

Turks, that is those Moslems who remained outside the ruling class, were also victimized by this system, but as the chief working force of the Empire, the *rayahs* had always paid the lion's share of the taxes. Now these were levied at whim by the ruling

9

vali (governor-general) of the Province, by the *mustasarif* (governor) of the Department, the *kaimakam* (subprefect) of the District, and the *mudir* (mayor) of the Commune. The more remote the province the more flagrant the abuses; but as tax collectors became bolder (having discovered that few in power cared in the slightest), illegal taxes proliferated in the larger centers as well, and if the collector came around more than once and insisted that the tax had not been paid, a *rayah* had no choice but to pay it again. The *rayahs* did more, however. They provided a handy scapegoat for the depressed and disgruntled Moslem populations, whose masses constituted an unemployed army—a potentially dangerous force indeed.

The time had come when the sultans no longer needed prodigious conquering legions, and so the tribesmen had returned to their nomadic life or were squatting on the outskirts of towns and villages, generally unprepared for any form of labor except fighting and plunder. Their lives were circumscribed by centuries of indoctrination whereby the order of the universe was seen to consist in an orgiastic cycle of violence, reward, and the profound afterglow of joyful contemplation, or *kef*—a condition that has traditionally enchanted Westerners. *Kef* is more gratifying as a response to spent energy than as a state of prolonged indolence, however, and having neither outlet nor hope of reward, the simple Turk, Kurd, Circassian, or Tartar became irritable and menacing. The ruling class made no provision for enhancing his productivity but encouraged him to turn on his Christian neighbors, who in most cases appeared to be enjoying a higher living standard.

Beginning in the fifteenth century, Ottoman policy drove the most unmanageable elements, such as the Kurds, into the six Armenian provinces in the isolated northeast. Thereafter, the Armenians were not only subjected to the iniquitous tax-farming system (applicable to the Moslem peasants as well), the head tax, and the dubious privilege of the military exemption tax, but also to impositions that gave the semibarbarous tribes license to abuse them. The hospitality tax, which entitled government officials "and all who passed as such" to free lodging and food for three days a year in an Armenian home, was benign compared to the dreaded *kishlak,* or winter-quartering tax, whereby—in return for a fee pocketed by the *vali*—a Kurd was given the right to quarter himself and his cattle in Armenian homes during the long winter months, which often extended to half the year. The fact that

Armenian dwellings were none too spacious and the Kurdish way of life exceptionally crude proved the least of the burden. Knowing that the unarmed Armenians had neither physical nor legal redress, a Kurd, armed to the teeth, could not only make free with his host's possessions but if the fancy struck him could rape and kidnap his women and girls as well.

Family sanctity was highly prized among Armenians and its violation was thus all the more hideous. Parents made frantic, often futile, attempts to protect their daughters. Until they reached puberty girls were dressed as boys, although chances of deception were slim in a limited area over a long period. Understandably, those families were considered the most fortunate who had the most unappetizing daughters, or better still, none at all.

In the last analysis their lives were in the hands of the ruling *vali*, who could, if he chose, exert a degree of control over the Kurdish chieftains. Thus in one province, under a relatively kind-hearted *vali*, the Armenians might have a period of respite, while in another their fate could be exceptionally cruel—as in districts such as Afyon Karahissar, where because a ruling official had at one time decreed that an Armenian could speak his native language only at the risk of having his tongue torn out, entire generations of Armenians learned to speak only Turkish.

The gradual dispersion of Armenians to other parts of the Empire was an inevitable result of such harassment, although Ottoman authorities discouraged a mass exodus by forbidding emigrants from taking their families with them. As more and more young men left the region to go abroad or to settle in larger commercial centers, and as the rulers moved more tribesmen into vacated land, the condition of those left behind became increasingly precarious.

In coastal cities the presence of foreigners offered a measure of safety to the lives and limbs of the *rayahs*, the majority of whom worked for European firms or supplied these firms with materials for export, while contributing to the demand for European goods. Foreign residents, on the other hand, were protected by a set of agreements known as the Capitulations, which dated back to Byzantine days and offered what amounted to diplomatic immunity to them and their descendants in perpetuity.

Those who were immune from the system, while profiting under it, were delighted with the status quo. A perspicacious English visitor, the painter Francis Hervé, had noted early in the nine-

11

teenth century, "On the whole I know of no part of the world where a man can settle with such advantage as he is not subject to the laws of the country nor to the imposts. Thus he may make a fortune; whilst the native subject can never be allowed to accumulate anything under the system of licensed pillage and extortion which at present is enforced by the different authorities to whom power is delegated by the Turkish government." In Hervé's untutored opinion, the Turkish government was "one which every philanthropist must wish to see dissolved."

There were few philanthropists among the prosperous foreigners in Smyrna and Constantinople, most of whom had been born and raised there. So long as the system remained deficient and discriminatory, the Capitulations were amply justified. As far as the European element was concerned, such a state of affairs could hardly be improved. As Hervé reported from Smyrna in 1840, "It appears a favorite system with many of the European inhabitants, indeed I may say with the best informed, to eulogize the institutions, the legislature, and the government of the Porte."

Smyrna's Greek population had returned to that region during the seventeenth and eighteenth centuries, when the trade routes eastward from Europe were reopened. They had become cultivators of the fine vineyards and highly prized tobacco of the Smyrna region, and had taken leading positions in the city's trade with the West. Since they had brought their language and culture with them more or less intact, Smyrna and its environs acquired a predominantly Greek character. At the end of the eighteenth century, numbers of enterprising Greek merchants left Smyrna and other flourishing Ottoman ports to establish commercial houses in nearly all the great trading centers of the West. Over the next decades they absorbed the liberating concepts of the French Revolution, then circulating through Europe, and dispersed these among their compatriots under Ottoman rule. Literary and political unions sprang up throughout the Ionian peninsula and the Peloponnese and became centers of revolt. After 1830, when a relatively small portion of Greeks gained their independence from the Ottoman Empire with the vital help of Russia, England, and France (each country joining in lest the other pre-empt the major influence) and made clear their intention of liberating more of their fellow Greeks, Moslem rulers began to look on the remaining Christians in the Empire as potential traitors and on European influence as perfidious. The vast majority of Greeks remained under Turkish rule, most of them along the Black Sea Coast and in the Mediterranean and Aegean regions which constituted the more prosperous centers of the Greek world. Of these, Smyrna was second only to Constantinople.

As was the case with the Ottoman Greeks, over the centuries numbers of Armenians moved abroad, prospered in trade, and kept in touch with their Eastern kinsmen. But it was the American missionary invasion of Turkey during the second half of the nineteenth century that "Westernized" the masses of Ottoman Armenians and aroused the wrath of the Moslem authorities. Eager to enjoy the educational benefits that the missionaries were offering, Armenians were not averse to "converting" from their established church to the more evangelical brands of Christianity. And so the missionaries—who had arrived in the Near East to convert Moslems only to discover that the penalty for such conversion was death, as sanctioned by Koranic law—decided to remain in Turkey, justifying their expenditure of funds and energy among Christians with the long view that "if it were possible to . . . instill them [the Armenians] with a lively missionary spirit, they would be the best and most effectual missionaries because native to the soil."

Oblivious of these motives, the Armenians welcomed the missionary influence. It extended far beyond the relatively small percentage of Armenians who actually converted to Protestantism, for it stimulated reforms within the Armenian church schools, promoted literacy among women as well as men, and exposed whole communities to Western literature and Western ideas. It brought enlightenment to remote, formerly primitive villages, and in so doing it fatally increased the resentment of local Moslem tribesmen and peasants by widening the gap between them and the Armenians.

Western ideas had meanwhile begun to penetrate a fragment of Turkish society as a growing number of prosperous officials sent their sons abroad to be educated. A Turkish intellectual movement was developing, including among its members some who recognized the urgency of internal reforms if the Empire was to remain intact. The Ottoman State had been considerably weakened by the defection of the Greeks after their successful revolution, and indeed had sunk so low that foreign ambassadors—known as *Elchis* —were in virtual control, the ambassadors of Great Britain, France, and Russia vying with one another to exert their wills over the dissolute sultans. They had no intention of encouraging reformers from within.

Convinced that the dissolution of the Empire was imminent,

13

Czar Nicholas approached the English in 1853 with the idea of bartering the Egyptian portion of the Empire in return for Russian domination over the Dardanelles. The Czar was partial to metaphor: "We have on our hands a sick man, a very sick man," he told Sir Hamilton Seymour, the British Ambassador to St. Petersburg. "It will, I tell you frankly, be a great misfortune if one of these days he should slip away from us before all necessary arrangements are made." He pressed his point in still another conversation. "If your government has been led to believe that Turkey retains any elements of existence your government must have received incorrect information. I repeat to you the sick man is dying and we can never allow such an event to take us by surprise. We must come to some understanding."

Sir Seymour replied by piously disclaiming any British designs on Egypt. Britain was at that moment virtually in control of the Ottoman Empire and had no incentive to share her with Russia. Her Ambassador to Constantinople, Sir Stratford Canning, known as the "Great Elchi," had an incomparable talent for bullying the Sultan with the utmost geniality. He took on a good deal of responsibility for setting his country's Near East policy. He and his government agreed that the cornerstone of that policy must be to oppose Russia.

Having been rebuffed in his attempts to parcel out the Ottoman territories between Russia and England, Czar Nicholas now pointed to the persistent mistreatment of the Christians and demanded that he be allowed to act as protector of the Greek Church throughout the Turkish dominions. Neither Sir Stratford nor England's foreign minister, Lord Clarendon, had any illusions about the plight of the Ottoman Christians. "The Christian subjects in Turkey," wrote Clarendon, "are made to experience in all their daily transactions the inferiority of their position as compared with that of their Musselman fellow subjects . . . seek in vain for justice for wrongs done, either to their persons or properties, because they are deemed a degraded race, unworthy to be put into comparison with the followers of Mohammed." The dilemma lay in the question of who was to introduce and enforce measures for their protection. Determined that it should not be Russia, Sir Stratford advised the Sultan to refuse the Czar's demands. His advice resulted in the Crimean War ("The only perfectly useless modern war that has been waged," as Sir Robert Morier characterized it), in which England theoretically came to Turkey's defense against Russia. Actually the

British assumed the brunt of the fighting, and their losses were heavy.

Having been defeated in a war she had ostensibly fought to protect the Ottoman Christians, Russia was determined to deny that privilege to England once peace was achieved. With a major assist from France, the right to protect these unfortunates was therefore entrusted to the very government that was responsible for their abuse. An impressive Edict—the *Hatt-i Humayoun*—supposedly "emanating spontaneously" from the Sultan's "sovereign will" and alleging the Sultan's solicitude for his Christian subjects, was inserted in the peace treaty, which explicitly forbade the major powers "either collectively or individually" from interfering in the relations between the Sultan and his subjects. An exceptionally bloody war had been waged, in effect, to give the Sultan license to mistreat his subjects.

Ironically, those responsible for the Crimean War were the most anguished by the consequences of the peace. "The Porte will never of its own accord carry the provisions of the Edict seriously into effect," Sir Stratford protested in a letter to Lord Clarendon. "The Treaty would therefore confirm the right and extinguish the hope of Christians." Lord Clarendon wrung his hands: "If you could have seen all that was passing when I got to Paris," he moaned. "The bitterness of feeling against us, the kindly (I might almost say enthusiastic) feeling toward Russia. . . . Peace had become a military as well as a financial and political necessity [for the French emperor]."

History repeated itself after the Crimean War, with few the wiser. Driven to the wall, a group of Ottoman Christians would revolt; barbaric countermeasures, another war, another pusillanimous treaty—and the Turks would treat their minorities with even greater ferocity.

The Serbs and Slavs rebelled in 1875, the Bulgarians a year later. The Bulgarian revolt in particular was countered with such an orgy of cruelty (in this instance the Turks unleashed the Tartars) that detailed accounts sent out by British journalists on the scene sent shudders through Victorian England. They left British officialdom unmoved. Disraeli was Prime Minister and so obsessed about Russia that he was avidly pro-Turkish. He scoffed at the Bulgarian horrors, calling them "coffeehouse babble." Whatever he accomplished for the glory of the British Empire, Disraeli's intransigent cold war policy in the Near East spelled disaster for a good many Ottoman Christians. He refused to support "The Berlin Memorandum," a proposal set forward by Russia, Germany, and Austria to insure reforms. He refused to help a small group of Turkish reformers, led by the liberal Vizier Midhat Pasha, who sought England's assistance and encouragement (Midhat's days were subsequently numbered); and he sabotaged the peace after Russia once again went to war with Turkey and this time won. British public opinion kept Disraeli on the sidelines during the Russo-Turkish war of 1877–79, but he sent Indian troops to halt the Russians when they reached the gates of Constantinople. He then insisted that the peace treaty which the Russians and Turks had signed at San Stefano be submitted to the Great Powers for review in Berlin.

The Treaty of San Stefano had liberated most of European Turkey from Ottoman rule. Thanks to Disraeli, the superseding Treaty of Berlin restored thirty thousand square miles of territory and two and a half million Europeans "to the blessings of Ottoman administration." In the northeast, where the bulk of the Armenians lived, the Russians had captured five provinces and promised to return one of these as soon as certain reforms were put into effect; until then Russian forces were to occupy the territories and protect the Christians. Disraeli succeeded in nullifying this provision. By an ironic reversal, Article 16 of the San Stefano treaty was superseded by Article 61 of the Treaty of Berlin, which saw to it that two Armenian provinces were returned to Turkey, with neither Russian forces nor an organization of European militia remaining to protect the subject population. Instead, Disraeli proposed to establish British consulates throughout the area as a means of restraining the Turks.

The result was predictable. Under the consuls' noses the Turks intensified their abuse, all the more as the British government made it clear that it would do nothing beyond protest. "Great Britain will spare no diplomatic exertion," Lord Salisbury declared bravely. Unheeded diplomatic exertion became increasingly embarrassing, however, and after two years most of the consuls were withdrawn.

In return for her favors Britain received from Turkey the island of Cyprus, whence she might leap to that nation's defense if Russia should threaten to attack. The disclosure of the secret deal was made at the Congress of Berlin, "to the amazement of the members."

Sultan Abdul Hamid II was on the Ottoman throne at this time. He had come to power masquerading as a liberal, but after his reform-minded Vizier, Midhat, failed to enlist British support for his proposed reform constitution, and after the Powers demonstrated at Berlin that they were sublimely indifferent to the fate of their fellow Christians, Hamid laid aside all pretense of liberalism and proclaimed himself absolute monarch. He had Midhat convicted of treason at a rigged trial, ordered him strangled in prison, and had his head delivered to the palace in a box.

After the Treaty of Berlin, Hamid defiantly gerrymandered the boundaries in the northern provinces, usurped Armenian lands, moved in more Kurds, and increased the proportion of Moslems. When the Armenians were driven to protest to Britain that the Porte was breaking the terms of the treaty, Hamid denounced them as traitors conspiring with foreigners to destroy the Empire.

Yet it was not until 1887 that a number of Armenian leaders, despairing of every other means, organized the first of two Armenian revolutionary parties—the second was organized in 1890. The Church discouraged revolutionary activity, fearing that it would lead to nothing more than intensified bloodshed, and the people were on the whole inclined to agree with their religious leaders. Small bands of Armenian revolutionaries nonetheless staged a number of demonstrations during the 1890's and gave Hamid exactly the pretext he sought. Declaring that "the only way to get rid of the Armenian question is to get rid of the Armenians," he proceeded to the task with every means at hand. He sent masses of unhappy Circassians, who had themselves lately been driven from Europe, into Eastern Anatolia—where the Armenian population had already been reduced by massacre and migration—and encouraged them, along with the Kurds, to attack village after village. He roused the tribesmen to the kill by having his agents spread rumors that the Armenians were about to attack them, then cited every instance of self-defense as proof of rebellion and as an excuse for further massacre. He sent his special *Hamidieh* regiments to put down "revolts" in such districts as Sassoun, where the Armenians were protesting that they were unable to pay their taxes to the government because the Kurds had left them nothing with which to pay.

"The slaughter of the Armenians was a joy to the Turks," a missionary eyewitness has recorded. "A massacre was heralded by the blowing of trumpets and concluded by a procession. Accompanied by the prayers of the mollahs and muezzins, who from the minarets implored the blessings of Allah, the slaughter was accomplished in admirable order according to a well arranged plan. The crowd, supplied with arms by the authorities, joined most amicably with the soldiers and the Kurdish *Hamidieh* on these festive occasions. The Turkish women stimulated their heroes by raising a gutteral shriek of their war cry, the *Zilghit,* and deafening the hopeless despair of their victims by singing their nuptial songs. A kind of wild, cannibal humour seized the crowd . . . the savage crew did not even spare the children."

While few if any educated Turks disapproved of Hamid's treatment of the Armenians, they chafed at the "suppression of everything original, energetic, honest and capable, and the artificial selection of the unfit," as one of their number expressed it. Excluded from the Sultan's tight circle, they observed that "the only efficient organization in the country was the huge spy system." The Sultan carried his obsession with insurrection to bizarre extremes. Not too surprisingly, "Onward, Christian Soldiers" was considered a seditious hymn. Constantinople could not be electrified because "the *Padishah* dreaded *dynamite* bombs and prohibited *dynamos* lest through a similarity of names they partake of the same atrocious nature." Censors were particularly energetic in screening textbooks, having discovered that certain books shipped from America to mission schools carried the subversive formula H_2O. The books claimed this to be the chemical formula for water, but the Turkish censors knew full well that it was a treasonable slogan indicating that Hamid II was good for nothing. Such paranoia merely increased the resentment of the more enlightened Turks and drove them to plot Hamid's downfall.

During the 1890's the Turkish medical school, that cradle of modern Turkish politicians, spawned the Committee of Union and Progress. This group of revolutionaries, later known as the Young Turks, gained the cooperation of dissatisfied elements in the Turkish army and ultimately engineered Hamid's capitulation. In 1908 a coalition of Young Turks and army officers headquartered in Salonika forced the Sultan to restore the defunct constitution and to establish a parliamentary system with elected representatives of the people. In return for having accepted the ultimatum, Hamid was allowed to remain on the throne as a figurehead. He was deposed a year later, after an attempted counterrevolution, and exiled with his army of wives to Salonika. His ineffectual brother, Mohammed V (whom Hamid had kept imprisoned for decades in the "cage"), was placed on the throne in his place. "A more flabby, pitiful, witless countenance it would be difficult to imagine," wrote an American official in Salonika.

The Young Turks came in on the slogan of "Freedom, Justice, Equality, Fraternity," and on a wave of jubilation from the *rayahs*. Joyous demonstrations took place in Athens, where parading Greeks carried Ottoman flags alongside their own. Armenians and Turks embraced one another on the streets, and Turkish delegations bore armfuls of wreaths to Armenian cemeteries. Armenian revolutionary party leaders were on close terms with members of the Committee of Union and Progress, for they had worked with the Young Turks to depose the Sultan and were eagerly prepared to support the new government. For the first time in history *rayahs* were given all the privileges of Ottoman citizenship, including the right to send representatives to Parliament and the right to bear arms in the nation's defense. Having achieved their furthermost objectives, the Armenians were in a euphoric state.

Theoretically the Committee of Union and Progress was to administer the nation in accordance with the will of the people. In reality it continued to operate as a conspiratorial organization. An unlikely pair emerged as its dominant leaders: Enver Pasha, a dandified army officer with intense pro-German leanings, and Talaat Bey, a ruthless boor who had achieved a meteoric rise from postal clerk and had only lately learned to use a knife and fork. Before long it became evident that the Committee's promises of equality and freedom camouflaged a fanatical chauvinism whose objective was to "Turkify" all the elements of the Empire, crushing resistance with terror. It was only a matter of time before the more sinister elements would oust the benign in the struggle for power; yet the most enlightened Turks were all the same committed to the policy of Turkification (along the lines expounded by the socialist philosopher Ziya Gökalp), and it outraged them to see Ottoman minorities forming their own clubs, propagating their own languages and literature, and naïvely defending their right to do so under the new constitution.

It may well be true, as Western and Turkish historians insist, that Western nationalism had so infected the subjects of European Turkey that they were beyond redemption. If so, the Young Turks did all they could to hasten their revolt. Between 1909 and 1911, in towns and villages throughout Macedonia and Serbia, Christian leaders mysteriously disappeared or were found murdered. Ironically enough, in almost all cases the victims had been active in the movement to depose Hamid. The American consul in Salonika, George Horton, witnessed the persecutions. "From the extermination of notables, the program extended to people of less importance," he wrote. "Bevies of despairing peasant women who had come to visit the *vali* and demand news of their husbands, sons, or brothers appeared on the streets of Salonika. The answers were usually sardonic: 'He has probably run away and left you,' or, 'He has probably gone to America' were favorite replies. The truth, however, could not long be hidden as shepherds and others were soon reporting corpses found in ravines and gullies in the mountains and woods. . . . The next step was the so-called 'disarming.' This meant, as always, the disarming of the Christian element and the furnishing of weapons to the Turks. That the object was not so much to collect hidden arms as to terrorize the inhabitants was soon made evident from the tortures inflicted during the search."

Such incidents were not reported in the European newspapers of the day. It may be purely coincidental that foreign investors were at this time seeking to renew with the Young Turks the exploitation rights they had not long before secured from Hamid. However, in 1912, when the Serbs, Montenegrins, Macedonian Greeks, and Bulgars united in a massive revolt to free Macedonia, the European powers anticipated their victory with a great show of sympathy for the rebels. The Balkan Wars apparently came as a betrayal to the Turkish people, who were anticipating kudos from the West for their "democracy," and the grateful allegiance of all their Christian subjects. The perfidy of the *rayahs* simply proved the Turkish leaders correct: coexistence was obviously an impossibility.

The Armenians felt relatively secure during these years; yet in 1909, when reactionary elements conspired with Hamid to effect a counterrevolution in Constantinople, the Turks massacred twenty-five thousand Armenians in Adana—ostensibly for siding with the reactionary forces. Since the Armenians despised Hamid and were actively supporting the Young Turks regime, the Adana massacre came as an incomprehensible blow. Even so, during the Balkan Wars they demonstrated their allegiance to Turkey by fighting so staunchly beside the Turks that their Turkish commanders publicly commended them.

But a staggering defeat in the Balkan Wars had left the new regime materially and politically bankrupt. The Ottoman Public Debt, which was applicable to Turkey's undeveloped oil and mineral assets, was firmly in the clutches of Western financiers. Local trade was almost entirely in the hands of Ottoman Greeks and Armenians. With thousands of disgruntled and destitute European Moslems on her doorstep, and with the conviction that an unassimilable minority was a potential threat, the Young Turk leaders resolved to do away with the Armenians and to confiscate their properties. More disciplined and better organized than their predecessors, they were content to wait for the opportune moment to present itself. Their scheme, methodically planned and carried out, would in another generation and in another place come to be called genocide.

CHAPTER II

What is this day supported by precedents will hereafter become a precedent.

THUCYDIDES
Annals, XI, 24

Turkey was uncommitted at the outbreak of the First World War, her leaders split in their allegiance to opposing camps. The army, under the natty little Minister of War, Enver Pasha, led the pro-German faction; but Turkey's pathetically backward navy was being modernized by the British, and Turkish public opinion appeared to favor the navy view that the British were their better friends. Turkey's financial situation was certainly conducive to neutrality: the Germans, after a setback during the Balkan Wars, were working away on a Berlin-to-Bagdad railway project that cut through Turkey; while the oil interests, whose agents scurried around the Mosul, were a mixed crew that included the British government, the German Deutsche Bank, and the Royal Dutch Shell.

In English shipyards two battleships were under construction for the Turkish navy: the *Reshadia* and the *Sultan Osman*. The *Osman* was the largest battleship on earth. The money for these

ships had been collected by public subscription amid great fanfare, and the people were awaiting their arrival with considerable pride. By the time war had become imminent, the great *Sultan Osman* had already been sumptuously outfitted with everything from crystal drinking goblets to oriental rugs and oriental-style latrines, and Turkish sailors had been ogling it impatiently for days from a small boat anchored near the shipyards. Then, on the eve of the transfer, Winston Churchill (in his position as England's First Lord of the Admiralty) suddenly refused to permit the ships' release on the ground that if Turkey was to side with Germany, they would be used against England.

The embarrassment and dismay caused by England's refusal to turn over the ships swung Turkish sentiment toward Germany. To hasten a commitment, the Germans rushed two of their own swift battleships to Constantinople. The British gave chase, unsuccessfully, and the German warships *Goeben* and *Breslau* were soon in Constantinople harbor flying the Turkish emblem—to the resounding cheers of the populace and the acute dismay of British observers. Despite British assistance the Turkish navy was still deplorably inept, and German officers and men remained on board to operate the impressive battleships. Soon afterward, the Russians were provoked into declaring war on Turkey when the German commander-in-chief obtained permission from the Turks to conduct maneuvers on the Black Sea and while so engaged took the liberty of bombarding Russian installations from ships flying the ostensibly neutral Turkish flag. This *fait accompli* delighted the pro-German clique in the Turkish cabinet as much as it did the Germans, and on November 1, 1914, the Turks were at war against the Allies.

Yet the Turkish people held the British navy in awed respect. They had no great appetite for fighting either the English or the French, and the unpopular war spewed one defeat after another: at Suez, at the Persian Gulf, at Basra, in the Caucasus. By March 1915 Constantinople was in a panic, for the fall of the Dardanelles appeared imminent. The government evacuated its treasures and prepared to set fire to the city before removing to the interior. "Thousands of Turks were secretly praying for an Allied victory," Lord Kinross, who obtained much of his information from Turkish sources, has written, "and the chief of police was sending gangs of unemployed out of the city for fear of revolution."

Then the unbelievable happened. On March 18, 1915, the British made a halfhearted attack on the Dardanelles and, astonishingly enough, did not follow through! Their diffidence not only spelled disaster for the brave Australian and New Zealand regiments which were all but annihilated a few months later at Gallipoli, but it signaled the doom of the Armenian people as well. An official of the U.S. Embassy at Constantinople, Lewis Einstein, commented: "The Allied fleet had failed to force its way through the Dardanelles, the Straits were impregnable, therefore they [the Turkish leaders] could do what they liked. The tragedy of their sinister policy was contained in that deduction, for 'what they liked' meant the extermination of the Armenians."

The strategy had already been rehearsed. In order to prove the rebelliousness of the victims it was necessary first to provoke them into acts of self-defense, which could then be labeled "insurrectionary." A campaign of terror such as had been practiced earlier in the Balkans was already under way in Armenian towns and villages near the Russian border, and had been ever since Enver's impetuous winter offensive against the Russians had turned into a disaster; Turkish leaders had publicly ascribed the defeat to the perfidy of the Armenians on both sides of the Russo-Turkish frontier. The Turkish Armenians, however, proved themselves perversely forbearing in the face of provocation. "The Armenian clergy and political leaders saw many evidences that the Turks . . . were [provoking rebellion] and they went among the people cautioning them to be quiet and bear all insults and even outrages patiently, so as not to give provocation," wrote Henry Morgenthau, American Ambassador to Turkey. " 'Even though they burn a few of our villages,' these leaders would say, 'do not retaliate for it is better that a few be destroyed than that a whole nation be massacred.' " The authorities were forced to intensify their efforts. One ruse was to requisition a number of fighting men from an Armenian town. These were then taken away and slain, and their bodies left where they could readily be found.

In February 1915 the citizens of Van, a town near the Russian border, suddenly found the friendly *vali* of the province replaced by one Jevdet Bey, who happened to be the brother-in-law of Enver Pasha. Jevdet lost no time in engineering the murder of four prominent Armenian leaders after luring them to a neighboring village with an "honor guard" for their ostensible protection. He boasted to an American missionary doctor that he would not leave a single Armenian alive in that village. "Not one so high!" he shouted, pointing to his knee. The citizens of Van thereupon refused to submit to Jevdet's demand for four thousand fighting men; instead they organized a defense and held siege in their walled quarter until an approaching Russian army arrived to save them. The American hospital was located within the besieged area, and its personnel were among the foreign observers who recorded the events.

A suitably inflammatory version of the Van "insurrection" reverberated through the Turkish press and provided the justification for the next stage in the solution of the "Armenian Question." During the night of April 24, 1915, the Constantinople police routed six hundred leading Armenian citizens of the capital from their beds, among them Zohrab and Vartkes, the two elected Armenian deputies to the Turkish Parliament, and imprisoned them on charges of treason. None could have been more startled than the two deputies. Both were on close terms with the Young Turk leaders; Vartkes had saved the life of one of the cabinet ministers during the counterrevolution of 1909, and Zohrab had been entertained at dinner by Talaat himself the night before his arrest. They were led away with the others, never to return. The Turks subsequently declared to interested parties that Zohrab had died of "heart disease" and Vartkes "from a fall from his horse." The stories were intended to be apocryphal. "It is altogether likely that, when murdered, he should fall from his horse!" an amused Turk chuckled to an American official.

In rapid succession the leaders of every Armenian community were seized, imprisoned, tortured, and ultimately put to death on charges of sedition. Simultaneously all Armenians serving in the Turkish army—these already were segregated into "labor battalions," on the contention that they could not be trusted to carry arms—were taken aside and killed. Once the leaders and fighting men had been disposed of, the final phase began. It was euphemistically referred to as "deportation," and it had been rehearsed in 1913 when the Turks had driven entire Greek villages out of Thrace and eliminated thousands of Greeks by starvation and exposure. By 1915, however, the leadership had devised more efficient means for accelerating the victims' demise in a day when the refinements for mass murder had not yet been devised and the job had to be done "by hand." Moslems along the routes of deportation were inflamed to slaughter—in many cases by the exhortations of the Moslem clergy and also by the Turkish press, which invoked in lurid detail crimes the Armenians had supposedly committed or were planning to commit against the Turks. This last contention subsequently bore a measure of justification, for those Armenians who escaped to Russia and joined the Russian army were undoubtedly prepared to avenge their murdered kinsmen at the first opportunity.

The deportation procedure followed a pattern which Lord Bryce, the British statesman and author of *The American Commonwealth*, summarized in the preface to his compilation of authenticated documents in a British Blue Book:

At one Armenian center after another, throughout the Ottoman Empire, on a certain date (and the dates show a sequence), the public crier went through the streets announcing that every male Armenian over age fifteen must present himself forthwith at the Government building. . . . The men presented themselves in their working clothes, leaving their shops and workrooms open, their ploughs on the field, their cattle on the mountain side. When they arrived, they were thrown without explanation into prison, kept there a day or two, then marched out of the town in batches, roped man to man along some southerly or southeasterly road. . . . They had not long to ponder over their plight for they were halted and massacred at the first lonely place on the road.

After a few days' interval, the Armenian women, children, and old men, were ordered to prepare themselves for deportation. Many were turned out on the road immediately, but in some towns they were given a week of grace which they spent in a frenzied attempt to sell their personal possessions for whatever was offered. Government orders forbade them from selling real property or stocks, as their banishment was supposed to be temporary. Scarcely were they out of sight, however, when Moslem refugees from Europe, who had been gathered nearby, were moved into their homes. Since the Turks of the interior were almost totally unskilled, a representative Armenian craftsman in each area—a shoemaker, a tailor, a pharmacist—was permitted to remain. Medical doctors and interpreters serving in the Turkish army were also exempted from the general orders. All the rest were set upon the roads leading to the deserts. According to Morgenthau, thousands "could be seen winding in and out of every valley and climbing up the sides of every mountain."

In the first six months alone, over 1,200,000 people joined this procession.

By now the story becomes chillingly familiar, especially when one remembers that the victims of this last, most hideous phase were almost exclusively women and children. They were marched south from the plains of Anatolia, through a region that is a no-man's-land of treacherous ravines and craggy mountains, forbidding to the most hardened traveler, and finally into the bleak Syrian desert, fiercely hot by day and frigid by night. On the way, they were beset by all the Moslem populations they encountered. First there were the Turkish villagers and peasants, who robbed them of their few provisions and their clothes, and took such of their women as they pleased; then the Kurds, who committed blood-chilling atrocities, first butchering any males in the convoy, then attacking the women. According to the Bryce Report: "It depended on the whim of the moment whether a Kurd cut a woman down or carried her away into the hills. When they were carried away their babies were left on the ground or dashed against the stones." Then came the *chettes*— brigands who had been loosed by the thousands from prisons and set in the victims' path—and the dervishes, who roared down from their monasteries in the hills and carried off children "shrieking with terror." And always there were the gendarmes, prodding the exhausted figures with whips and clubs, refusing them water when they passed wells and streams, bayoneting those who lagged behind, and committing increasingly perverted attacks.

Apologists have claimed that these atrocities were simply the work of barbaric and fanatic tribesmen, but Ambassador Morgenthau has shown that they were a matter of deliberate policy. Thus, an educated Turkish official told the Ambassador with some pride that "all these details were matters of nightly discussion at . . . headquarters. . . . Each new method of inflicting pain was hailed as a splendid discovery, and the regular attendants were constantly ransacking their brains in an effort to devise some new torment. He told me that they even delved into the records of the Spanish Inquisition and other historic institutions of torture and adopted all the suggestions found there."

Nor can there be any doubt that the policy of extermination as a whole was planned by the central government. The official record includes the following orders, sent on cipher telegrams and in all but one case addressed to the provincial government of Aleppo (the lightning advance of Allenby's forces prevented the Turks in Aleppo from destroying these compromising documents):

September 3, 1915
We recommend that the operations which we have ordered you to make shall first be carried out on the men of the said people, and that you shall subject the women and children to them also. Appoint reliable officials for this.

(signed) Minister of the Interior
Talaat

September 15, 1915
It was first communicated to you that the Government, by order of the *Jemiet*, had decided to destroy completely all Armenians living in Turkey. Those who oppose this order and decision cannot remain on the official staff of the Empire. An end must be put to their existence, however criminal the measures taken may be, and no regard must be paid to age, or sex, or to conscientious scruple.

(signed) Minister of the Interior
Talaat

November 15, 1915
From interventions which have recently been made by the American Ambassador in Constantinople on behalf of his government, it appears that the American consuls are obtaining information by secret means. In spite of our assurances that the Armenian deportations will be accomplished in safety and comfort, they remain unconvinced. Be careful that events attracting attention shall not take place in connection with those who are near the cities or other centers. From the point of view of the present policy it is important that foreigners who are in those parts shall be persuaded that the expulsion of the Armenians is in truth only deportation. For this reason, it is important that to save appearances, for a time a show of gentle dealing shall be made, and the usual measures taken in suitable places. It is recommended as very important that the people who give such information shall be arrested and handed over to the military authorities for trial by court martial.

(signed) Minister of the Interior
Talaat

January 10, 1916
Enquiries having been made it is understood that hardly ten percent of the Armenians subjected to the general transportation have reached their destinations; the rest have died from natural causes, such as hunger and sickness. We inform you that we are working to bring about

the same result with regard to those who are still alive, by using severe measures.

(signed) Abdullahad Nouri

As a result of this policy, over one million Armenians died. Despite the pretext that the banishment of Armenians was dictated by military considerations, the deportations took place in every hamlet, village, town, and city in Turkey—with the exception of Smyrna and Constantinople, where the presence of so many foreigners required "gentle measures to save appearances." Talaat himself admitted more than once that the exigencies of war had little to do with his policy. "He said I must not get the idea that the deportations had been decided upon hastily, in reality they were the result of prolonged and careful consideration," wrote Morgenthau. And German Ambassador Wangenheim, a towering, steely-eyed aristocrat who to the day of his death remained indifferent to the murder of the Armenians, reported to the German Chancellor in June 1915: "It is obvious that the banishment of the Armenians is not due solely to military considerations. Talaat Bey, the Minister of the Interior, has quite frankly said to Dr. Mordtmann of the Embassy that the Turkish government intended to make use of the World War to deal thoroughly with its internal enemies, the Christians of Turkey, and that it meant not to be disturbed in this by diplomatic intervention from abroad."

In Palestine the Jewish colony—by now eighty-five thousand strong and including many recent immigrants—nervously took heed of the Armenian fate as Turkish authorities closed down Zionist schools, newspapers, and clubs, encouraged the Arabs to turn on their Jewish neighbors, and exiled Ben Gurion and other leaders. The Armenian example did not deter an ill-starred band from forming a spy network to help the British, but Zionist leaders abroad, as well as Jewish residents of Palestine—like the Arabs, they were suffering enormously from famine—forswore actions that would provoke the wrath of the Turkish authorities.

In the Smyrna region the energetic protests of Liman von Sanders, Commander of the Fifth Army, helped prevent the mass deportation of Armenians from that area. Without bothering to consult Berlin, he notified the Smyrna *vali* that German forces would interfere physically if the deportations were carried through. The threat suited the *vali*; he enjoyed the hospitality of the wealthy Armenian colony and was pleased with this excuse to leave the populace alone. In order to pacify the ruling clique in Constantinople, however, he was forced to deport Armenian revolutionary party leaders from the city.

In the hinterlands of the Smyrna district it was the Greeks who bore the brunt of the Turkish policy. In June 1915 a violent campaign against the Greeks burst into the Turkish press, while posters exhorting the Moslems to murder appeared suddenly on the walls of schools and mosques. Murders of from ten to twenty peasants each day culminated in a massacre of the Greeks at Phocia, in the deportation of several hundred thousand others, and the destruction of their homes and carefully tended vineyards in the region north of Smyrna. "There is no doubt that the people who were expelled to the interior from the coastal towns were robbed and malevolently maltreated and that many girls were violated," George Horton, the American consul in Salonika, wrote, adding that "many Greeks from the coast escaped to nearby islands where they have since been nursing their vengeance."

Diplomatic pressure from both Greece and Germany, whose statesmen nurtured hopes of gaining Greece as an ally, prevented the anti-Greek movement from becoming generalized. The Germans further demonstrated their ability to intervene when they successfully prevented the molestation of Armenian employees on the Berlin-to-Bagdad railroad by arguing that the efficiency of their operations would be seriously endangered. Later, even such protests as these were ineffective, for they were so tentative and so obviously intended merely to mitigate world opinion that the Turks realized they had a free hand. In refusing to take a firm stand for fear of incurring the resentment of their Eastern ally, German statesmen resisted considerable pressure from their own missionaries and from humane officials and military commanders in Turkey. Count Wolff-Metternich, who succeeded Wangenheim as Ambassador to the Porte, wrote to his Chancellor: "In order to have success in the Armenian question we must instil into the Turkish government the fear of consequences." But those at the helm obdurately refrained from imposing effective measures, and the count was later recalled at the behest of the Turks. The deportations as such did not trouble them; according to Morgenthau it was in fact the Germans who had originally suggested the deportations, and Julius Kaliski, a German Social Democrat, responded to appeals for saving the Armenians on grounds of economic expediency by suggesting that "the business talents of the Armenians might be adequately replaced by those of the Jews." But the policy of extermination caused hand-wringing at the Wilhelmstrasse. German financiers, with their enormous interests in Turkey's development, could not have been entirely unaware that a genuine deportation of an enterprising population into the interior promised certain developmental advantages for themselves. Extermination was seen as a waste of resources. German officials lamented, "The worst of the matter is that the whole world will attribute the guilt for the Armenian horrors to Germany."

The worst of it was being described in detailed reports by horrified Germans as well as by other foreign eyewitnesses, and world opinion was already incensed. Protestant and Catholic churchmen in Germany as well as in all the Allied nations issued protests. The Vatican was aroused. The governments of Great Britain, Russia, and France issued a joint declaration warning that all members of the Ottoman government would be held responsible for "this crime against humanity and civilization." And in England Lord Bryce, "in the interests of historic truth and with an eye to the questions which might arise when the war came to an end," undertook to compile the evidence with the assistance of historian Arnold Toynbee.

The American people were meanwhile responding generously to appeals from the Committee on Armenian Atrocities (later renamed the Committee for Armenian and Syrian Relief, and still later, the Near East Relief). The agency had been formed at the behest of Ambassador Morgenthau after his repeated protests to the Young Turks* and his requests to the State Department to take effective countermeasures had proved equally unavailing. Cleveland Dodge, a trustee of Robert College in Constantinople and a close friend of President Wilson, had convinced the President to avoid any measures that might antagonize the Turks into expropriating American properties. In Anatolia alone the American Board of Missions had three hundred and fifty-three primary and secondary schools, eight colleges, and three hospitals. The relief committee, representing all the American missionary and educational interests in Turkey, enlisted the help of the American press and proceeded to campaign from coast to coast on behalf of "the starving Armenians." In sermons laden with cant, churches and

---

* Talaat ignored Morgenthau's repeated protests but expressed interest in the victims' insurance policies. Since many Armenians had their lives insured by American firms, and since their beneficiaries were also dead, Talaat thought it only right that the State should collect.

Sunday schools portrayed the Armenians as Christian martyrs suffering persecution unto death because of their faith. Children were encouraged to collect their pennies and were force-fed on the principle that to leave food uneaten on one's plate was a disservice to the Armenians.

The starving ones were those who had escaped to nearby countries and were expiring there from lack of food, as well as a number of emaciated orphans whom the missionaries had managed to rescue, and in rare instances to protect, in improvised orphanages. Local officials were occasionally benign enough to allow the missionaries to feed the deportees as they filed through towns and villages, and there were instances when compassionate Turks themselves hid Armenian children and adults. Exceptional administrators refused to obey the general orders and consequently suffered dismissal, or worse. But such humanitarian acts were rare, and rarely tolerated under a policy that aimed to exterminate a race. Not only the neutral American flag but even the German flag was frequently violated, as Turks stormed buildings suspected of harboring Armenians and killed or forcibly removed the inmates over the pleas of the foreigners in charge. Some of the missionaries accompanied their charges a part of the way; a few heroically stayed to the end and perished with them.

Since messages and reports could be safely forwarded only through diplomatic channels (and sometimes not then), the relief committee had from its inception maintained strong connections with the Department of State. In 1917 the group prevented the United States from declaring war on Turkey. Wilson yielded to the missionary lobby in the face of pressure from Great Britain, France, Italy, and Greece, and from a good many American legislators and Armenian leaders in exile. The relief group's protestation that a declaration of war would mean abandoning the Christians of Turkey undoubtedly swayed Wilson, but this was a secondary consideration to Protestant leaders—most of their charges had perforce been abandoned long since. Such help as could be given in Turkey during the war was admittedly minimal and largely ineffectual. In view of the attitude these missionary leaders manifested after the war, it is fair to assume that they were as concerned about their real estate as about their fellow Christians.

CHAPTER III

We have been moved already beyond endurance, and need rest.

JOHN MAYNARD KEYNES
The Economic Consequences of the Peace.

At the war's end in November 1918, the Allies gathered their bargaining forces in Paris and proceeded, or so they thought, to ordain the peace. Chroniclers of the Paris fiasco have been numerous, for in addition to the usual bevy of professionals, many of the participants were driven to record their own observations. At least one historian used the culinary metaphor, noting that "most of the cooks in the Paris broth, after spoiling it, were unable to control the impulse to tell the world why it was not their particular fault." In view of the complicated nature of the feast, there were not too many cooks. Indigestibility was rather the result of incompatible ingredients; of political expediency neutralizing farsighted statesmanship; of clashing temperaments spicing irreconcilable interests. Furthermore, the Big Four chefs—Clemenceau, Lloyd George, Wilson, and Orlando—invited censure and suspicion by brewing some of their most crucial formulas in secret conclave.

33

Ensconced as king of the conference was the old French Premier in his incongruous and archaic dress: square-tailed coat; thick, buckled, country-style boots; hands invariably gloved. This intransigent cynic, as John Maynard Keynes described him, "had one illusion—France; and one disillusion—mankind, including Frenchmen and his colleagues not the least." He had the advantage over his colleagues of understanding and speaking both French and English, and although he manifested boredom when his interests were not directly involved (no less than his electorate, he was single-mindedly concerned with imposing a costly and debilitating peace on Germany), even when he pretended to doze, his colleagues learned that he was in control and might at any moment shatter a victim with his malicious wit. On occasion, as in an encounter with the long-suffering British Foreign Minister, Lord Curzon, Clemenceau was capable of driving his opponent literally to tears.

Devious and ingratiating, in contrast to Clemenceau's testy eccentricity, Signor Orlando ("a white, weak, flabby man," wrote Harold Nicolson) was no less determined, at whatever cost, to enforce his nation's demands; notably to press for the fulfillment of certain secret agreements that the Allies had made during the war and that Russia—a defected ally—had recently announced to the world. The trouble with these secret treaties was not only that some of them contradicted others, but that in sum they also contradicted the lofty principles for which the war had allegedly been fought, and which the American President, for his part, was determined to uphold.

Wilson had arrived at the Peace Conference armed with his ideals as embodied in the concept of a League of Nations and the Fourteen Points that set forth his principles of international justice. These had been widely publicized, deservedly acclaimed, and would have comprised a sufficient contribution had the President been able to count on the support of his European colleagues —or for that matter of his own legislators. Unfortunately, the President was not prepared to suggest practical means of implementing his ideas. "He had no plan, no scheme, no constructive idea whatever for clothing with the flesh of life the commandments he had thundered from the White House," Keynes noted. Wilson had gone to Paris over the objections of a number of his advisers, including his Secretary of State, Robert Lansing, who later disclosed that he had objected to Wilson's departure because he considered the President ill-prepared to deal in detail with the problems of the peace. (Lansing also confessed that he was himself against the League of Nations, against foreign mandates, and that the President distrusted such legal arguments as Lansing was prepared to advance.) Wilson did not appear to be in top form on his arrival in Paris. Keynes, who considered the Conference a disaster and resigned from the British delegation before it was over, described Wilson as a "blind and deaf Don Quixote . . . entering a cavern where the swift and glittering blade was in the hands of the adversary"; as slow-thinking and insensitive to his environment, in contrast to Lloyd George's "unerring, almost medium-like sensitivity to everyone immediately around him." To the brilliant Keynes, the American President manifested the intellectual limitations of an evangelical preacher.

Lloyd George was the most controversial of the contenders at the conference table. This magnetic, impetuous Welshman with the shock of silvery hair and eyes that wrinkled at the corners when he laughed was a courageous, imaginative leader to his fans; a conniving, untrustworthy demagogue to his political adversaries. No one has denied his gift for eloquence, his mercurial wit, and his political shrewdness. Yet even his supporters have admitted that his judgment was clouded, on occasion, by his need to reconcile public consensus with national interest. Wishful thinking sometimes guided his hand and led to disastrous miscalculations.

Still, none of the statesmen gathered at Paris can be credited with an abundance of insight, or foresight. While imposing a Carthaginian peace on Germany, they procrastinated a settlement in the Near East, the more willingly as their respective designs in that area were irreconcilable and their pledges had been thorny indeed.

The European allies had summarily agreed, early in the war, that Turkey would be divided among them. France had her eye on Syria and Cilicia. In exchange she had offered England a free hand where England most wanted it—notably wherever there was oil. But during the war, France had not been notoriously helpful in the Eastern theater. In May 1916, after General Townshend and a force of eight thousand men were defeated by the Turks at Kut-el-Amara, the British tried to induce the French to participate more actively in the Turkish theater to relieve the hard-pressed British troops, offering as bait "all the land eastward as far as and beyond the Euphrates, including the town of Mosul."

The French never rejected the offer but put forth no more effort than before, and the resulting military exigencies drove England to promise independence to some of the Arab factions in return for their help.

In her anxiety to retain Mosul, England would have been delighted, in 1919, to settle French claims on Syria and Cilicia; but now, alas, there were those knotty pledges to the Arabs to contend with, and these conflicted with her promise to France. There were other nagging promises as well: a homeland for the Jews, as Lord Balfour had pledged in his famous Declaration; a promised homeland for the Armenians in northeastern Turkey. And both Greece and Italy, at various times, had been led to expect identical portions of the west coast of Anatolia, including Smyrna.

The Russian Revolution, followed by that nation's unforeseen withdrawal as a contender for Turkish territory, provided still another complication by canceling all the promises the Allies had made to Russia and thereby increasing the rivalry of the remaining Powers. Moreover, while the United States had refrained from going to war with Turkey, certain powerful business interests were looking enviously at the economic spoils and insisting that America exert her influence in the Turkish settlement.

These interests had the support of an emerging elite among American advisers on foreign policy, a group including the Dulles brothers, Elihu Root, Colonel Edward House, and a tight little circle of Yale professors, some of whom hovered on the fringes of the Peace Conference and found American diplomacy painfully wanting, in contrast to the self-serving European model. Their disenchantment led to the forming of an august "club," The Council on Foreign Relations, whose members—leading financiers, directors of giant corporations, and the heads of the more prestigious universities, foundations, and news media—would unofficially direct and expound American foreign policy in the coming years. It would take nearly half a century for the Council to emerge as more or less synonymous with the "establishment" and for its members to realize what most of their European counterparts had meanwhile been forced to learn: that self-interest cannot forever be couched in humanitarian terms. Still, those who were in Paris in 1919 had reason to find their President's idealism embarrassingly inadequate.

Wilson's Fourteen Points promised self-determination to indigenous populations and rejected a settlement based on prearranged deals between Powers, but when applied to specific areas their ambiguous wording sometimes provoked a dilemma. Point Twelve, for example, assured "Turkish portions of the present Ottoman Empire . . . a secure sovereignty" and "the other nationalities an undoubted security of life and unmolested autonomous development." Secret treaties aside, how could Wilson's vision of an independent Armenia (which alone might provide security of life and unmolested autonomy) be reconciled with the sovereignty of the "Turkish portions"? Even before 1915 the Armenians had been so dispersed and decimated that they no longer constituted a clear majority in any but two northeastern provinces. Were "sovereign" portions to be determined historically, or on the basis of self-determination of the existing majority? In the absence of definition Point Twelve became a dangerous instrument, signifying one thing to the Turks, another to the Armenians.

Greece was prepared to claim the Smyrna region on the basis of population, although it had also been held out as a plum to entice her into the war against the Central Powers. In January 1915 England and France, with Russian approval, had offered Greece "large concessions on the coast of Asia Minor." A month later Clemenceau had dangled hints that Greece might even be given control of Constantinople, at a moment when England and France were privately agreeing that its control would be given to Russia. Eleutherios Venizelos, then Prime Minister of Greece, had replied that Constantinople should be internationalized. A hardy and worldly Cretan, Venizelos was all the while chafing to join forces with the Allies; he felt certain that they would win and dreamed of expanding Greek territory at Turkey's expense. King Constantine, however, wanted no part of the war, and his persistent neutrality led to Venizelos's resignation. In September 1915 Venizelos established his own revolutionary government in Crete, and in November he declared war on the Central Powers and Bulgaria. He then worked with the Allies and waited for an opportune moment to stage a coup in Athens.

King Constantine's refusal to join the Allies, added to the fact that his wife was the Kaiser's sister, led to Allied charges that the King was inordinately pro-German, despite the fact that he just as persistently resisted his brother-in-law's overtures and occasional threats. In this instance the Germans were more scrupulous than their opponents in respecting Greek neutrality, perhaps because neutrality was the most they really expected. France and

England had a history of intervention in Greek internal affairs (they had in fact acted like proverbial mothers-in-law ever since Greek independence); if the King could not be cajoled into entering the war, they were determined he would be provoked, or compromised.

In 1916 Athens was flooded with secret agents and became the scene of cloak-and-dagger dramas bizarre enough to read like those parodies in which the end frequently becomes lost in the means. The memoirs of certain intelligence agents disclose so much bungling, intriguing among the Allies, and slinking around to relatively little purpose that they provide a fetching commentary on the espionage business itself. In his *Greek Memories,* Compton Mackenzie conveys some of the fun-and-games spirit that was only slightly tempered in wartime Athens. On the eve of his departure from London, he writes, an agent he calls "C" presented Mackenzie with a swordstick that C had always carried in peacetime spying expeditions. "That's when this business was really amusing," he told Mackenzie. "After the war is over we'll do some amusing secret service work together. It's capital sport."

In Greece the sport aimed to create incidents that would embarrass the Constantine government. Since the English had made an enormous fuss over German violations of Belgian neutrality, their higher echelons counseled a restraint not always practiced in the field. French agents were even less inhibited and went so far as to plan to kidnap their own minister and carry him off into the mountains to create trouble for Constantine. On occasion, intrigue between French and British agents was no less imaginative or premeditated, for although both nations were engaged in attempting to topple the Constantine government, each mistrusted the other's influence on Venizelos and sought to minimize it. A third ally, Italy, mistrusted both France and England and preferred to keep Constantine on his throne.

Eventually France and England obtained the right to pass their troops through Greek territory. They then tightened their demands on the King by insisting on the surrender of Greek artillery, the demobilization of certain forces, the control of police and railroads, and the right to occupy certain strategic points in Athens. Finally, they righteously demanded Constantine's resignation after French and British marines landed, marched on the capital, and were fired upon. The King resigned, Venizelos returned to Athens, and Greece entered the war on the side of the Allies on June 30, 1917.

Venizelos's political platform rested on essentially one premise: that by joining in the fight, Greece would be permitted to "liberate" the Smyrna region, with its large Greek population, from Turkish rule. As a poor country, already financially and militarily drained by the Balkan Wars, Greece had no other justification for entering this war. So it was that when the war ended, the Greek leader hurried to Paris to claim his country's portion.

Since they had promised substantially the same area to the Italians, France and England were in no great hurry to tackle the problem. When the Greek government (but not Venizelos) had ignored the original offer in 1915, the west coast of Turkey had been offered to Italy and helped to induce that country into the war. The Allies moreover confirmed the bargain with Italy and defined the area specifically to include Smyrna, under the April 1917 agreement of St. Jean de Maurienne. The Italians were seeking a share in the Near Eastern jackpot so firmly controlled, heretofore, by England and France. Beset by overpopulation and a lack of arable land, they viewed fertile Anatolia with longing. They saw Greece as England's vassal, the Greek claims as a British ruse to block Italian influence in the Near East, and were the more convinced because Lloyd George showed a distinct partiality for Venizelos.

Every aspect of the Near Eastern question provided a dilemma. There was universal agreement on the question of freeing Armenians from Turkish rule, but by 1919 the opinion even here was divided between those—like Wilson—who favored an independent Armenia under United States mandate, and those who for various reasons, not the least of which were economic, insisted on an American mandate over the whole of Turkey. Torn between the intransigence of the Arabs and that of the French on the question of Syria, the British were for scrapping the wartime treaties if they could keep such strategic areas as Mesopotamia for themselves.

Wilson recommended that all decisions in the Near East be postponed pending inter-Allied investigations; the United States had already begun organizing an investigating team and at least one of its members had already left for Turkey. In the ensuing confusion he was never formally recalled, but simply found himself in a kind of official limbo. A second group of appointees had a similar experience when they were superseded without notice by a third group. Knowing full well that the Arabs wanted no part of the French, the French wanted no part of an investigation, although they did not come right out and say so; while Prince Feisal, son of King Hussein of Mecca, was threatening an Arab revolt if an investigating team did not arrive forthwith. The Italians, like the French, preferred to settle matters behind the scenes. The Zionists opposed an investigation because they considered their claim to Palestine already settled by the Balfour Declaration. The British hesitated to join an investigating team for fear of offending the French, but thought that there should be one.

In the end, and after several months' delay, a new American team unofficially tagged the King-Crane Commission went off alone. President Wilson found Messrs. King and Crane (the president of Oberlin College and a retired plumbing tycoon, respectively) admirably suited for the investigation of Syria since they knew nothing about the place and presumably would therefore be unbiased. Crane, as it turned out, did little beyond dissuading the Commission from visiting Mesopotamia by contending that the Iraqi unquestionably favored British rule. (According to William Yale, another member of the Commission, "Crane had no intention of permitting the Commission to go to Iraq. It seems likely that Mr. Crane got his idea that the Iraqi favored British control of Mesopotamia from leading Britishers in Paris.") While other members of the Commission were at work Crane frequently wandered off to pass the time of day with Arab sheikhs and to visit the Constantinople Women's College (of which he was a trustee), whose president, Mary Patrick Mills, was militantly pro-Turk.

The Commission included a number of knowledgeable advisers and their report—to which Crane, one member said, "contributed the geniality"—recommended a small, independent Armenia, discouraged Greek control in Anatolia, and confirmed that the Arabs were inexorably opposed to French rule in Syria. The report was suppressed and in the end all of its recommendations were ignored.

While the King-Crane and other investigating teams were shuffling about the Near East, finding out what the experts already knew and conducting, as Winston Churchill has written, "a roving progress in search of truth through all the powder magazines of the Middle East with a notebook in one hand and a lighted cigarette in the other," the peacemakers were by no means lethargic over the question of demobilization. The one political urgency in France, Italy, and Great Britain, no less than in the United States, was to "bring the boys home." The British were singlehandedly shouldering the burden of the Turkish occupation as they had earlier the fighting, and Lloyd George now hastened to please his electorate. "In January, 1919," Churchill noted, "the war office had still nearly three million men abroad under its orders. By March it had two, and these in a rapid process of demobilization. By midsummer 1919, apart from the forces on the Rhine, we had hardly any troops at all." But in the East it was clearly the conquerors and not the conquered who were war-weary. While the British forces in the Ottoman territories were melting away, the Turks were preparing to fight as they had not fought before, to avoid the consequences of their defeat.

The Young Turks had by the end of the war lost favor with their countrymen. Failure rarely sustains admiration and their wartime gamble had brought the country to the brink of partition. Shortly before the Armistice, the ruling triumvirate—Talaat, Enver, and Djemal—fled Turkey in a German warship. Enver was killed in subsequent fighting in the Caucasus, Djemal by an assassin in Tiflis. Talaat remained in Berlin until 1921 when a young Armenian named Soghomon Tehlirian shot him to death in broad daylight. (A German court acquitted Tehlirian on the grounds of temporary insanity brought on by Talaat's crimes against the Armenians in general and Tehlirian's relatives in particular.) A truce was hastily negotiated between Admiral Calthorpe, the British Commander of the Mediterranean fleet, and Rauf Bey, the Ottoman Minister of the Marine. The agreement included "immediate demobilization of the Turkish army" except for "troops required for the surveillance of the frontier and maintenance of internal order," and gave the Allies the right to occupy "strategic points" which were not defined.

It became obvious that to the British "strategic points" were those that offered commercial as well as military advantages: Mosul, the seaports of Alexandretta, Constantinople, and Samsun, and that vital gateway, the Dardanelles. It was at these points that they therefore concentrated their dwindling forces while supervision elsewhere evaporated. France sent token forces to occupy Cilicia and Syria when the British made it clear that they were not going to guard those regions on her behalf. But in the hinterland there were virtually no foreign troops at all by

41

the beginning of 1919, and in the Caucasus a vast Turkish army was left entirely to its own devices.

A complex political situation had developed in this Russo-Turkish frontier area, a portion of which Russia had ceded to Turkey when the two nations had signed a separate peace in March 1918. The peace brought renewed anguish to the surviving Armenians, thousands of whom had earlier fled for their lives to join their Russian-Armenian kinsmen on territory the Soviets were now proceeding to hand over to the Turks. The otherwise preoccupied Czarist army had in fact deserted this territory in 1917, and the Armenians had at that time joined Georgia and Azerbaijan in a tentative Trans-Caucasian confederation. But after signing the peace treaty of Brest-Litovsk with Russia, the Turks encouraged the dissolution of the confederation, recognized an independent Armenian Republic—on condition that Turkey should provide the militia to "protect" it—and proceeded to attack it by force of arms. With their meager supply lines cut off by the Moslem Azerbaijanis, who supported the Turks, the Armenians were simultaneously hit by famine and epidemics that wiped out 180,000 persons in the last six months of 1919. A half million more would have perished but for massive aid from American relief agencies—primarily the Near East Relief—between 1919 and 1923. The Turkish army was nowhere stronger, better organized, or better equipped than in this Caucasus region where the decimated Armenians were struggling to stay alive. In the face of the armistice injunction to reduce his forces, the Turkish military leader in the area (a Turkish army officer named Kiazim Karabekir) was busily expanding them by distributing arms to the Turkish population from the ample stores the Allies had left behind.

Elsewhere the Sultan's army had disintegrated into anarchy. By the end of the war five hundred thousand men had deserted, taking with them their arms and ammunition. They formed outlaw bands and roamed the interior, robbing and in some areas virtually controlling entire villages. Outlaw, or *chette*, bands were nothing new to Turkey; young men intent on evading conscription had traditionally found refuge in the mountains and resorted to banditry. But never before had there been so huge a population of able-bodied men, armed and ready for whoever might come forward to lead them.

The emergent leader was the thirty-eight-year-old Mustafa

Kemal, hero of the Dardanelles and in fact the only Turkish hero of the war. A superb strategist, self-assured and intensely ambitious, Kemal had become increasingly disdainful of the blundering Young Turk leadership during the war, and had come to Constantinople right after the Armistice to try to wangle his name onto a new cabinet list. The reinstituted Turkish Parliament, however, voted to support the Sultan—still the enfeebled brother of Abdul Hamid—who soon dissolved the Parliament and named his own brother-in-law, Damad Ferid, as Grand Vizier. Kemal, sulking over his defeat and his nation's ignominy, and temporarily out of a job, spent the winter plotting against the Allies and intriguing with his friends Ismet Pasha, Hussein Rauf, and Ali Fethi, all of whom held influential posts in the Sultan's government (indeed Rauf, as chief officer of the Marine, had signed the armistice). Imposingly tall, blue-eyed, dashingly uniformed and bemedaled, Kemal made himself conspicuous in the splendid Pera Palace Hotel, a rendezvous of Allied officers, Bolshevik spies, and assorted agents of intrigue who were often indistinguishable from the diplomatic colony. Here Kemal made contacts that would enhance his ambitions. Once he attempted (unsuccessfully) to land a post with the British through the intercession of G. Ward Price, a sympathetic English journalist.

Constantinople in 1919 could have provided the setting for a dozen monumental spy thrillers. Those were the days when White Russian colonels, their toes sticking out of their boots, stood begging outside the U.S. Embassy and Red spies drank champagne at the Pera Palace bar. "What a pleasantly diverting place it was!" a nostalgic reporter recalled, year later. "Always a crowd of flashing uniforms, three deep, at the little bar (and only one bartender who could mix a decent cocktail); the orchestra always playing 'Ain't We Got Fun?'" An American intelligence officer described the colorful Caucasian tribesmen who provided comedy: "Their belted grey wool wrappers, astrakhan caps with orange crowns, curved swords and straight daggers, chink eyes, top boots and the row of cartridge holders like filigree pepper pots across their bosoms, adorn the Grande Rue of fleshpots," he reported. "But when the Tartar delegation hesitated here on their way to Paris, at least one of the Azerbaijan 'commissioners' was found unable to write his name. He is still here executing his barbaric dances in the midnight dives."

A prominent and evidently irresistible member of the defunct

Young Turk party, who was wanted by the Allies for his part in the Armenian murders, was found by the French gendarmes hiding out in oriental splendor on—of all things—a French warship in the Golden Horn, under the protection of a French ladyfriend whose husband had large holdings in Ottoman mines and spirit factories. In waterfront dives waiters served "American Skoch Misky," that sailors recall later made the stateside bootleg variety seem like the balm of Gilead. And in the shuttered upper rooms of cafés, languorous beauties doubled as agents—some for the Reds ("the *désenchainée* who may have persuaded you to open a bottle of German champagne or beer in a box at the Petit Champs show, will begin to fear a Bolshevist advance toward the city in order to persuade you of its inevitability"), some for the respective Powers, who were tormented by mutual suspicion. "Much of the work," wrote the American agent, "consists of keeping tabs on the maneuvers of the Allies themselves, none of whom is in the other's confidence, but all secretively watch one another like hawks. The French and the Italians are the most tightmouthed; it is impossible officially to get any information of value from their representatives. . . . The British alone are freehanded with information, particularly if it reflects ill upon the French or Italians' territorial ambitions. They are tightmouthed mainly regarding their commercial plans."

Convinced that the British would favor Greek claims in Turkey, the Italians—while putting up a united front—decided to gamble on their own. Count Sforza, the shrewd Italian High Commissioner in Constantinople, began conducting secret meetings with potential Turkish rebels who might be counted on to defy the Allies and, if they succeeded, show their gratitude to those who had helped them. Kemal's defiant newspaper articles aroused Sforza's interest. Through Turkish journalists and other intermediaries, he encouraged Kemal's plans for a militant nationalist movement. Sforza went so far as to offer Kemal arms as well as moral support, and at a face-to-face meeting he even offered Italian protection: "You may be sure," he said, "that if you are in trouble this Embassy is at your disposal." A year later, when British suspicions were thoroughly aroused, the Italians heatedly denied any dealings with Kemal. Lord Curzon did not believe them: "They have been intriguing everywhere," he said.

Kemal had already connived with Kiazim Karabekir, the leader of the Turkish Caucasian forces, when Kiazim had passed through

Constantinople on his way to assume the northeastern command. Kiazim was to "prepare the ground" for Kemal's arrival while Kemal was seeking a legitimate excuse to join him; their mutual aim would be to prepare to defy the rumored peace terms, particularly the prospect of an independent Armenia sanctioned by the Great Powers.

Kemal's chance came early in the spring of 1919, when lawlessness in the Caucasus and on the Black Sea, where the Greeks had a considerable population, had reached alarming proportions. Despite reports that the Turks were attacking the Christians in these areas, and despite the fear of widespread massacre, the Allies were unwilling to supply the personnel required to bring about order. Instead, they resorted to their age-old policy of leaving the matter to the Turkish government, whose only effectual leadership at that moment consisted of a number of Kemal's fellow conspirators. Not too surprisingly, Kemal was chosen as the man to go to the Caucasus and limit Kiazim's authority. His orders, which Kemal himself had helped to draw up, enjoined him to restore law and order, confiscate and store all arms and ammunition, disband groups under unofficial army protection, and prohibit further recruitment and distribution of arms. In order to do this he was to have virtual control over ten provinces. By the time certain Allied quarters decided that Kemal might not be the most reliable man for the job, he was already on his way to the northeast, armed with his passes and, according to his latest biographer, Lord Kinross, "biting his lips with excitement at his indescribable luck." If the Italians had not actually instigated Kemal's selection, they had most assuredly encouraged it; the pass in his pocket had been issued at Count Sforza's request.

As Kemal was joyfully charting his trip, Italian claims were disturbing the peace at the Peace Conference back in Paris, where the Italian and American chiefs of state tangled over the disposition of Fiume. The Adriatic port city had been promised to Italy under the secret Treaty of London signed in 1915 by England, France, Italy, and Russia. Finding himself in still another bind when the question came up in Paris, Lloyd George, according to Harold Nicolson, "had been able with charming evasiveness to throw upon President Wilson the brunt of the controversy." The President saw the disposition of Fiume as an issue critical to his principles: A surrender to Prime Minister Orlando would be a surrender to the secret treaties. "In America there is disgust with the old order of things," he declared on April 19, 1919. He rejected Orlando's maneuver to claim Fiume on the principle of self-determination, countering that "Fiume is only an island of Italian population," and that if the suburbs were taken into account the city would be predominantly Slav. The American President was "ready to fight" for his position that if Trieste went to Italy, Yugoslavia was entitled to Fiume.

Faced with an impasse, Orlando and his no less obstinate Foreign Minister, Sonnino, threatened to walk out of the Conference. Colonel House wrote in his diary: "The whole world is speculating as to whether the Italians are 'bluffing' or whether they really intend going home and not signing the Peace unless they have Fiume. It is not unlike a game of poker." On April 24 Wilson appealed to public opinion by releasing his views on Fiume to the press and publicizing Italian intransigence. Enraged, Orlando and Sonnino stalked out of the Conference the next day. By the time they returned, Italian moves in Turkey had advanced enormous mischief.

The Italians had been engaged in some unauthorized maneuvers even before their Paris walkout. On March 12 an Italian battleship, the *Regina Elena*, slid into the harbor of the Turkish Mediterranean seaport of Adalia—about two hundred and twenty-five miles southeast of Smyrna. The ship's commander called on the governor of the town and announced that because of bandit activity in the area, the Italians had come "to take charge of the security of the town." The governor's rejection of this explanation was followed, the same night, by a mysterious explosion in a building adjoining the home of an Italian bank director. Three hundred Italian sailors thereupon disembarked and occupied Adalia. Five days later these detachments were replaced by swift-footed Italian marines (*bersaglieri*) from the island of Rhodes. The Italian diplomats had scarcely left Paris when word reached the Conference that Italian forces were moving up the coastline toward Smyrna, occupying town after town along the way.

Of the Big Three, Lloyd George and President Wilson were by now disturbed, and Wilson thoroughly angered, by the high-handedness of the Italian moves. The Council had as yet made no disposition of the Turkish coastal area, nor for that matter of Adalia, which the Italians had now seemingly pre-empted, apparently in alarmed response to the fact that Venizelos had laid his case for Greek control of Smyrna before the Council on February 3 and had impressed his audience favorably. It was now the Council's turn to be alarmed. Seven Italian warships already lay at anchor in Smyrna harbor, and as Italian forces advanced, the prospect of their occupying that city appeared imminent. There were not many alternatives by way of counteraction. Lloyd George's suggestion that all the Allies send forces into Smyrna was greeted apathetically. Clemenceau was not about to volunteer French troops. The American President politely refused, explaining that he could not volunteer American aid, since his country had never been at war with Turkey.

At this juncture Lloyd George proposed that the Council authorize the Greeks to occupy Smyrna in the name of the Allies. His suggestion had a precedent: A few months before, when French naval forces had mutinied at the prospect of fighting Bolshevik troops in Odessa, the Allies had sent Greek troops to do the job. In Churchill's words: "Mr. Lloyd George asked for a decision that M. Venizelos might be authorized to send troops to be kept on board ship at Smyrna ready for landing in case of necessity. President Wilson asked why the troops should not be landed at once since the men did not keep in good condition on board ship. Lloyd George did not demur."

But diplomacy requires discretion. Providentially, three weeks before, on April 12, Venizelos had presented to the Council a letter and accompanying documents protesting Turkish mistreatment of Greeks in the Smyrna region. The diplomatic pretext was thus conveniently at hand: The Greeks were ostensibly being authorized by the Allies to land forces in Smyrna in order to protect the Greek population of the area. As this was the same pretext the Italians had used—without authorization—at Adalia, they had little choice but to accede to the Greek landing when they returned to Paris. Yet the real purpose of the move was never in doubt. Moments after he had been informed of the decision, Venizelos telegraphed to Athens: "The occupation is activated because the Allies were informed that the Italians who have occupied Macri and Marmarisee [Makri and Marmaris, opposite Rhodes] intend next to occupy Bondroum [Bodrum]. Our ships will be escorted by English warships."

Surprised though he may have been when the offer suddenly was thrust upon him, Venizelos was nonetheless elated and hastened to assure the Big Three leaders that his troops would swiftly comply. On the same day, May 6, 1919, he telegraphed to the Greek High Commissioner at Constantinople: "Kindly inform very confidentially the French High Commissioner that I was advised today by the ministers of England and France, and by the President of the United States, that they had resolved among themselves immediately to occupy Smyrna by the Greek army." The Chiefs of State had indeed agreed to the matter "among themselves." Fearful of losing time and afraid that word might leak out to the Italians, they had not troubled to consult their advisers; but most diplomatic and virtually all military experts in every allied camp were skeptical of the venture. Captain Dayton of the United States battleship *Arizona*, anchored off the coast of Smyrna, later acknowledged that like most of his colleagues he had been nervous about the Greek landing. More than once he had urged at a conference of Allied naval officers that the city be occupied and policed by inter-Allied detachments, at least to insure order before the Greeks should be permitted to land. But the English, it appeared, "were for letting the Greeks run the whole show alone." As it happened the Greeks were eager, and no one else was willing.

CHAPTER IV

The whole responsibility was thrown on the Greeks, who landed among a population, as far as the Turks were concerned, more insulted by their advent than the white citizens of Mobile would be if it were given over to a mandate of Negro troops.

GEORGE HORTON
The Blight of Asia

The show began at eight o'clock on the morning of May 15, 1919, when Captain Dayton sighted a British destroyer leading two Greek destroyers, six Greek transports, and the Greek battleship *Kilkis* into Smyrna harbor. The transports soon moved into piers and began disembarking Greek troops, to the applause and cheers of the majority who thronged the quayside.

The civilians were in a holiday mood and many were dressed accordingly. Most appeared to be Greeks, but among them were Armenians, Jews, and even some Turks, although the Turks were not cheering. The Greek Metropolitan, Chrysostomos, was there, too, venerably bearded and arrayed in the richly embroidered robes and mitre of his office. He blessed the troops, a Greek company performed a national dance—a needlessly tactless gesture, in the opinion of some foreign observers—and the troops proceeded toward the government house shouting "Viva!" and followed by an enthusiastic crowd. As they approached the Turkish barracks where several hundred Turkish soldiers and officers had been confined, on Allied orders, since the night before, and reached a point where some small Turkish boats were moored near the shoreline, a shot rang out and the spectacle diffused into panic. Civilians scrambled for safety as Greek soldiers began firing indiscriminately and a number of Greek civilians took advantage of the melee to round up Turks, or those they took to be Turks, and to club, kick, and abuse them. Turkish soldiers were marched out of the government barracks and some were likewise attacked. Random shots killed and wounded a number of bystanders. Within an hour a squall came up and a drenching rain cooled and dispersed the crowds. Violence meanwhile erupted in the Turkish quarter and in outlying villages, where a number of Greeks decided to settle old scores by robbing, raping, and killing Turkish civilians. When the reports were in, it appeared that from two to three hundred Turks and a hundred Greeks had been killed, and an undetermined number injured and molested.

There is little discrepancy among the recorded eyewitness accounts of the noonday scene, although there is a considerable variation in attitude. General Ali Nadi Pasha, the commandant of the Turkish army corps confined to the government barracks and later marched to a Greek steamer, was understandably indignant about the violence directed at his men (he reported forty fatalities), and especially outraged at the "terrible flow of insults that were thrown at us" and by the fact that the Greeks forced his men to shout "Long live Greece, long live Venizelos," as they were marched along the quay. American observers were distressed that the violence had broken out but relieved that it had been quickly arrested. "That no more serious trouble occurred than actually did occur is a matter for congratulations," wrote an American resident. He was not alone in finding it incredible that the Allies should have sent Greek troops "to occupy or police a town with such a large inimicable population." Consul Horton agreed: "What is very evident to me is that the acts of savagery and violence committed by the Greeks immediately after their landing are so natural that they could have been foreseen by anyone familiar with human nature," he wrote. "These people had been driven from their homes, their relatives had been murdered, their women violated; very probably in the army of occupation there were many who had either resided in Asia Minor or who had relatives or friends here." The violence in outlying districts, Horton noted, was committed by Greeks who had been horse-whipped, whose daughters had been raped, and who until that day "had no recourse whatever but to endure." Joining in praise for those Greek community leaders who immediately went about counseling restraint and order in the villages, Horton noted: "That it could be so restored was nothing less than a miracle when one considers the persecutions which the Greeks had so recently suffered."

No one could be certain who had fired the first shot on the quay and thus instigated the fracas. "Reports indicate it was fired by the Turks from some concealed position," wrote Captain Dayton. Some Americans believed it had come from a small Turkish boat anchored by the shore. The chief of the American hospital, who had been riding along the quayside on horseback and, much to his embarrassment, receiving an ovation from onlookers mistaking him for an exalted Greek official, stated that the Greek soldiers had responded to the initial shot by firing in panic. "Every minute or so through excitement one would discharge his gun and then the rest would start to fire indiscriminately," he reported. "Twice I rode up to the end of the line and commanded them to cease firing, which they did."

The Greeks insisted that the Italians had precipitated the violence, noting that the smoke had scarcely cleared before the senior Italian naval officer was knocking at the British Admiral's door, exulting that the Greeks were obviously incapable of maintaining a peaceful occupation. No one could deny that criminal elements might easily have been involved, after investigation disclosed that all the prisoners in the Smyrna jail had mysteriously been allowed to escape the night before the Greek landing.

Within three days of the occupation the Greek command had forced restitution of a large portion of stolen property, offered payment of one thousand Turkish gold pounds to the *vali* in recompense for his temporary confinement (the *vali* is said to have indignantly refused the sum), and had rounded up and tried fifty-four persons, largely Greeks, who had been active in the disorders. These were tried and sentenced in a military court—three to death, four to hard labor for life, and the rest to hard labor for a number of years ranging from two to twenty. The penalties were severe and the executions conducted in public to provide a harsh example to the Christian population. An inter-Allied investigating team, however, later held this punitive action against the Greeks, on the ground that it constituted a tacit admission of guilt.

Scarcely a week after the landing, on May 21, Venizelos appointed a fellow Cretan named Aristedes Sterghiades to the post of civil governor of Smyrna. A stern, humorless man with unbending reserve and a flinty temper, Sterghiades proceeded to refuse all social engagements and to live in seclusion lest he be accused of partiality toward his countrymen. Since any Greek ruler would have been anathema to the Turks, Sterghiades' behavior had no favorable effect on their attitude but only served to alienate his fellow Greeks, for his zealous impartiality often led him, in cases of conflict between a Turk and a Christian, to lean toward the Turk. His well-known temper and tactlessness, moreover, led to spectacular, though relatively minor, crises—as when he slapped a Greek priest in the face one day as the cleric was being formally presented to him in a country village. It seemed that during the journey to the village someone had told Sterghiades about a priest who had refused to officiate at a child's funeral because the family was too poor to pay the fee. Sterghiades had wrongly concluded that this was the priest in question, and had acted on his assumption. He was not, however, a man to apologize. On learning of his error he simply ordered one of his aides to "give the man a hundred drachmas for his poor."

One of Sterghiades' first acts was to close the houses of prostitution; if these were run by foreigners, over whom he had no jurisdiction, he posted sentries at the entrances to take down the names of all the patrons. The zeal with which he suppressed gambling as well did not endear him to Smyrna's sportier natives. But he did institute a number of popular reforms, among them the organization and improvement of sanitary conditions. He was markedly generous and cooperative toward educational institutions, and he gave an unprecedented impetus to Turkish primary education in Smyrna. Although one secondary school building was taken over for use as a court of law, the Greek administration supported a polytechnic school at Smyrna for over two hundred poor Moslem children and opened another Turkish high school as well. Still, periodic murders of Greek officials in outlying villages, and the retaliatory burning of Turkish homes when the Turks refused to name the assassins, marred the Greek occupation, and the Turks grew increasingly implacable.

Their reaction to the Greek occupation had manifested itself first in stunned disbelief. Many Turks had assumed—some had even hoped—that the British would come to rule them. ("If we must be punished let it be by our old friend England.") "We *wanted* them to come," a merchant in the Turkish quarter moaned to his Armenian employee on the morning of the occupation. He had once visited Egypt and been forever impressed with British rule. "We *wanted* them to take over the country! But they sent the Greeks! This is impossible!" The Sultan stumbled from his Council chambers in tears when he heard the news, and as shock gave way to outrage, his Interior Minister's exclamation, "By God, what an impertinence!" struck the keynote of Turkish sentiment from palace to hamlet.

Unchecked by the Allied censors, the news of the Smyrna landings and of the bloodshed at the docks and in the countryside reverberated wildly throughout Turkey, until the numbers of Turks allegedly massacred by the Greeks on May 15 swelled into the tens of thousands. The front pages of Turkish newspapers, heavily outlined in black, reprinted Wilson's Twelfth Point day after day (back in Paris the President confessed that he had forgotten exactly what he had proclaimed in that clause), and everywhere but in the Smyrna region the Turkish flag hung in crepe of mourning. Crowds gathered daily in the squares of towns and villages; priests intoned prayers for the Smyrna martyrs; and fiery speakers aroused the masses into hysterical mobs in scenes reeking with melodrama. Two hundred thousand swore vengeance at the Sultan Ahmed Mosque in Constantinople, while a French general standing by—"A Frenchman by birth but a Turk at heart"—wept unashamedly. A young man cried out "My nation, my poor nation!" and fell to the ground in a dead faint. And everywhere Turks armed themselves. Six months later an American intelligence report noted, "The Smyrna affair as a clarion call to Turkish nationalism has been worked to the limit."

During these months the handful of British officers supervising the execution of the armistice terms in the interior were, in Churchill's words, "first ignored, then insulted, then chased for their lives or flung into arduous captivity. The 'dumps' in which the equipment of considerable armies had already been gathered passed in a week from British to Turkish control." Arriving in Samsun four days after the Greek landings in Smyrna, Kemal found the situation riper for a massive rebellion than he could have dreamed. For his purposes, the Council's action in sending the Greeks to Smyrna had provided the ultimate gift.

In Smyrna province Turkish guerrillas were meanwhile harassing the Greek forces. Horton reported that on June 15 "strong and well armed" Turkish forces had driven the Greek garrison of eleven thousand men from Bergama, about fifty-five miles from Smyrna. The Greeks had retreated to Menemen but had been so badgered along the way that only six hundred had reached that city alive. The Turks, Horton wrote, appeared to be operating with "perfect liberty."

The Allies found themselves more concerned with restraining Greeks than Turks. While giving Venizelos its hasty approval for the landings, the Council had not yet, unbelievable as it seems, defined the Greek zone of occupation. After the Italian delegation returned to the fold, the Council set the Greek limits of occupation at within three kilometers of the city. By then the Greek forces had fanned out in three directions, toward towns and villages which had considerable Greek population.

By mid-June Venizelos was pleading with the Supreme Council to formally extend the Greek zone so that his forces might repel Turkish attacks. The Greek leader continued his protests after signing an agreement with Italy which defined Greek and Italian areas of influence. Turkish attacks, he insisted, were being launched with impunity from Italian-held territory and with considerable material and moral encouragement from the Italians.

Ignoring his pleas, the Council responded with alacrity to the mounting indignation of the Turks by appointing four representatives to an Inter-Allied Commission of Inquiry on the Smyrna Landings. As fate and power politics would have it, the inquiry placed the Greeks in the position of the accused and the Italians among the judges already predisposed against them. Because the Greeks were neither permitted to hear the charges against them nor to present witnesses of their own, pressure from Lloyd George caused the Commission's report to be suppressed. Its conclusions were nonetheless leaked to the Turkish press, where they appeared in variously distorted versions. Even in their original form the conclusions were sufficiently damning to the Greeks. The landings were deemed unjustified because the Commission had uncovered no evidence to support Venizelos's charge that the Smyrna Greeks had been mistreated by the Turks. Since such evidence exists, there is some doubt as to whether any serious attempt was made to uncover it; since in any case the charge had merely provided an excuse for the landings, the Commission's accusation—in effect—of an unwarranted invasion let the Council neatly off the hook and saddled the Greeks with the blame for having landed at all.

The Commission condemned the Greeks for showing "all the manifestations of an annexation" in their occupation, although it did not explain how an annexation, as opposed to an occupation, was manifested; and it went on to concede that if the Greeks were permitted to occupy the area they had to be allowed to "annex" the territory and the Greek commandant given "freedom of action vis à vis Turkish forces." Whenever it found the Greeks guilty of instigating violence, as in two instances, the Commission did not hesitate to say so. In three instances when it absolved the Greeks, however, the writers were careful not to put responsibility on the Turks but merely on "hatreds which existed for centuries between Turks and Greeks." In this vein, the Turkish authorities were not held responsible for the mass exodus from the jail the night before the Greek landings, but were gently rapped for "taking no steps to prevent" the wholesale escapes. As for violence which erupted during the landing itself, the Greeks had acknowledged their guilt when they punished the culprits.

The writers of the report, Admiral Mark L. Bristol and his chief intelligence officer, had evidently expended considerable effort in wording the conclusions, and the Admiral was so pleased with the results that he urged the United States Secretary of State to give them wide publicity "to insure accurate information to our people and not information colored by European interpretation of the true facts." The Admiral, who was chairman of the Commission and about to be appointed U.S. High Commissioner at Constantinople, had scarcely needed an investigation to determine the true facts. Three days after the Greek landings at Smyrna he had already made up his mind in Constantinople: "The actions of the Greeks came as no surprise to the people in this country who know the character of the Greeks," he had noted in his diary of May 18, 1919. In a letter to a naval colleague he was even more explicit: "To me it is a calamity to let the Greeks have anything in this part of the world. The Greek is about the worst race in the Near East."

CHAPTER V

He who owns the oil will own the world.
HENRI BERENGER
Letter to Clemenceau
December 12, 1919

Genial, self-assured, and zealously committed to serving his country's interests, Admiral Mark L. Bristol was the prototype of the dedicated American diplomat of his day. In certain navy circles it was snidely rumored that the Admiral was better suited to State Department duty than to naval strategy or command, but his navy connection was eminently appropriate in the Near East, where American naval power provided the aristocratic right arm of American diplomacy. The American position had emerged Januslike from the war, with two faces determinedly fixed in opposite directions. One, bearing a remarkable resemblance to Miss Liberty, gazed benignly on her own shores and righteously disclaimed foreign entanglements. The other, eagle-eyed, searched out opportunities abroad for economic penetration.

Before the First World War the United States had not officially concerned itself with a Near Eastern policy, other than to nod support of British policy on the principle that what was good for

Britain could not be bad for America. But the war brought about a technological revolution and threw industrial leaders into a position of intimacy with government. The result was that by 1919, encouraged by a vastly strengthened United States Chamber of Commerce, the State Department had adopted an aggressive policy on behalf of American business. The effect in certain quarters was prodigious, as the official history of the Standard Oil Company (New Jersey) testifies: "For years American businessmen had practiced their 'dollar diplomacy' abroad in the face of indifference to their ventures on the part of the State Department. The year 1919 marked the end of this period. . . . The fact that the State Department commenced to extend its active support to American businessmen abroad is not only of utmost significance to this period of Jersey Standard's history, but is fundamental to an understanding of the Jersey Company today." The jackpot was purported to be immense. "The opportunities for the expansion of American interests in the Near East are practically unlimited," the United States Chamber of Commerce for the Levant announced in 1919. "In fact, with the conclusion of peace, there is the economic structure of an empire to be developed." The postwar American policy toward Turkey was based on the disarmingly simple proposition that the economic cake could be both eaten and had, by disclaiming political responsibility while insisting on equality of opportunity. Success, it was reasoned, lay in exploiting the American advantage, which was considerable.

Countries that had been overtly imperialistic throughout the Victorian age were by now at pains to rationalize their position, if only because past performance and future aspirations were hard to reconcile in modern times. As Harold Nicolson noted of the British, "After 1919, the issue of imperialism was stated in terms of democratic theory, and in such terms it could not be logically defended. Once we substituted a political theory for benevolent autocracy we were lost. . . . It was unfortunate that we should have tried to substitute a democratic justification for what was in fact an imperial need."

No such conflict of principle troubled the United States in those days. Her spokesmen could, and often did, invoke her very existence as proof of her anti-imperialism—any hanky-panky indulged in on her own continent had yet to plague her. She alone of the victorious Powers was unsullied by revelations of self-serving treaties and questionable alliances, and her President was living

57

proof of her dominant concern for the welfare of small nations. Where others were exposed in the act of clawing at the remains of the Turkish empire, Americans had a trail of mission schools, hospitals, and orphanages to show that their concern was pure philanthropy. Moreover, the United States was the one victorious Power which had refused, at the behest of the missionary interests, to declare war on Turkey, so she could not be counted among that country's enemies.

Admiral Bristol's efforts, as American High Commissioner at Constantinople and ranking United States diplomat in Turkey, were directed at maintaining his country's beneficent reputation among the Turks. One of his first acts was to convince missionary and relief personnel in Turkey that it was the better part of wisdom and Christian charity to extend alms to the Turks as well as to their victims. There was no denying their need—the war had left unprecedented numbers of Turkish widows and orphans who were obtaining no assistance from their own government. When some relief workers protested that their funds had been gathered in the name of those who had been victimized by the Turks and that diverting this money would amount to misappropriation, Bristol suggested that they return to the States and bone up on their Bibles. The Admiral grinned when one outspoken lady threatened to publicize the new policy on her return to America. She was to understand why when she repeated her design to the executive director of the Near East Relief. "Not a newspaper in the country will print your story," he told her. The agency was by now working under Congressional charter and continued to maintain close ties with the press as well as with the Department of State.

Much of the Admiral's time was devoted to persuading key missionary personnel to join forces with the business community. If they expected to remain in Turkey they would have to realize, he said, that their "interests depend very largely upon our American business interests." Bristol was inexorably opposed to accepting an American mandate over Armenia. The Europeans, he wrote, "are going to try to get a division of the spoils, and then force us into taking the mandate for the so-called Armenia. This would . . . give us a territory practically desolate, without natural resources and with practically no railroad communication or real seaports. To use a slang expression, 'we would be given the lemon.'"

Bristol advocated an American mandate over the whole of Turkey. In urging this policy on the philanthropists, educators, and missionaries, he adopted a benevolent outlook: "It is a task worthy of America to stand up for the big idea of cleaning up the whole of the Ottoman Empire by once and forever destroying all European influences and concessions and, therefore, European intrigue in this unfortunate country, and then giving all these people good government. . . ." With his business contacts he used a more direct approach: "It [Turkey] is practically a virgin field for American business and American financial exploitation. The Turks want us, the Americans, because they believe we have no political string tied to our operations."

A number of educators had been independently altering their views on the mandate question, although not altogether for the reasons Bristol advocated. After an extended tour through Asia Minor in the spring of 1919, President Caleb Gates of Robert College feared that the delay in setting up peace terms, and the intransigence of the heavily armed Turkish population "that is in no sense repentant for its deeds and has not undergone any change of mind regarding the Armenians" would spell disaster if Armenians were put in charge of an area where Moslems predominated, as they now did in the area contemplated. After what the Turks had done, they feared the Armenians, "and a malefactor who is afraid for his life is always the most dangerous kind of criminal." Gates had no great hope that sufficient troops would be made available to guard the entire region and he therefore feared that the Armenians would be butchered before any Allied or American troops could rescue them. He, too, urged a protectorate for the whole of the Turkish Empire and trusted that as Armenians began to return to their provinces and their numbers increased, the Turks and Kurds would move away, the Armenians' affinity for industry would lead to prosperity and strength, and home rule might eventually be practicable.

Bristol gave himself credit for this change of view and did his best to propagate it along diplomatic as well as missionary channels. He was pleased to note that "as time goes on I find that this idea is becoming more or less universal." A believer in "pitiless publicity," he urged business contacts to promote his views in the United States. (To L. I. Thomas, a director of Standard Oil, he suggested: "I have tried to get our business men to reconcile the differences with the benevolent institutions and in the same way have pointed out to the missionaries, educators and philanthropists that their interests depend very largely upon our American business interests. I have met with a good deal of success in this but at the same time would suggest some work along the same line in New York.") Wilson remained adamantly against the idea of an American mandate over all of Turkey, but many of his advisers were soon converted.

Since American businessmen were not universally enthusiastic about investing in Turkey's future, Bristol spent a good deal of his time squiring prospective investors around Constantinople, urging them to gain the good will of influential Turks or assuring them through the mails that the jackpot was immense. "The Turks do not understand the way in which we hang back," he wrote to an exporter, "and if we do not seize the opportunity it will pass to the nationals of other countries." He put up, as he said, "a constant fight to get our Americans to go and do their own business and not link up with foreigners and especially with foreigners in this part of the world." He fought for "one hundred per cent American investment" and "one hundred per cent American personnel." He was all the more opposed to Greek influence in Turkey when he observed that in Greece, British firms were being favored with business concessions. This he did not consider "fair and square." ("My policy is simply, in a nutshell, working for a fair deal to everyone.") "I am," he said, "for the U.S. first, last and always."

After hours the Admiral plunged into a busy social life. His magnetically deep, ringing voice and candid manner captivated his Turkish friends. "Yet there were moments, and subjects, that made him reserved," wrote an admirer, "when his eyebrows drew together and one had to walk delicately or draw one's own conclusions and let it go at that. There was never an instant's doubt where one stood with Admiral Bristol."

Nor was there any doubt where Admiral Bristol stood on certain subjects. He was not alone in regarding the Greek occupation of the Smyrna region as a British trick to extend that country's influence in the Near East, but he was more forthright than most. "We fought to destroy the Prussian power, we may still have to fight to destroy the British power," he wrote. He made no attempt to get along with the Allied High Commissioners or to hide his opinion that the European Powers were commercial opportunists. Although the United States was ostensibly uncommitted, he also aired his opinions on the relative worth of the Near Eastern peoples with little inhibition.

"The Armenians are a race that deserve small consideration," he liked to write; or, "Armenians are a race like the Jews; they have little or no national spirit and have poor moral character." To prove his impartiality he sometimes claimed that he was equally prejudiced toward all Near Easterners: "I am holding no brief for any race in the Near East. I believe that if the Turk, the Greek, the Armenian, the Syrian, etc., were shaken up in a bag you would not know which one would come out first, but probably the Turk is the best one of the lot. . . . I have not so much hope for these other races." The Armenians and Greeks, he insisted, "have many flaws and deficiencies of character that do not fit them for self-government," while "the Turk has some individual traits of character that are so far superior to those of other races that one is led to sympathize with the Turk even though you never forget the bad traits of his character that are illustrated by the acts committed against subjugated races."

The Admiral showed that he was informed about these acts in disarmingly candid discourse with his Turkish friends. He warned them that if they did not practice more forbearance it would be impossible to change the attitude of the American people toward them. When Suad Bey, a Turkish aristocrat, "tried to claim that the Christian races had been treated in a tolerant way, I pointed out to him that the Christian races, ordinarily spoken of as 'rayah' were really slaves in the country and so long as they behaved as slaves they were allowed religious freedom and treated by their masters very well. They did not allow the Christians to serve in the army and thus further degraded them. When a Christian died the head of the community had to get permission to bury him and the letters granting such permission were in the nature of orders written by a Moslem official, who took occasion in these letters to make the Christian understand that he was a vile infidel of unclean carcass and even used the words, 'the carcass of an unclean swine, etc.' It was only natural that the Christian races under such conditions would resent their treatment."

Within a year the Department of State was forced to ask him to restrain himself. It did so gently: "The Department feels confident that the reported attitude is wrong and has been unintentional on your part but you are nevertheless requested to make no expressions whatever which may be construed as unfriendly toward the Greeks or show favoritism to the Turks." The Admiral was unperturbed. "I am even accused of being pro-Turk," he confided to President Gates, "but such things do not bother me fortunately because I believe there is only one correct road to follow and that is the right road." Thereafter the Admiral presumably allowed his eyebrows to carry his message in public and was more restrained in his correspondence with a host of business acquaintances, writers, and friends.

As news filtered to Constantinople that violence against Christians was on the increase, Bristol found it expedient to discount or minimize such reports as "propaganda from unreliable sources" and to counteract by urging "pitiless publicity as to the true facts." It mattered little that the reports had come from American consular officials, relief workers, or United States military intelligence officers, and that there was no evidence to contradict them. He didn't put much stock in these reports, the Admiral insisted, and indeed at times his own reports and correspondence bore little resemblance to the eyewitness accounts he had received. Recognizing his selective preference, certain of Bristol's subordinates went so far as to play to his prejudices, at times so blatantly that in June 1919, the Commander of the United States (Naval) Forces in European Waters was forced to rebuke the tone of certain reports emanating from Bristol's command. He took particular offense at a report concerning the Greek occupation of Smyrna, and its references to the work of the Paris Peace Conference. Not only was the style flippant and improper, the Commander complained, but the remarks about the Peace Conference were "of a nature to deserve a worse characterization than that." To be sure, Admiral Bristol had no great use for the views of some of the American delegates in Paris. An American contact in that city wrote him, confidentially, that he could count more on the French to work "unconsciously" for his policy than the Americans.

Bristol took special pains with writers and journalists. He exchanged some anti-Semitic guffaws with Kenneth Roberts, and congratulated Arnold Toynbee for "preaching one thing all the time, and that is that not one of the Eastern nationalities is civilized in the Western sense."* He briefed newspapermen generously as to who was and was not reliable "in this part of the

---

* After a trip to Anatolia where he viewed the Greco-Turkish hostilities from the vantage point of the Turkish Red Crescent, Toynbee's attitude had undergone a traumatic reversal. The shock of seeing Turks as victims when he had envisioned them as monsters led him to repudiate his earlier writings condemning them for their actions against the Armenians.

world [where people] falsify the information they give out." "Today I had a long talk with Richard Eaton, who is writing a book on the Balkans," he wrote in his diary. "He said he was going to see Meletios, the Armenian Patriarch. [Meletios was actually the Greek Patriarch.] I warned him that he is a native of one of these races and like the rest of them probably doesn't know the difference between truth and falsehood." He urged writers to visit areas where, in the course of the fighting, Greeks were inflicting damage on Turks. His influence was considerable. American newsmen could not hope to get much beyond Constantinople without their High Commissioner's blessing, and the High Commissioner made it clear that his blessing was contingent on their efforts to "protect my interests." The majority had no choice but to agree. They needed passes for travel into the interior; to some areas the only means of conveyance was by American destroyer.

In the course of carrying relief supplies to starving Armenians in the Russian Caucasus, these destroyers plied their way between Constantinople and Batum carrying selected journalists, intelligence officers, American businessmen, and oil prospectors. Never before had the Navy been put to such active peacetime use: "The Navy not only assists our commercial firms to obtain business but when business opportunities present themselves American firms are notified and given full information on the subject," a Navy source disclosed. "One destroyer is continuously kept at Samsun, Turkey, to look after American tobacco interests at that port. By utilizing the wireless of destroyers in Turkish ports, at Durazzo and elsewhere, commercial messages have been put through without delay. . . . Destroyers are entering Turkish ports with business 'drummers' as regular passengers and their fantails piled high with American samples. An American destroyer has made a special trip at thirty knots to get American oil prospectors into a newly opened field."

The oil race—soon to become the oil war, albeit a cold one— was the most crucial of Bristol's concerns. He had assumed his duties in Constantinople just as it was dawning on American ruling circles that the British had outwitted them, hands down, by staking out the untapped oil resources of Persia and the Mosul (Mesopotamia)—a find truly as wonderful as Aladdin's—while in the United States the domestic oil supplies that had been smugly regarded as inexhaustible were running alarmingly short of a rapidly accelerating demand. The motorcar had already begun to prove its thirst for the liquid fuel (and the American public its yen for the motorcar), and there was the more vital matter of fuel for industrial machines and for a new oil-driven United States merchant fleet.

A generation before, only a handful of visionaries had foreseen the supremacy of oil. One, a peppery British naval captain named Fisher, had in the 1880's so persistently proselytized his belief that the future of the British navy hinged on converting the coal-driven fleet to oil that his skeptical colleagues had dubbed him "the oil maniac." Fisher's clairvoyance served his country well when he became First Lord of the Admiralty, in 1904, and set about propagating his doctrine in terse memos that converted some crucial industrialists and statesmen to his point of view. Said Fisher:

"It is an economic waste of good material to keep men grilling in a baking fire hole at unnecessary labour and use three hundred men when a dozen or so will suffice."

"It is a criminal folly to allow another pound of coal on board a fighting ship."

Not only did the oil engine provide economy of storage and labor, but, as Winston Churchill perceived long before he came to head the Admiralty, it also provided enormous naval advantage in time of war. Oil-driven ships could travel faster, since oil gave seventy per cent more heat than coal, and an oil fleet could sail for fifty-seven days without stopping to refuel, in contrast to fourteen days for coal-driven ships. Great Britain's fleet was supreme because she owned coaling stations along the world trade routes where ships could refuel only with her permission. For the same reason she could charge lower freight rates and beat her rivals to world trade. But from the moment that ships began to use oil rather than coal, the balance could shift. Before the turn of the century Britain had virtually no oil at all, while the United States controlled eighty per cent of the world's supply.

Grasping the situation, Churchill disclosed to the House of Commons in 1913 a ploy whereby the Admiralty would "become the owners, or at any rate the controllers at the source, of at least a proportion of the supply of natural oil which we require."

In 1914 the British government took possession of the Anglo-Persian Oil Company, a corporation created just after the turn of the century when one William D'Arcy, an English prospector, obtained from the Persian Shah the Arabian Nights promise (it turned out to be no fantasy) of what amounted to all the oil in Persia. D'Arcy had been staking his claim at about the same time —1898—that Sultan Abdul Hamid was promising his Mesopotamian oil to both the German Kaiser and a friendly American Admiral, Colby Chester.

Chester had been sent by the State Department to present an official protest to Hamid and to demand compensation on behalf of the American Board of Missions for certain properties destroyed in the course of the large-scale massacre of Armenians; but in the course of his visit he modified his mission considerably. As one of his business associates later boasted, the Admiral was well aware that these "unimportant" missionary claims "were whipped up by foreign interests . . . . Admiral Chester proved to Abdul Hamid and the Turkish officials that the American government and people were not inclined, as other nations were, to take advantage of the excuses afforded by the massacres of 1896 . . . and similar upsetting conditions, to 'hold up' the Turkish government in various ways." His humanitarian mission thus completed, the Admiral retired from the Navy and returned to Turkey with the official blessing of the United States Chamber of Commerce to 'hold up' the Sultan himself, or at least to collect a reward for his tact. No less shrewd than the Admiral, Hamid magnanimously offered Chester the exploitation rights to the Mosul oil fields and to the lands stretching for thousands of miles along the route of the incipient Berlin-to-Bagdad railway; in fact the very same rights he was simultaneously offering to the German Kaiser. Oblivious of this formidable competition, Chester returned home elated and began whipping up interest among American investors.

By 1912, three years after Hamid's downfall, it was apparent to all but Chester that the German interests had won out. These, with the help of Sir Ernest Cassel (German-born, though a British citizen) and an intermediary named Calouste Gulbenkian, formed the Turkish Petroleum Company, with the German Deutsche Bank, the Royal Dutch Shell, and the National Bank of Turkey as partners, and with half of Turkey's share coming from Cassel. In 1914, only months before war erupted, the government-owned Anglo-Persian company took over Cassel's share in Turkish Petroleum and bought out Turkey's share as well from the Young Turk government. When war came, the British confiscated Germany's share in the venture and promised it to France. Thus, when the war

65

ended, the British, together with the French and the neutral Dutch, had a tight hold on the greatest oil find in history. Royal Dutch Shell was American Standard Oil's greatest competitor.

"The Allies floated to victory on a wave of oil," Lord Curzon proclaimed in November 1918. The Americans had perceived the technological advantage in time to construct an oil-driven merchant fleet before their entry into the European theater. But even when the price of oil had risen at a rate genuinely alarming to the United States Navy, American dedication to Free Enterprise had been intense enough to prevent any serious effort at government control, much less governmental entry into the oil business. And while America had stubbornly refused to declare war against Turkey, the British had directed their military strategy in the eastern theater with the oil fields very much in mind. Their dwindling forces in Turkey were now concentrated in such key areas.

Because it was the transportation of oil that made the fuel prohibitively expensive to market, old John D. Rockefeller had himself tapped a gold mine some years before when he devised the idea of putting down pipelines. His Jersey Standard Company's activities abroad had been primarily concerned with transporting and refining the crude oil of other producers. It was not until after the war, when pipeline technology and tanker fleets abounded, that the Standard Oil Company of New Jersey committed itself to hunting down sources of crude oil wherever they could be found, with the result, as its historians have noted, that "all phases of the Company's foreign activities became complicated in the web of international and political intrigue."

In February 1919, while the peace settlement hovered uneasily over the conference tables in Paris, Standard Oil president Walter Teagle, still unaware that the British had long since pre-empted him, was writing a memorandum to his directors from New York: "In the settlement of the division of Turkey, consideration should be given to the oil possibilities. . . . I am wondering if there is any way we can get into the oil producing end of the game in Mesopotamia." Company representatives were sent to Paris, where they confronted the ominous possibility that the British might be planning to dominate that end of the game to the exclusion of American interests; a prospect that the company officials considered "a greater menace to Jersey's business than a German victory would have been."

Standard Oil Company prospectors, who had meanwhile been

sent out to scour the globe, reported that they were being denied entry into strategic areas in Persia, Mesopotamia, and wherever the British were in control. A company agent was arrested in Jerusalem for attempting to prospect in Palestine. The British government countered American protests by insisting it had enacted similar prohibitions against its own geologists and those of Royal Dutch Shell, but the Americans were not reassured, and with good reason: Shell later acknowledged possession of detailed maps and charts of areas their geologists were ostensibly forbidden to enter. American oil men were all the more incensed to discover that the British were quietly buying their way into what Americans considered their own territory by obtaining controlling shares in certain companies in Central and South America.

Admiral Bristol's Anglophobia was in no way soothed by reports of these machinations, nor by the discovery that the British would no longer guarantee to fuel his ships. As a Navy man he had warm feelings for the precious fuel and warm contacts, besides, with officials of Standard Oil. Early in 1920, E. J. Sadler—a company director—made a special trip to Constantinople ("where his Annapolis background stood him in good stead") and briefed the Admiral at length on the Mesopotamian situation. Sadler suggested that "until the situation is entirely clear, and all interested parties have had an opportunity to explore the territory, we feel it would be the greatest injustice to allow any concessions to be taken . . . . We believe that no concession taken since the beginning of the War in 1914 up to the present should be held valid."

Concurring wholeheartedly, Bristol forwarded Sadler's views to the State Department with his strongest endorsement. It arrived, propitiously enough for Standard Oil, at a moment when alarm over the dwindling domestic oil supply was reaching a climax. (In May 1920 oil reserves were so low that Secretary of the Interior John Payne suggested that the Navy convert American merchant and fighting ships from oil back to coal. Secretary of the Navy Josephus Daniels rejected the idea as "an impossible step backward.")

Then in July 1920 came the stunning disclosure that England and France had during April of that year secretly signed an agreement at San Remo, Italy, dividing between them Turkey's oil-rich territories. (On the same day that they had signed the San Remo Treaty, France and Britain had appealed to the United States to take a mandate over Armenia; the State Department found the request ill-timed, to say the least.) In dividing the prize, they had not felt bound to consult the United States because she had not chosen to enter the fight against Turkey. Besides, the British said, citing examples in the Western Hemisphere, the United States wasn't opening any doors herself.

The disclosure of the Anglo-French oil deal created a public stir in the United States, although there was no lack of admiration for Great Britain on the part of certain congressmen, senators, and the officialdom of the petroleum industry, who suddenly felt a lessening of their devotion to Free Enterprise and began clamoring for more government help. The State Department sprang into action and a full year before the Harding administration—with its notorious partiality for the oil business—came to office, the "open door" had become the official objective of American foreign policy.

CHAPTER VI

What valid work was ever for itself wrought solely, be it
war, art, statesmanship?

JOHN DAVIDSON
Smith

In Smyrna foreign businessmen, British included, were downcast
about having the Greeks in control of the area. The city was to all
practical purposes still run by foreigners. Of the two great railway
lines that branched north and east from the city, one was owned
by the British, the other by the French. Power and lighting were in
British hands; the waterworks were Belgian. The quay of Smyrna
and the tramway lines were French concessions. The important
licorice and tobacco interests were American, as were the oil depots
standing on the north end of the shoreline that curved to face the
city. The carpet, grain, mineral, and dried-fruit businesses were
largely run by British firms. The agent of a foreign company expressed the consensus when he told Consul Horton: "In Greece
proper you see few foreign companies working. Send away the
Greeks from here and leave us to exploit the Turks."

The Greeks had more influential opposition on the continent.
French financiers, although not displeased at efforts to undermine

Italian expansion, held sixty per cent of Turkey's prewar debt and recognized that a viable Turkey could more easily repay the debt. French bankers were unhappy, too, with the prospect that the contemplated peace treaty would internationalize control over the Berlin-to-Bagdad railway. They had held a thirty per cent share in the line when it was still under German control, and they saw no reason why they should not now dominate the works. (French investors were traditionally fond of ploughing their money into foreign enterprises. This did little either for the French national economy or for its labor force; it did wonders for their pockets with a minimum of effort.) Envisioning international control as British control, these French magnates favored a strong and independent Turkey that could call its terms—with their help.

In Britain, too, there was strong Conservative opposition to Lloyd George's Near Eastern policy. It was led by Sir Edwin Montague, the Secretary of State for India. Sensitive to the feelings of the Moslems in India, who were rallying behind the Hindus in Mahatma Gandhi's call for independence, the powerful India lobby wanted deferential treatment accorded the Moslem Turks. Wrote Winston Churchill, "Lord Curzon, mounted upon the Foreign Office, rode full tilt against Sir Edwin Montague whose chariot was drawn by the public opinion of India, the sensibilities of the Mohammedan world, the pro-Turkish propensities of the Conservative party and the voluminous memoranda of the India Office." Curzon had not approved sending the Greeks to Smyrna, but he considered England committed and was essentially behind Lloyd George's policy. He was especially insistent that in the peace settlement the Turks yield Constantinople to some sort of international control.

Most of the British military were on Montague's side. There were, as Churchill said, "the pro-Turkish inclinations of the British military mind." There was also the rampant opinion that Greece could not conquer the tide of increased Turkish resistance, for the military men saw better than anyone that the Greeks were very much on their own.

The Turkish rebels were meanwhile receiving some surprisingly deferential visitors from countries on whose behalf the Greeks were supposed to be operating against them. Traffic was heavy at Erzerum, where the rebellious Kiazim Karabekir was convening a Congress in July 1919 on behalf of his friend Kemal. The delegates had scarcely accepted a Declaration of Principles that would soon

70

become the Turkish National Pact, and elected Mustafa Kemal as President, when a telegram arrived from Constantinople ordering Kiazim to arrest Kemal on charges of disobeying orders. The timing of the order came as something of a joke.

Colonel A. Rawlinson of the British army was in Erzerum at about this time enjoying, or so he at first thought, Kiazim's cooperation in confiscating military equipment under the terms of the armistice and attempting to transfer by rail huge mounds of abandoned guns and ammunition across the Turkish frontier to two English army units awaiting them on the Russian side. It was not long before an inordinate number of "accidents" and "holdups" on the railway made the Colonel realize that Kiazim had no intention of yielding the stores. This discovery appears to have increased Rawlinson's admiration for the old fellow. After a number of bantering tête-à-têtes (Rawlinson: "Do you know how many dreadnoughts the British have?" Kiazim: "Every Turk is a dreadnought in himself. How can millions of dreadnoughts be taken under a mandate?" Rawlinson: "Your coffee is excellent. May I have another cup?") the Colonel returned to London, where he tried, we are told, as unsuccessfully as had Admiral Calthorpe, a signer of the original armistice, "to awaken the British government to the future potentialities of the Nationalist movement."

Americans were also courting the rebels. At the Congress of Sivas, which Kemal convened in September 1919 to set up the *de facto* Nationalist government, Louis Browne, an American newspaperman, appeared as the private emissary of Mr. Crane of the famous King-Crane commission. Kemal's chief propagandist, a fetching, emancipated Turkish lady named Halide Edib, was herself close to both Crane and Admiral Bristol, and it was she who had suggested Browne's visit. Her idea, as communicated to Kemal, was that an American mandate over the whole of Turkey might be "the least harmful solution." This, she noted, was the feeling in Constantinople.

A week after the Congress of Sivas had adjourned, U.S. Major General James G. Harbord arrived to visit the rebel stronghold in the course of his mission to investigate the possibilities for an American mandate over Armenia. To Harbord, Kemal insisted that the Turks would resist anything more than a "slight exercise of authority." Harbord, after reminding Kemal of Turkey's record in dealing with its minorities, said that a nation could hardly be expected to take on the responsibility of a mandate without the corresponding authority. According to Kemal's biographer, Lord Kinross, the Turkish leader then engaged in a metaphorical pantomime that converted Harbord to his side. He jerked apart a string of prayer beads, then proceeded to gather them from the floor, illustrating his intent to "draw the pieces of his country together, to save it from its various enemies, to make of it an independent and civilized state. . . . 'If we can't succeed,' he said, as he slowly closed his upturned palm, 'rather than fall into the palm of the enemy, like a bird . . . we prefer, being the sons of our forefathers, to die fighting.' "

Says Kinross, "Harbord was impressed with his resolution, his spirit. 'I had taken everything into account,' he said, 'but not that. Had we been in your place we should have done the same thing.' " Harbord has offered a more clinical version of the incident: "He was apparently under considerable strain and continually drew a string of prayer beads through his rather good-looking hands, never keeping them quiet for a minute. I learned later that he had recently been suffering from malaria and had fever at the time of our interview."

While the rebel chieftain was impressing his visitors, Vizier Damad Ferid, Turkey's legal representative, was pleading his country's case before the Peace Conference in Paris and being summarily dismissed. The Vizier expressed regret at Turkey's crimes, which he admitted had, during the last war, "been such as to make the conscience of mankind shudder with horror forever." The former regime was, however, now properly discredited, he said. In rejecting this apology the Council unconsciously gave a clue to a more pragmatic attitude when it stated that Turkey could not evade the consequences of having entrusted her affairs "into the hands of men who, utterly devoid of principle or pity, *could not even command success*." (Italics added.) In the political arena failure is, ultimately, the worst crime of all.

The Nationalists could not have failed to take a lesson from these encounters. There was the Grand Vizier, traveling all the way to Paris, humbly acknowledging that Turkey had sinned, and being rebuffed for his pains. Here, on the other hand, was Kemal, outlawed both by the Grand Vizier and the Great Powers themselves, acknowledging his defiance of both and being approached by Western luminaries, hats in hand.

French forces began replacing the British in the southeastern portions of Turkey in November 1919, and shortly afterward

Kemal received an impressive visitor in the person of Georges Picot, the French High Commissioner in Syria. Picot, allegedly without his government's blessing, announced himself as representing France and asked for Kemal's cooperation in Cilicia. Kemal's reply (in Kinross's words) that "unless the French show that they had no designs against the Turks in Cilicia they would fight there to defend their independence," seems to have impressed Picot as "a positive attitude." Soon afterward, the French press began to show signs of sympathy for Kemal's movement.

French political maneuvers became murkier as the new year, 1920, dawned and Millerand, with the backing of French financiers, replaced Clemenceau as Premier. The British had by then withdrawn the last of their forces from southeastern Turkey (Cilicia) and the French had reluctantly taken charge of this area, as well as the Ottoman lands farther southeast that now comprise Syria and Lebanon. In this last sector the British had left Emir Feisal behind as governor. Feisal had helped the British during the war by organizing and commanding an Arab revolt against Turkey (in return for which he had been promised an independent territory) and he now began to give the French no end of trouble. For their part, the French suspected that the English were encouraging Feisal, if not actually instigating him, to new revolts.

With their hands full in Syria, the French had little energy to spare in Cilicia. Here, Armenians who had escaped the 1915 genocide had been induced to return to their homes under promises of French protection. In order to limit the need for French forces, the French now armed an Armenian legion along the lines of their Foreign Legion in North Africa. (The United States at this point waived its ban on service in foreign forces and allowed naturalized citizens of Armenian origin to serve.) Oblivious of the fact that the Turks, who could not countenance Greeks in control, would be even less willing to tolerate Armenian policemen, the French corralled the willing Armenians into service.

Late in January 1920, bands of Turkish guerrillas attacked Marash—a town with a large Armenian population—and set a pattern for the region. They set fire to the houses, shot at the inhabitants as they fled into the streets, and burned alive thousands who sought refuge in schools and churches. From his office in Constantinople Bristol tried as best he could to counteract on-the-scene reports. Although driven to admit that there was some truth in them, Bristol maintained that the eyewitness reports were exaggerated and unreliable: "In the outlying districts of Marash murders of Armenians are steadily going on, but I do not believe that these are systematic or in the form of massacre," he cabled the State Department, displaying his penchant for semantic distinctions.

In some towns—as in Marash—entire French garrisons were wiped out along with the Armenians. In others, orders were secretly given the French to evacuate in the dead of night. Armenians who got wind of the flight in time followed on the heels of the French army, but the Turks annihilated thousands more, and others perished from exposure in the snowbound mountains.

French agents were all the while pressing their negotiations with Kemal, although news of these meetings did not leak out for a year, and passing French arms along to support his cause. The insurgent leader was also receiving abundant arms from the Italians, who had of course assisted him from the start; they were also providing help in transporting these arms through Allied checkpoints. In view of all this left-handed assistance while right hands were preparing a stringent peace treaty and professing to back the Sultan's government in Constantinople, it is not surprising that the Allies rejected the Grand Vizier's plea for help in fighting Kemal's rebels. Instead, the British proceeded to withdraw their few remaining troops from Samsun and Eskishehir in western Anatolia. This action, in effect, left the rim of the western plateau in Kemal's hands. Vizier Damad Ferid resigned.

The British next tried to conciliate the Nationalists by encouraging the new Turkish Vizier (Ali Riza Pasha) to hold elections for a new Parliament. An overwhelmingly Nationalist Chamber of Deputies was elected, and it proceeded immediately to endorse Kemal's National Pact. The Turkish press simultaneously began to publish inflammatory statements in open support of the rebel cause.

The British now began to fear that the Capital itself might fall into Nationalist hands, and that such a coup would leave them with no bargaining position whatever. On March 16, 1920, General Milne of the British forces, acting in the name of the Allies but without their enthusiasm, marched his troops into Constantinople before dawn, took over all public buildings and telegraph offices, and established a belated censorship of the press. A large number of Nationalists in the city were deported to Malta. (In reprisal Kemal arrested the handful of British officers left in the interior, among them Colonel Rawlinson, who had returned to Erzerum.) The Italians joined in the occupation, after it was initiated, but passed along Kemal's vigorous protests to their colleagues. Soon after this the Sultan reappointed Damad Ferid as Vizier and dissolved the Parliament. The Sultan's forces then began what turned out to be a desultory effort to put down the Nationalist forces.

In May 1920 Venizelos disclosed the terms of the impending treaty (it was signed in August at Sèvres) that would set the Allied peace terms with Turkey. Venizelos had undoubtedly disclosed it to hearten his countrymen, but in view of all that had transpired since the Armistice, the treaty was an astonishing document, produced by men who seemed hermetically sealed from reality. It gave the Smyrna area to the Greeks. It established a free Armenia and an autonomous Kurdistan. It partitioned Anatolia into French and Italian zones, maintained the Capitulations, and reduced the Turkish army to a "token force under Allied supervision." It provided for international control of the Bagdad railway, the Dardanelles, and the Russian port city of Batum. These last two provisions, according to some historians, provided the stimulus that turned Russia irrevocably toward Kemal, or at any rate hardened her resolve on his behalf; for under these terms Russia's southern flank was exposed to the attacks of any state that might be at war with her. The Italians were displeased with the treaty because it gave so much to Greece that they felt rightfully belonged to them. The French financiers were disconsolate that the Bagdad railway and other Eastern goodies would have to be shared equally. In all, the Treaty of Sèvres was taken seriously only by the Armenians, the Greeks, and some but by no means all of the British.

"At last, peace with Turkey," Churchill has written, "and to ratify it, war with Turkey!" But none of the great powers had any intention of going to war, and the Turks knew it.

The disclosure of the treaty's terms outraged the Turks to the point that thousands more joined in the Nationalist cause. In Angora, newspapers far from the censors' eyes warned France and Italy to stop their shilly-shallying and commit themselves to Kemal—or "the worst for them." Kemal reacted by attacking British forces within the Dardanelles zone at Ismit. As was its habit when thoroughly alarmed, the Supreme Council once again called on Venizelos. If he were permitted, the Greek premier assured the members, "he could guarantee that within a few weeks he would sweep the Kemalists from the zone of the Straits, both in Europe and in Asia, and remove from the minds of the Supreme Council all further anxiety regarding the Turkish Nationalist movement."

In the face of opposition from their military advisers, the members of the Council once again bowed to Venizelos's optimism. Greek forces immediately moved north from the Smyrna region and, to almost everyone's astonishment, routed the Turks at the first blow. Within weeks the Greeks had occupied Bursa, surrounded and defeated the Nationalists in Eastern Thrace, and occupied Adrianople. "Greece had saved the Allied positions both in Asiatic and European Turkey," Nicolson wrote. "It remained to deal with Kemal himself."

Lloyd George was ecstatic: "They are beaten and fleeing with their forces toward Mecca."

"Angora," said Curzon.

"Lord Curzon is good enough to admonish me on a triviality," said the Prime Minister, "nevertheless . . . !"

In the lull that followed, Kemal retreated to the fastness of Angora to lick his wounds, organize his forces, rout rebellion within his ranks, and dispose of the feeble assaults of the Sultan's armies. In the autumn, although he felt ready for the Greeks, they again routed him and advanced to the strategic railway lines connecting Constantinople with Konya. Lloyd George was able to announce to the House of Commons, "The Turks are broken beyond repair."

This last turn of affairs proved too much for the French and the Italians. They insisted that the Greek advance be restrained, and enjoined the Supreme Council to order the Greek army to stop in its tracks. French, British, and Italian forces rode out to confront the Greeks, halting them at a position far more precarious, strategically, than the one they had abandoned in order to rush to the Allies' rescue in June. "At the eleventh hour Kemal and his recruits were thus rescued from destruction," Nicolson has noted. In the ensuing months the major Powers began, one by one, to desert Greece in earnest.

Soviet Russia was the first. Having already turned over her southern territory to Turkey, the Treaty of Sèvres incited her to side openly with the insurgent Turks. The Nationalist cause became a people's fight against foreign capitalist domination. In December 1920, after a two-month drive, the Nationalists suc-

ceeded in liquidating the fledgling Armenian Republic in Cau-
casia—which the Allies were pledged to support and expand
under the terms of the Sèvres treaty, but to which they in fact
gave no assistance whatever; the Soviets (with the approval of
a good many Armenians who saw the alternative as domination
by Turkey) thereupon took over the tiny remaining province of
Yerevan and signed a treaty of friendship and peace with Turkey.
After this, Soviet aid came freely to Kemal.

The Soviet-Turkish pact gave the Nationalists still another bargaining point, one their propagandists exploited to the hilt. "We
are the only possible obstacle to the great wave of Bolshevism,"
the threat went. "We would have been the only buffer state if
they had treated us decently. Now we will let it inoculate us and
pass the germ to the West." The Soviets were not fooled: "Never
for one moment do we forget that the movement headed by Kemal
is not a Communist movement. We know it." But the British
cabinet was alarmed enough to send agents of the Secret Service
to Anatolia to sound out the Nationalists on peace terms. "They
presumably have no credentials, so they can be disavowed if they
are unsuccessful," Bristol reported to the Secretary of State.
Churchill sent a frantic memorandum to Lloyd George: "The
Turks will be thrown into the arms of the Bolsheviks. Mesopotamia
will be disturbed at this critical period of the reduction of the
army there; it will probably be quite impossible to hold Mosul and
Bagdad without a powerful and expensive army." At this juncture, political events in Greece provided an excellent excuse for
withdrawing the last pretense of Allied backing from the Greeks.

The protracted war, and Venizelos's two-year absence from his
country, had plunged Greece into turmoil by late summer of
1920. Riots erupted in Athens, a Greek deputy was assassinated
—reportedly by a Venizelist—and the Premier determined to return to Greece. He was at the railway station in Paris, two days
after the Sèvres treaty was signed, when two young Greeks fired
fourteen shots in his direction. Venizelos was only superficially
wounded, thanks to a bulletproof vest, but he arrived in Athens
in poor physical condition and found affairs even more turbulent
than he had feared. Disillusionment was rampant; some of the
men had been away ever since the Balkan Wars. The Treaty of
Sèvres notwithstanding, there was no noticeable improvement in
the Greek position; in fact, the contrary. To top it all, the premier's subordinates had been abusing his authority during his

long absence. At this juncture, on October 25, King Alexander of Greece died as the result of a bite from his pet monkey. The King's brother Paul, who had been living in exile with his father, King Constantine, was offered the throne but refused on the grounds that since his father had never abdicated, the offer was illegal. The question of Constantine's return was then put to a vote, and at a general election the populace voted to return him to the throne.

Here, Nicolson writes, was the Allies' "heaven-sent opportunity of ridding themselves of that irksome moral obligation." Constantine was anathema to the Allies for his purported pro-German affinity during the war. "For the sake of Venizelos much had to be endured, but for Constantine nothing," Churchill has written. "In England, the feeling was not resentment [at the election] but a total extinction of sympathy or even interest." Only Lloyd George stood fast, insisting that the elections would produce no change in Anglo-Greek relations. His statement blatantly contradicted a note sent by his Foreign Office to Athens scarcely two weeks before: "The governments of Britain, France and Italy . . . do not wish to intervene in the interior affairs of Greece, but they find themselves constrained to declare publicly that the reestablishment on the Greek throne of a sovereign whose attitude and disloyal conduct toward the Allies during the War has been for them a source of grave dangers and difficulties . . . will create another unfavorable situation in the relations between Greece and the Allies. . . ." Britain, France, and Italy, joined by the United States, further agreed that Greece would receive no financial support whatever. This effectively abrogated Allied loans extended during Venizelos's tenure that had not yet been paid.

No one has yet convincingly explained why Constantine chose to continue fighting in Turkey. His decision appears all the more inscrutable considering the fact that the Greek people had overthrown Venizelos primarily because of their dismay over the interminable war. Equally enigmatic is the attitude of those who condemn Venizelos for prolonging the fight despite Allied rebuffs, but who do not appear to question why his successor prolonged it in the face of outright opposition. The pro-Constantine argument insists that to withdraw was unthinkable, as it would have left the Anatolian Christians at the mercy of the enemy. The hindsight argument rebuts that to persist in fighting a losing battle visits as much suffering on innocent victims. One answer may well lie in the verity that it is easier to enter wars than to quit them; another, in the fact that Constantine received confidential hints from the British minister at Berne that British support of his return was contingent on his promising to continue Venizelos's policy. Lloyd George's open encouragement confirmed the notion, Churchill tells us, that "the great man is with us, and in his own way and in his own time and by his wizardry he will bring us the vital aid we need."

Actions spoke otherwise. In February 1921 the Supreme Council gave Kemal's Angora government what amounted to *de facto* recognition when it invited him, as well as the Sultan, to send delegates to London for a peace conference with the Greeks. The Conference did not end the hostilities but it did enable French and Italian emissaries to push forward negotiations with Kemal's men. The Italian Treaty was ratified on March 21, 1921. News of an Anglo-French deal leaked out in the spring, when a French deputy and former Propaganda Minister named Franklin-Bouillon turned up in Angora, much to the consternation of the British. The French government pooh-poohed rumors of a peace treaty with Kemal, but M. Franklin-Bouillon signed one all the same with the Nationalist minister for Foreign Affairs on October 20, 1921.

In return for her promise to yield Turkey's French-held territories to Kemal, the Nationalists promised France exploitation rights to the region's mineral resources, and investment priorities in "Turkish banks, ports, waterways and railways." The Nationalists had long since been receiving French armaments, but now shells from heavy artillery and bombs from French planes began to hit the Greek positions at a moment when Greece was on the verge of bankruptcy and her army destitute. And in the waiting room of the Paris Foreign Office, according to Churchill, "Two disconsolate suppliants" paced the floor: the Greek Prime Minister and the Greek Minister for Foreign Affairs. Their pleas were unavailing: "Not a gun, not a shell, not a soldier, not a shilling was voted in support of the Greek enterprise."

CHAPTER VII

*The public weal requires that men should betray, and lie,
and massacre.*

MONTAIGNE
Works, Book III

After Venizelos's downfall and the return of King Constantine to
Greece, the Supreme Council declared (on August 10, 1921) that
Greece and Turkey were engaged in a private war in which England, France, Italy, and Japan would remain strictly neutral.
Neutrality in this instance meant that French and Italian ships
could supply war materials to Kemal with impunity, while the
Greeks were prevented from applying blockade rules the Allies
themselves enforced when they were fighting Turkey. Despite this
advantage, Kemal's troops at Afyon Karahissar were forced to surrender that city to the Greeks, after some fierce encounters with
attendant atrocities on both sides, and to retire to the north, where
they held the line at Eskishehir. Here they sat, comfortably
equipped, for almost a year.

The Greek army of two hundred thousand men was in desperate
straits in the Turkish interior. It had been at war with one or
another country for ten years. Greece was virtually bankrupt,
with Allied and American loans canceled. The winter was

severe, clothing and food exceedingly scant, equipment decayed, leadership demoralized. The men were isolated and abandoned in a hostile land. "For upwards of nine months . . . the Turks waited and the Greeks endured," wrote Churchill.

In the spring of 1922 reports that the Nationalists and their friends had managed to suppress for over a year began to appear in English newspapers. They revealed still another death march in the interior. Ottoman Greeks and Armenians were being marshaled out of towns and villages held by Kemalists in northwestern and central Anatolia and set on roads leading eastward through the mountains and toward the desert beyond Diyarbakir. Once again gendarmes were forcing men, women, and children, barely clothed and foodless, to march at sword's point until they dropped from hunger, thirst, exhaustion, and exposure to the bitter cold of the Anatolian highlands. The local authorities permitted American relief workers in some towns along the line of march to pass out a few days' supply of bread. The *vali* of Diyarbakir countermanded orders from Angora and allowed the survivors to remain until the worst storms had passed. But these were isolated cases. After the winter snows had melted, the gentle Anatolian spring laid bare the evidence: alongside the roads, row upon row of trenches heaped with human remains.

For a year and a half the story was hushed. Directors of Near East Relief, who were now working closely with the State Department, extracted from each relief worker a signed statement that he would reveal nothing of the deportations. There was nothing to prevent a man's publishing his evidence after he had left the organization—nothing except, as it turned out, the reluctance of the American press to touch it.

Suddenly, in May of 1922 the report of a man named Yowell, former director of the Near East Relief in Harput, sprang into headlines of the *London Times* and caused a furor in both England and America. Admiral Bristol and Florence Billings, the Near East Relief agent at Constantinople, joined the Turkish press in branding it a lie; but Yowell's heartrending account was soon confirmed by others, among them Dr. Mark H. Ward, whose diary was published in England after American newspapers turned it down, and *Chicago Tribune* reporter John Clayton. Clayton's testimony did not appear in his newspaper; he sent a copy to the American consul in Aleppo, who passed it along to Bristol in Constantinople. Clayton had seen a good deal himself. He had also taken the trouble to find out where Yowell's successor

—a man named Applegate—kept his official diary, had "borrowed" it overnight with no one the wiser, copied it, and returned the original to its place before dawn. It showed that Yowell, if anything, had understated the case.

The State Department's dismay at Yowell's public revelation, and its concern lest Clayton's confirmation should appear in the *Tribune,* was matched by Admiral Bristol's. Earlier, the Admiral had warned Yowell "against giving these facts to the public," on the ground that "such propaganda" would only hurt the minorities. He had taken it upon himself to assure Kemal's foreign minister that he would absolve the Nationalists of all responsibility for these acts—though they ruled the area; now, in the face of Clayton's confirmation, he kept insisting that "Yowell's yowl" was exaggerated propaganda, calculated to enhance British political aims, and urged the Department to do everything within power to hold firm against any shift in American public opinion. The Admiral had felt especially close to the Department since his First Secretary, Allen Dulles, had left for Washington in April to take charge of the Near East Division. "I was absolutely delighted to have someone in the Department [of State] thoroughly familiar with the conditions out here and also absolutely in accord with our policy," he noted in July. A month later, he wrote to a friend: "It was a fine thing to have Dulles go to the Department in charge of this division. He had been long enough here so that we were in complete agreement and it is like having a section of the Commission out there in the State Department to have Dulles there."

More attuned to the complexities of the situation, Dulles tried to explain confidentially to the Admiral that the State Department was in a bind: its task would be simple if the reports could be declared untrue or even exaggerated, but the evidence, alas, was irrefutable—and if the Armenians and Greeks were here and there retaliating against Turks they could scarcely be blamed. The Department's position was complicated by the fact that aroused American churchmen were joining the British government in pressing for an investigation of Kemalist atrocities. Although Bristol might insist that the United States refuse to take part in such an inquiry, to decline was all the more difficult since the evidence came primarily from American sources. As Dulles explained, the Secretary of State wanted to avoid giving the impression that while the United States was willing to intervene actively to protect its commercial interests, it was not willing to move on behalf of the Christian minorities.

The murders of a number of American relief workers in Nationalist-held territory did not make headlines and do not appear to have ruffled either the State Department or the relief agencies for whom the victims had been working. Dulles himself was more disturbed about the mandate arrangements proposed for Syria and Palestine. He bemoaned the agitation on behalf of the Greeks, the Armenians, and the Palestine Jews; he had been kept busy, he complained, trying to ward off congressional resolutions of sympathy for these groups.

The dilemma over whether to join an investigation confounded President Harding, who had to make the ultimate decision. "I am wondering," he wrote in his inimitable style, "whether the possible manifestation of our impotence [in the event the reports proved to be true] would not be more humiliating than our non-participation is distressing." He ended by offering to decide in favor of the investigation if the Secretary of State would guarantee that he would have no regrets. Secretary Hughes politely declined to accept the buck. He regretted, he said, that he could not give such an assurance, "but I suggest that the real difficulty will be due to the fact of the atrocities rather than to our joining the inquiry." To his great relief the problem was resolved when the British, "in deference to the desires of France," suggested that the International Red Cross undertake the inquiry. In the end that, too, was abandoned. In the early summer of 1922 another Nationalist campaign, this time to annihilate about one hundred thousand Greeks on the Black Sea coast, was well under way. The British press may have been less reticent than the American about revealing the atrocities because Kemalist newspapers were coincidentally conducting a virulent campaign against the British.

The official organs of the Nationalist government were the *Yeni-Ghun* and the *Hakimiet-i-Millie,* both published in Angora, beyond the pale of Allied censorship. *Yeni-Ghun* began to show Kemal's hand in April 1921, when Talaat's assassination in Berlin led it to forget its occasional—and relatively mild—diatribes against the Young Turk regime, and to reveal itself in eulogies that would be unmatched until Kemal himself was laid to rest. "Our great patriot has died for his country," the newspaper declared. "We salute his fresh tomb and bow low to kiss his eyes. Talaat was a political giant. Talaat was a genius. History will prove his immense stature and will make of him a martyr and an apostle. Talaat was a revolutionary but he was, above all, a man of justice. . . . Despite all the calumnies Talaat will remain the greatest man that Turkey has produced."

Among the distinguished personages—for the most part retired German and exiled Turkish officials—reported by *Yeni-Ghun* as present at Talaat's funeral was the Director of the Deutsche Bank. With such connections as this, the article concluded, Talaat had so threatened England's peace of mind that he had had to be annihilated. "We announce to the world: It is England that armed the hand of the miserable Armenian assassin. . . . But Machiavellian England has not succeeded in ruining the work of the Young Turks. We, the heirs of the great patriots of 1908, shall continue their work in the same spirit, in the same tradition and with the same energy."

Kemal's newspapers were no less menacing toward the Christian minorities. If the Turks had erred, *Yeni-Ghun* declared on May 10, 1922, it was in having been too good to their minorities. The warning was clear: "Beware! We have no intention of repeating the same mistake!"

By midsummer of 1922 the Turks were thoroughly rested and equipped, and their passions properly inflamed to a fever pitch. At the same time the Greek leaders, realizing that their army could not survive another winter, devised a plan whereby they would amalgamate their forces and make a quick thrust for Constantinople. It was, as Churchill has written, "a shrewd stroke," which would allow them a safe retreat. They knew full well that their occupation of the capital would be only temporary; in fact they wanted nothing more than to be asked to withdraw. Their request for Allied cooperation got no further than General Harington, the commander of the Allied military forces and an Englishman Admiral Bristol admired. "You of course have read of the Greeks attempting to take Constantinople," Bristol wrote to a friend on August 31. "I think they would have done it if it hadn't been for General Harington, who acted on his own hook and blocked the game. So thus the Allies, with Turkish gendarmes, are facing their own ally, the Greeks, on the Chataldja line. It is a ridiculous situation." Thanks to the General's initiative the last desperate gamble had failed, leaving the Greek position the weaker by two divisions.

In the greatest secrecy Kemal prepared to seize the moment. Beginning at the end of July, he moved around the Turkish fronts on the pretext of attending a football match at one place, meeting with a British general at another. On August 6 he returned to Angora, and when he left again, on August 13, only his closest associates knew that he was gone. "They had even to publish in the papers that I had given a tea at Chankaya," he said later.

In mid-August Kemal and his generals had their plans coordinated. On their military maps were plotted the positions of all the Greek forces: regiment by regiment, division by division. By feinting attacks to the north and south of the Greek line at Afyon Karahissar, he weakened the main line and prepared to attack along a fifteen-mile front. The order of the day for August 26 began: "Soldiers, your goal is the Mediterranean!"

They struck at dawn, taking the Greeks unaware and smashing their lines with such dispatch that the headquarters troops, caught between the Turkish First and Second armies, never had a chance to fire their guns. The Turks annihilated five Greek divisions and captured fifty thousand prisoners. To the north, the Third Greek Corps fled toward Mudanya, where ships awaited them on the Sea of Marmara. There they were met by the French, who blocked their escape on the pretext that they were in a neutral zone. This was untrue, and the commanders of two Greek regiments, who knew it, managed to lead their men through the hills to Bandirma. The rest surrendered to the French, who turned them over to the Turks.

South of Afyon Karahissar, the Greek Commander-in-Chief, General Tricoupis, tried vainly to lead a counterattack and was captured by Turkish cavalrymen on September 2. The Greek retreat had by then turned into a rout, and his men were already in flight. There was no longer any pretense of organization or command as demoralized Greek officers thought only of escape. Soldiers threw down their ammunition and pushed blindly toward the sea, gathering tens of thousands of Greek civilians in their wake.

Kemal had once declared to his followers: "If it is the will of God that we are defeated, we must set fire to all our homes, to all our property; we must lay the country in ruins and leave an empty desert." Now the defeated Greeks, in their panicked flight through a detested land, set the torch to their own villages, killed and maimed some of the Turkish inhabitants, and took to the roads. For one hundred miles, until they caught up with their enemy in the suburbs of Smyrna, the pursuing Turks came upon one smouldering town after another.

85

CHAPTER VIII

He who has dwelled there longs for her in other lands and sighs for the vineyards and olive groves, the villas and ruins, the delicious breezes and the star-eyed maidens of Smyrna.

> S. G. BENJAMIN
> *The Turk and the*
> *Greek* (1867)

The harbor of Smyrna, as perfect a crescent as emblazoned the Turkish flag, held an imposing display of Allied might at daybreak on Saturday, September 9, 1922. Besides twenty-one warships—two British battleships, three cruisers, and six destroyers; three French cruisers and two destroyers; an Italian cruiser and destroyer; and three American destroyers—the harbor was massed with virtually every sort of vessel that could float, from tiny Levantine caïques to massive freighters bearing the flags of all the maritime nations on earth—except Greece. The last Greek ship had pulled down its flag and slid away before dawn.

The men on the U.S.S. *Litchfield*, which was moored with her stern to the quay exactly in dead center of Smyrna harbor, opposite the motion picture theater, were confined to shipboard. They spent a good deal of time looking across at the broad paved roadway that curved with the shoreline of the inner harbor. Imposing stone villas—many of them foreign consulates or the

homes of wealthy European merchants, judging by their flags—
faced the water, while behind these buildings the city sprawled
up the hillsides. Day by day traffic became more congested along
the quay, which was piled high with crates, bundles, trunks, rolled
carpets, furniture, and sewing machines. All week long, ships
packed with such freight and with hundreds of passengers had
been steaming out of the harbor, but only a few boats were
taking on passengers or freight this morning and whole families
were squatting on the pavement beside their baggage. Men wearing fezzes (the fez merchants appeared to have done a brisk business in the last few days) were milling about as distractedly as
the abandoned horses, mules, and camels that jogged into sight,
then disappeared down narrow side streets. Some of the animals
were still trailing carts. Some had gear strapped to their backs.
No one was making a move to round them up.

On the American destroyer *Simpson*, moored to a buoy off the
Standard Oil works on the north side of the harbor, some of the
men had interpreted the lowering of the Greek standards as a
sign of mutiny. They knew that Turks and Greeks had been fighting in the interior and that the signs of Greek defeat were unmistakable. They had been in port three days watching the exhausted, maimed remnants of the Greek army hobbling along the
waterfront in search of transport. Allied officials referred to these
ragged creatures as "deserters," but the Greeks appeared themselves to have been deserted as they limped up the quayside looking for ships to carry them to safety. They were a pitiful sight
to the crisply uniformed, well-fed American bluejackets who had
never before seen an army in defeat. No one had enlightened the
sailors about the international complexities, but they had heard it
rumored that the British were somehow to blame for the plight
of the Greek army, and as the last Greek transport pulled out before
dawn, leaving hundreds of stragglers on the docks, some sur-
mised that the British were preventing the Greeks from covering
their own retreat. If so, it seemed natural enough that the Greek
sailors should try to resist orders to abandon their own troops.
Although they sensed that something momentous was going on,
many of the American seamen wondered why they were there.
After all, their country was neutral in whatever was at hand. This
they had been told, and repeatedly. Unlike her European allies,
the United States had not been at war with Turkey.

The sailors stationed ashore were no less confused than their shipmates. "We were doing guard duty, but I still don't know what we were supposed to be guarding, to tell the truth," said Melvin Johnson during an interview many years later. According to the retired seaman, it had been good duty up until that September—all over the Mediterranean, up through the Dardanelles to the Black Sea, over to Rumania, Bulgaria, Russia, and down again to Constantinople. You couldn't beat Constantinople for liberty. "Only place could beat it was Saigon. That's over and finished too, now," Johnson added wistfully. Then, on this September day, his ship had suddenly shifted course and headed for Smyrna, and within hours Johnson found himself standing guard at a movie theater. An odd turn of events, he had thought.

The sailors could not know how reassuring the sight of their armed ships was to apprehensive Smyrneans that morning. Now that the Greek forces had left, the life-and-death question in the mind of every Ottoman Christian was whether the foreign warships would remain in port to protect them if the Turks took over the city.

In spite of the war raging in the interior, life in Smyrna had been curiously unaffected, even carefree, until the last days of August 1922. The city was the center of the nation's commercial and agricultural life, and although trade with the interior was diminished the harbor bustled with traffic. The presence of the Greek military gave an illusion of safety and permanence to the political scene, in contrast to the virtual state of anarchy in many sections of Turkey. Greek officers enhanced Smyrna's abundant social life, and the weather was consistently benign. There had been no showers since May and dust hovered during the day like a low fog over well-traveled roads; but the nights were cool and fragrant, thanks to the sea breeze and the profusion of courtyard gardens.

The markets testified to an abundant harvest. Smyrna fruit was known for its incomparable fragrance and the open markets exuded a tantalizing variety of aromas: grapes, fresh figs, apricots, melons, cherries, pomegranates—all so plentiful that the poorest villager could live on fruit and cheese. In season, baskets of rose petals lined the streets; rose-petal conserve and paper-thin pastries heavy with rose-flavored syrup were favored delicacies served to guests—in the more fashionable homes on a silver tray with a glass of cold water. In some streets the smell of freshly baked bread overpowered the roses. The bake shops were open to the streets, with the ovens just over the counter; pedestrians cultivated the habit of ducking when passing by, for the bread was shoveled in and out the oven with a long-handled implement.

The countryside diffused its own special perfumes. There were the almond trees, the laurel, the mimosa, the oleander bordering the banks of streams with luxuriant clusters of delicate pink flowers, and the rich-scented jasmine. Those who lived within sight of the railway station at Basma Hane, at the edge of the Armenian quarter, could sniff the air and know that the train from suburban Bournabat had arrived, for its passengers invariably carried armfuls of jasmine to their friends in the city.

Bournabat and Boudja were the most fashionable of Smyrna's suburbs. Here, in the seventeenth century, English traders had built imposing homes. "Never was I so struck with any village," Francis Hervé, the wandering English artist, declared of Bournabat in 1837. He found it "one entire bower." Cheerful white villas with trellised balconies gleamed amid a profusion of stately trees and formal gardens. Flanking the garden gates would be a pair of immense stone seats where families gathered in the evening to feast on the sunset.

Both the bizarre and conventional aspects of Smyrna life had arrested Hervé, as they were to captivate subsequent travelers, and had tempted him to linger for some time. One major temptation of the city was its veritable army of marriageable ladies, the offspring of European traders whose ancestors had settled in Smyrna during the seventeenth and eighteenth centuries. Since that time, residents of mixed lineage were referred to as "Levantine," those purely European as "Frank." As both varieties of parents were intent on making suitable matches for their daughters, few cities could beat Smyrna for hospitality toward Western gentlemen. "Most strangers who have visited Smyrna can testify to that effect," Hervé wrote, "particularly officers of whom they are particularly fond. I verily believe if an uniform was hung upon a jackass and a pair of epaulettes clapt upon the shoulders that if he did but bray at the windows he could get asked to walk in and invited to dinner if there were any young ladies in the house."

Thanks to its leading position in trade (the city surpassed Constantinople and every other Near Eastern seaport in exports until World War I), Smyrna was a cosmopolitan city. "The inhabitants speak nothing but Italian, French, English or Dutch here," Louis Pitton de Tournefort, a botanist and court physician to Louis XIV, had noted approvingly. (Hervé reflected that "a regular Levanter is supposed to speak several languages badly and none well.") Tournefort, visiting Smyrna in the seventeenth century, had already found it "the richest magazine in the world." The city, he wrote, was "better enlightened, better paved, and the houses better built than in many cities on the continent." The waterfront was lined with two-story villas, which were built around spacious courtyards and boasted such amenities as a covered gallery leading from the main dwelling to "a sort of pleasure house over the water." Warehouses were conveniently located on the ground floor, and the harbor was deep enough for boats to land at the merchants' doors. Even before Tournefort's visit, an Englishman named Aaron Hill had found traffic in and out of Smyrna harbor "great and advantageous." An English merchant's life in Hill's day (1700) was precarious, but not without dividends. One Englishman who suffered terribly from gout had fallen into an argument with a Turkish officer and been severely bastinadoed. "The joke is," wrote Hill, "that it cured his gout."

Over the centuries, between October and June caravans arrived daily from the East, carrying thousands of bales of raw silk, dyes such as indigo, and spices—cinnamon, clove, ginger, nutmeg—for shipment to Europe. There were the famous figs and grapes from the local vineyards and, from somewhat further away, cotton, frankincense, "Turkey" carpets, rhubarb, and opium, as well as mohair from Angora. Into Smyrna from the West poured satins, woolens, serge, tin, steel, enamels, and—to provide all the amenities and more—wines and liquors from France, Italy, and Spain, although the local wines rated high praise from travelers, who marveled at the rate of consumption among Smyrna's motley inhabitants.

Since the city was a center for the most dazzling variety of native dress—Turkish, Armenian, Persian, and Egyptian, not to mention the assortment of colorful costumes worn by the Greek islanders—the residents were well equipped for masquerades. Each evening during the Mardi Gras, bands of masqueraders, accompanied by musicians, went calling from house to house attempting to remain incognito. The young ladies of the town were "eternal dancers" and during the carnival week their days began early, often with breakfast aboard a frigate. They cavorted until seven or eight at night after which, Hervé wrote, "the same young ladies then change their dress and repair to the *Casin* [Casino] to dance all night. Certainly to see them creeping to their homes, one would say it had almost been the dance of death with them."

Smyrneans were famous, too, for their addiction to card games and gambling, and for their love of clubs, for they were inveterate joiners. Until the nineteenth century, the *Casin* had been restricted to Franks and Levantines; the Greeks, after vainly trying to gain admission, had opened a club of their own before the rules of the "Frank Casin" were relaxed. Thereafter, Greeks and Armenians were freely proposed and admitted to membership, over the protests of more conservative members, who snorted, "What! Admit a man who only a few years since wore a calpac and long robes?"

Europeans, Jews, Greeks, Armenians, and Turks continued to live each in their own quarter of the city, but over the years these contiguous districts had grown to overlap one another. The wealthiest of every nationality had homes in the European quarter, which encompassed the area closest to the seafront. In their luxurious "salons" they held teas, dances, and musicales. Smyrna was known for its orchestras, called *politakia* and composed of zithers, mandolins, and guitars; these frequently played in private homes and clubs, the musicians singing Greek songs and often improvising words to their own accompaniment. By 1914 there were four clubs, including a country club with magnificent golf and race courses. Schools had likewise proliferated by then and included two large institutions run by the American Board of Commissioners for Foreign Missions: the Collegiate Institute, for girls, located in the heart of Smyrna's Armenian quarter, and the International College, for boys, a prestigious institution situated four miles away in a suburb named Paradise. By 1922 the American YMCA and YWCA were burgeoning with wholesome activities for their patrons who, like the students in the American schools, were predominantly Armenian and Greek.

East and West met head-on at Smyrna. At one extreme was the American colony at Paradise: "A veritable little corner of America, set down in Smyrna," a delighted faculty wife reported to her family in the States. At the other extreme were the camel caravans that still arrived bearing the famous figs. At the head of each string of camels rode the driver, astride a donkey, turbaned and with an enormous sheepskin cloak flung over his shoulders, kicking his donkey's sides to the jangle of the bells fastened to the pack-saddle of the lead camel. The procession would move slowly past the American homes in Paradise and down through Smyrna until a string reached the appropriate courtyard, where with much ado the beasts would be made to kneel and deposit their cargoes. Then the pulpy fruit would be steeped in salt water and heaped on the paved floor to be processed and packed, a procedure that caused more than one visitor to swear off figs for life. "I verily believe if persons could see the operation of arranging the figs they would never eat another," Hervé wrote. "There are the filthiest set of women that can be raked together . . . the sight of them is so disgusting that whilst this work was going on and I had to pass the merchants' yards I used to run through as fast as I could tear, without looking either to right or left." The fig workers of a later day were no more fastidious as they worked over the fruit with their fingers while their children—barefoot, bare-bottomed, and badly in need of a wash—chased each other over the figs. "It is a very amusing sight to those who do not intend to eat the product," an American visitor noted.

As was the custom in Ottoman cities, the Turkish quarter of Smyrna commanded the highest point of the town. It nestled against Mount Pagus to the south and east, lying directly below the old Byzantine fortress that crowned the summit of the mountain. The quarter was a labyrinth of narrow, crooked, vine-covered streets dotted with ancient fountains that exuded the flavor of the Arabian Nights. Fezzed Turks puffed at their hookahs and professional letter-writers sat at tables recording whispered love notes.

An English traveler arriving in Smyrna on August 29, 1922, found the weather bright and the city's mood relaxed. Greek soldiers and officers mingled with the natives and visitors who strolled on the quay—or *Cordon,* as the French called it—among merchants going to and from work, porters bearing figs and raisins toward the docks, and laborers waiting to load these on barges to be towed toward freighters standing offshore. In the evening well-dressed customers filled the outdoor cafés. The Opera House was sold out; an Italian company was in town. The city's three theaters were, as usual, doing a lively business.

On August 26, when the Greek front collapsed at Afyon Karahissar, two hundred miles to the east, scarcely a soul in Smyrna was aware of imminent catastrophe despite the city's twenty-three newspapers, representing every conceivable attitude toward the Greco-Turkish war. For months conflicting rumors about the fighting had gone the rounds with telegraphic speed and come to rest in one or another of these journals. Finding them in print in his favorite paper, virtually every resident could consider a favorable rumor substantiated as fact, and could ignore all others as fatuous. Even when the defeat at Afyon was officially confirmed in a Greek communiqué, Armenians and Greeks accepted the setback as temporary. But on September 1 came the word that the Greeks had abandoned Ushak, one hundred and forty miles east of Smyrna. This news was ominous; Ushak was the center of the nation's carpet industry and had heretofore been considered impregnable. The British Consulate became nervous enough to alert its citizens in outlying districts. English residents at Boudja and Bournabat sipped gin and bitters on their clubhouse veranda and debated whether to stay or leave, while their sons and daughters played tennis. Wealthy Armenians and Greeks decided to take an impromptu holiday abroad.

It was on this first day of September, too, that the Greek wounded began arriving. They came in interminable trainloads, the carriages and freight cars so tightly packed that men were sitting and lying on the roofs of the cabs. The trains rattled on far into the afternoon; against the fading sun the bandaged figures appeared eerily silhouetted. Their destination was an embarkation point at Chesme, the tip of the peninsula that extends into the Aegean Sea and almost touches the Greek island of Chios.

Fleeing soldiers arrived next, on every possible mode of conveyance: ox-carts, huge-wheeled chariots common to the Near East since Assyrian days, trucks, camels, horses, mules, handcarts; and many thousands on foot, dragging one after the other if they had two to drag, or one man leaning on another, the stronger bearing the brunt. Most headed toward Chesme, but it soon became clear that the flight was massive and disorganized, as thousands more who had lost their way to the embarkation point poured directly into Smyrna. George Horton, the American consul, wrote that they were ragged, dusty, and ghostlike: "They looked neither to the right nor to the left but straight ahead, like men walking in their sleep." They stumbled to the doors of residents in the Greek quarter begging for food, and were handed bread, cheese, and grapes to sustain them until they could find a ship.

Civilian refugees from the interior began to flood the city next —Americans estimated that by September 5 they were arriving at the rate of thirty thousand a day. Most came on foot with their children, their draft animals, and all the household goods they were able to carry. Some were taken in by relatives and friends, some by strangers, but the streets were massed with them and the roads leading from the east were choked with thousands more. Bizarre convoys of men, women, and children formed the sort of numbed procession that witnesses have testified atrophies the hearts of observers, the kind that Ernest Hemingway, then a *Toronto Daily Star* reporter in Turkey, called "a silent procession." George Horton never forgot the sight of an old woman stumbling along "with an emaciated, feverish son astride her neck. The son was taller than the mother, and his legs almost touched the ground." They shuffled through the streets, bent double with the weight of their burdens and covered from head to foot with the dust of countless arid miles. At night they camped in churchyards, cemeteries, schoolyards, walled gardens. Those who found no shelter or enclosure at all camped in herds outside the town or in the streets of the city, arranging their bits of furniture so as to give a few square yards the illusion of a room. Places nearest the water were at a premium, since those close to the docks were the most likely to find passage on a departing steamer. They besieged the steamship companies with bags of drachmas and piastres and stormed the foreign consulates pleading for visas.

Later arrivals bore fewer possessions and looked even more destitute and distraught, as though they had left their homes moments before a tornado. Within days the panic spread to the local Greeks and Armenians and touched the foreign colony as well. Consular officials cabled their governments for more ships to take away their nationals if such a move became necessary. At the same time the British, French, and Italian consuls gave formal assurances to the Armenians and Greeks that their lives were in no danger. Only George Horton refused, in good conscience, to do so. He had been in the East too long and knew the West too well to feel sanguine. "Therefore," he wrote later, "I could not assure the Armenians and Greeks that they would be perfectly safe."

CHAPTER IX

There was perfect order and quiet in Smyrna up until the arrival of the Turks on Saturday, September 9.

CONSUL GENERAL GEORGE HORTON
Testimony at Senate Committee on
Immigration and Naturalization, 1923.

The city was quiet.

CAPTAIN A. J. HEPBURN
Diary, Sept. 9, 1922

For two days after the Greek High Commissioner and other officials departed, there was no government and no control. It was during this time that the robbing, looting, and murdering began.

ADMIRAL MARK L. BRISTOL
Report to the Secretary of the Navy
March 27, 1924

Allied officials in Smyrna had all along been more concerned about the retreating Greeks than the approaching Turks. On September 3 the British, French, Italian, and American consuls called on the Greek Chief of Staff, General Hadjianestis, a tall, patrician-looking man with a reputation for mental instability; there were days on end, it was said, when he refused to walk, under the delusion that his legs were made of glass. He now had the notion that a Greek regiment was on its way from Thrace to defend the city and maintain order. The delegation asked if the General would assure them that the Greek army would refrain from acts of violence—the thought seemed ludicrous since the exhausted soldiers could scarcely drag themselves to the waterfront. "They went through like beaten dogs," said Horton, "in a state of extreme fatigue and many of them without arms"; but in the interior they were said to be burning villages along their way, and Greek officers in Smyrna had been heard to say not long before

95

the rout that they would never give up the city except in cinders.

Hadjianestis asked the Allied governments to arrange some sort of understanding with the Turkish forces so that his men could retreat in an orderly manner. Barring an amnesty, he said, the retreating army was obliged to set fire to its rear to slow down the Turkish advance. Sterghiades, the civil governor, repeated the request for an amnesty to the American consul during a conversation the same evening.

Horton cabled to Admiral Bristol the next morning, begging him "in the interests of humanity and for the safety of American interests to mediate with the Angora government for amnesty sufficient to allow the Greek forces to evacuate. Amnesty will avoid possible destruction of Smyrna," he added. An unequivocal No from the State Department was relayed through Bristol, reaching Horton two days later. The Department "was not inclined to do more than send destroyers to Smyrna to assist in the protection of American lives and property. The situation would not appear to justify this government assuming the role of voluntary mediator."

When this message arrived, on September 6, the Greek General Staff and the entire Greek civil administration were already packing to leave Smyrna. The Allies faced the possibility of uncontrolled panic raging through the city after the Greek authority had withdrawn and before the Turks had arrived to take control. With over two hundred thousand local Christians and an equal number of homeless refugees in a state of panic, and the Turks in a frenzy over their victory, to allow a period of anarchy seemed unthinkable. Yet the consuls had no orders to guide them in such a situation, nor were the Allied navies prepared to work together. The commanding officer of the British naval force was determined to look out for British citizens only. "I will not land one sailor for any other purpose," he said. French Admiral Dumesnil, convinced that the Greeks would raise mayhem once the administration withdrew, was disgusted with the British attitude. He had no intention, he said, of sitting still and letting the population be massacred and the town burned. If the Greek authorities allowed looting and destruction, said Dumesnil, "I will refuse to let their transports leave this port but will keep them here until the Turks enter."

For his part, Bristol had issued strict orders to his officers: under no circumstances were they to appear to be cooperating with Turkey's enemies. Beyond that, they were more or less on their own.

Higher echelons in Washington heartily agreed with Bristol's view. The Departments of State and Navy concurred that it was "infinitely better not to send from here special instructions with regard to landing at Smyrna. If, therefore, American forces are landed, it would be entirely on the responsibility of the Commanding Officer." In short, the Commanding Officer would be the scapegoat if a landing should have unhappy consequences.

Two American destroyers, the *Litchfield* and the *Simpson*, steamed into Smyrna on September 6 with Lieutenant Commander J. B. Rhodes, Captain of the *Litchfield*, in charge. Admiral Bristol had briefed Rhodes the previous day in Constantinople. There would be a number of Allied ships in port, Bristol told him, "and these Allies were at war with Turkey while the United States was not." Rhodes, he said, must be careful "not to cooperate with the Allies, while at the same time coordinating his work with them on a purely humanitarian basis." How Rhodes was to coordinate without cooperating, Bristol did not say. However, he clearly defined the limits of humanitarianism: Rhodes was to take action "only in defense of American lives and property." If guards had to be landed, "it should be with the consent of the local authorities, whether Greek or Turkish, and especially they should not be in the position in any way to be operating with the Allies, the enemies of the Turks."

Among his men Rhodes had a reputation for eccentricity, but he now acted with understandable caution as requests poured in for the protection of American buildings. After receiving speedy approval from the Greek authorities, he landed a force of fifty-five men and distributed them at American institutions throughout the city: the consulate, the two American schools, the YMCA and the YWCA, the waterfront theater that Horton had designated as the gathering place for Americans who wanted protection, and the Standard Oil Company enclave.

The British had larger forces available and they nervously landed two hundred marines, concentrating these at their consulate, at the fire station (the insurance companies underwriting Smyrna properties were British-owned), the telegraph company, and the oriental carpet factory. The French landed marines to guard their own consulate, schools, and the Credit Lyonnais bank. The Italians were preparing to cooperate with the Turks in patrolling the city.

Only the Americans gave a thought to the refugees. Horton convened a meeting of leading American citizens and on the initiative of a businessman and former consul, Rufus Lane, organized a committee to distribute food among the destitute. A YMCA worker managed to obtain a supply of food from the Greeks and store it in a large home on the quay entrusted to him for safekeeping by a departing Greek merchant. Someone discovered six thousand bags of flour in an American warehouse and the committee took possession of this as well. Money was collected at the meeting, businessmen volunteered trucks and automobiles, the group hired bakers, and within a day Americans were distributing food among the refugees. When the relief group cabled Bristol for funds, the Admiral cautiously suggested that the State Department transfer $50,000 to the American Red Cross in Constantinople for this purpose. "I am sending this in code," he cabled, "in order that it may not be advertised at large that we intend to undertake relief work in Smyrna, and for the same reason I recommend that no funds be allotted by the Red Cross to other institutions for this work."

A day before the Greek withdrawal, the directors of the relief group—Caleb Lawrence of the International College and "Jake" Jacob of the YMCA—rented the Greek orphanage at Boudja from the Greek High Commission for five liras, thereby placing the children under American protection. A young American teacher from the College, Raymond Moreman, volunteered to take charge of the orphans and on his arrival at Boudja hoisted the American flag over the compound. The Greeks left funds at the American consulate to maintain the children.

American businessmen had criticized the British for having precipitately advised the evacuation of their nationals on September 4. Such action, they thought, was in bad taste, a blatant sign of the jitters and an ignominious example to the local populace. As tactfully as he could, therefore, Consul Horton suggested that all American citizens who wanted to leave the city gather at the theater on the Smyrna quay. About one hundred naturalized Americans wanted to leave immediately and at their expense Horton chartered a steamer to take them to Mitilini (the island of Lesbos). "We shall be glad to see them go tomorrow morning," Bristol's intelligence officer, Lieutenant Merrill, reported in his diary. "They would very likely swear at the Turks in Greek, behind

American flags, were they staying on for the big show." Merrill, like his chief, was contemptuous of the luckless Greeks and prepared to believe the worst of them.

When they discovered that the Greek administration was preparing to abandon the city, the Greeks and Armenians swarmed to their churches and besought their clergy for reassurance. In a state of apprehension themselves, the archbishops addressed an appeal to the Archbishop of Canterbury, pleading that he intercede with the British cabinet to arrange an armistice with Kemal outside the city, or at least to assure the protection of the minorities if the Turks were to enter Smyrna. "In the name of Christ, hasten to prevent imminent catastrophe," the message ended.

Charles Dobson, the British chaplain, carried the message to the British authorities, where it got no further than the Naval Chief of Staff—an Admiral with the dashing name of Sir Osmond de Beauvoir Brock. In spite of his avowal of the previous day to look out for British citizens only, the Admiral promised to "give all the protection in his power to all sections of the community," and authorized the chaplain to give this message to the local press.

On September 7 the harbor was ringed with warships. Word spread that the Allied powers were delimiting a neutral zone around the city to forbid access both to Greek and Turkish forces. The French and Italian consuls announced that the minorities were in no danger whatever, and in the newspapers there appeared a proclamation from Mustafa Kemal announcing that Turkish soldiers found molesting a noncombatant of any nationality would be summarily executed. The most affluent Armenians and Greeks had already left the city, and panic began to subside as the prevailing mood turned to one of resigned apprehensiveness. Then, on the morning of September 8, all official business stopped and the Greek High Commissioner announced that the Greek administration would cease at ten o'clock that night.

Throughout the nervous week, Greek gendarmes had continued to patrol the streets day and night and were effectively keeping order. Unwilling to set their own men to the task, the Allied representatives asked Sterghiades to leave the police at their posts on the assurance that they would be permitted to leave, unmolested, after the Turks arrived. "The Greek High Commissioner did not grant this request," Horton reported, adding, "I did not join in it."

Sterghiades, whose unbending character had made him so unpopular with his people, was the last Greek official to leave Smyrna. After handing the keys of the *Konak* to the French consul, he walked stiffly through a hooting crowd to the ship that was to take him away. He appeared to have aged ten years.

The city was stilled, as though it were holding its breath. "The interregnum of a city without a government began," Horton wrote, *"but nothing happened."* No one patrolled the streets, there was no one to maintain order, but despite all the gloomy predictions Smyrna was silent as a tomb. "Everything quiet," Lieutenant Merrill reported at eleven o'clock in the evening and again at four in the morning. He had seen no one walking about save the marines guarding their respective posts. The familiar tap-tap-tapping sound of the Greek police as they passed was unpleasantly missing. "I thought the hollow sound of my footfalls on the paved streets could be heard all the way to Constantinople," he wrote. It was a dark, moonless night and even the refugees appeared to have melted away. Like everyone else, they were hushed and waiting.

The U.S.S. *Lawrence* pulled into Smyrna harbor at seven o'clock on the morning of September 9. Admiral Bristol was growing concerned about Smyrna. He sensed a note of hysteria in Horton's dispatches. Should disaster strike, there was no one in the city besides Merrill—who had no command—on whom he could positively rely to avoid antagonizing Turkish officialdom. On the *Lawrence* was his Chief of Staff, Captain Arthur Japy Hepburn.

The Admiral had been trying to keep his misgivings to himself. On September 7, when two young ladies had visited him to ask where they might go on a holiday jaunt, Bristol, amused that they should come to him to settle the question, had suggested that they wait a week and go to Smyrna. That same day he had re-assured an official of the Gary Tobacco Company that his firm's holdings were in no danger whatever—the man had asked whether his company ought to raise its insurance on the tobacco in Smyrna. But at a British consulate luncheon on September 8, an unexpected guest had turned up in the person of Lord Beaver-brook, and that shrewd publisher had disconcerted Bristol into blurting out what was really on his mind.

Bristol was taken aback as much by Beaverbrook's appearance as by his manner. He was a short man, with a head rather too large for his body, and a habit of firing direct and embarrassing questions and very often refusing to listen to the answers.

"What do you think of Rumbold?" his Lordship had snapped at the outset. As it happened, there was no love lost between the Admiral and Sir Horace Rumbold, British High Commissioner in Constantinople. The two had been feuding steadily on the question of tariffs. Rumbold found Bristol disagreeable and pushy, and complained about him frequently in dispatches to London. Bristol thought Rumbold "impertinent." On his guard, Bristol refrained from answering the question, only to be greeted by an enigmatic smile.

"I like Rumbold very much personally and find him a very good chap," Bristol murmured.

"He's a very good chap but he has very little brains," Beaverbrook said. (Rumbold's intelligence was again to be called into question in 1933, when as British Ambassador to Germany directly after Hitler's coup, he conveyed to London his suspicion that the Führer was determined to conquer Europe, and was promptly recalled for his pains.)

The conversation turned to General Harington, the Commander-in-Chief of the British forces, whom Bristol could honestly say he liked very much. "And the fact that he was promoted during the war shows he is a man of ability," he stumbled on.

"The war wasn't won by generals," Beaverbrook snorted, "nor by prime ministers."

"He has a very good reputation," Bristol persisted.

"The war wasn't won by generals," Beaverbrook said again. The Admiral found him unnerving.

Beaverbrook volunteered that he had come to Constantinople pro-Turk and that he had always been pro-Turk, but he was very quickly becoming sympathetic to the Greeks. Bristol found this hard to understand—his Lordship had been in Turkey only a few hours. "The Greeks have had a rotten deal," Beaverbrook went on, talking more to himself than to Bristol. "They were supported by us and we let them be wiped out by the Turks. Lloyd George backed them up in every way except that he couldn't give them money, and now they are left in the lurch." He turned to Bristol: "And what are *you* people doing?"

Bristol replied that the United States was standing on the sidelines looking on, "because, although we had been associated with the Allies in the war we had not declared war on Turkey; only diplomatic relations were broken, by the Turks."

"Why don't you have a legation here, a minister?" asked Beaverbrook.

"Because we have no diplomatic relations," said Bristol. He was by now thoroughly rattled. Was it possible that Beaverbrook did not know who he was, or was the man dissembling?

The English lady seated between them injected the explanation that the Admiral was the American High Commissioner, with the rank of Ambassador, and that he was representing the United States in Turkey. Unfazed, Beaverbrook asked what could be done about the Turkish mess. "I told him that it could be settled, I thought, if they approached the question on the ground of giving fair play and a square deal to everyone concerned," Bristol noted in his diary. "I then went on to discuss the situation to avoid saying anything more on the subject of what would be a square deal for everyone."

"The Admiral is doubtless laughing up his sleeve at our position," the lady said.

"I became serious at once," Bristol wrote, "and I said, No, it was nothing to laugh about. I had been here for three and a half years and I had seen this horrible war going on in Asia Minor where men were being unnecessarily sacrificed in war and all kinds of horrible crimes and atrocities being committed together with cities and villages being destroyed and thousands upon thousands of people driven into exile, so that it seemed to me one of the most horrible crimes in the modern civilized world."

Lord Beaverbrook had perked up. He was going on to Smyrna, he said. What did the Admiral think of conditions in Smyrna?

Bristol told him that his reports indicated conditions were very bad: the Greek troops were in a panic, refugees were pouring into the city, and there was a danger that the city might be burned. He dispatched the *Lawrence* that night.

Aboard the destroyer, with Hepburn, were two relief officials— Major Claflin Davis of the American Red Cross, and H. C. Jacquith, the Director of the Near East Relief. Also aboard was one Mark Prentiss, advertised as Bristol's relief representative but professionally a representative of the United States Chamber of Commerce for the Levant and a propagandist for expanded foreign trade. Prentiss had signed up with the Near East Relief ostensibly out of compassion for the suffering minorities. Within a week he would be acting, as well, as a special correspondent for the *New York Times*.

Bristol had the newspaper angle well in hand with John Clayton and Constantine Brown aboard the *Lawrence*, and, as far as the Admiral knew, no other journalists in Smyrna. (Although Bristol did not know it, Ward Price, correspondent of the pro-Turk *Daily Mail,* had hitched a ride down on the *Iron Duke.*) He made his position clear before allowing them to embark: "I told them they must remember that going on my permission and on one of our destroyers they must always keep in mind that they were not free to report in the same way as if they went on their own resources. I would trust them to protect my interests along this line. They both stated that they understood exactly what I meant and I could count on them."

By eleven o'clock Saturday morning the new arrivals were gathered in the American consulate at Smyrna with Consul Horton and Lieutenant Merrill, discussing relief measures. They had just selected the YMCA as relief headquarters because of its central location, but with some misgivings about the word "Christian" in its title, when piercing screams outside the building roused them to their feet and drove them to the balcony.

A mob of terror-stricken women was stampeding the entrance to the consulate and being pushed back by the sailor guards. The building was on the Parallel, one short street up from the quay, and from the terrace the Americans could see a column of Turkish cavalry proceeding slowly down the shorefront toward the *Konak,* to the south. "Not a sane face was to be seen in the mob dashing past in the street below," Merrill reported, "but the cavalry paid no more attention to the excitement they were creating than if they were riding through the lonesome hills of Asia Minor. At the head of the first company was gallant little Cherefeddin Bey. He was in Captain's uniform and from his red cheek down he was drenched in fresh blood."

Sailors on the *Litchfield* were among those who witnessed the unexpected appearance of General Murcelle Pasha's celebrated cavalry regiment at the Point—the northern tip of the quay. To them, the Turks seemed "a hard, dusty, seasoned-looking bunch of men." To the refugees they appeared formidable. Many of the horsemen had the northeastern Mongolian features reminiscent of Genghis Khan and seldom seen along the Mediterranean. They loomed high on their horses, their curved, gleaming sabres drawn and raised in their right hands. On their heads they wore high black fezzes emblazoned with the red crescent and star. They rode at a dignified pace, and as panicked refugees shrieked and

103

scattered in their wake they called out, *"Korkma! Korkma!"* "Fear not! Fear not!"

Suddenly a grenade struck the leader a smart blow on the cheek. Although it failed to explode, it drew a stream of blood. The cavalrymen directly behind him drew their rifles and aimed into the crowd, killing seven or eight people. Observers could not tell who had thrown the grenade, or whether he had escaped or been killed. Then, as though nothing had happened, the regiment proceeded down the quay with a growing throng of Turkish civilians running alongside, shouting, cheering, waving flags. At the *Konak* the Turks encountered some Greek soldiers—the last stragglers of the retreating army—and exchanged a few shots before rounding them up. Soon afterward the Turkish flag was flying on the building.

Allied military representatives hurried to the *Konak* to congratulate the Turks on their victory and on their spectacular forbearance in the face of provocation. "I did lose my temper when I saw a British patrol standing close by making no attempt to stop the assassin," the spunky Cherefeddin told them. He was nonetheless in splendid humor. He had washed his face and wore a small bandage by which the foreigners now readily identified him. In excellent French, he told Lieutenant Merrill his story.

From the time he arrived in the outskirts of Smyrna, until he reached the *Konak*, he had had three bombs thrown at him by Armenians—probably fanatics who had sworn to get the first Turk who entered the city. The first bomb had killed his horse. Ten minutes later five Armenians had thrown two bombs, killing his second horse and wounding three of his men. These Armenians were all shot down. Then, in the main street of the city, along the quay wall, a third bomb had struck him a violent blow near the right eye. The little Captain said he had not even drawn his revolver, he was so thankful the bomb had failed to explode. (Two years later, under oath, the Captain gave a somewhat different version of his experience; the first two attacks, he said, consisted of rifle fire, "by persons we could not see." As to the source of the missile that struck him, "It was a uniformed, armed Greek soldier who threw the bomb.") The worst appeared to be over. "I had a feeling of relief that some proper authority had come to take charge of the city," the Reverend Dobson noted. Foreign officials recorded the same sentiment in dispatches to their capitals. Again, Horton remained the exception.

CHAPTER X

My brother said we ought to leave the city. But my parents said, "What can happen with all those battleships guarding the harbor? Nothing can happen with so many witnesses standing by."

ROSE BERBERIAN CACHOIAN
Interview, February 22, 1967

On Saturday afternoon the Turkish quarter of Smyrna was decked out as if for a carnival. Every available scrap of red cloth had been used to decorate shops and houses, carriages and street lamps. From dozens of balconies blared a cacaphony of Turkish music. On narrow labyrinthine streets ecstatic throngs laughed and sang, shouted greetings, kissed one another, congratulated themselves. They carried scarlet flags marked with the star and crescent, and pictures of Kemal—some as big as life. Women and children bore armfuls of flowers, while men who had not dared show a weapon in three years of Greek occupation jostled their way to the markets, armed to the teeth.

Kemal and his entourage had halted in the hills at Nif, some miles away, in a makeshift headquarters still hung with photographs of Venizelos. Here he had condescended to meet the French and Italian consuls, but communications had been roundabout, his message had been slow in reaching them, and by afternoon the roads to the city were choked with his advance troops. Lieutenant Merrill and the two American newsmen, driving toward a hoped-for rendezvous and interview with Kemal, came face to face with a Turkish officer who bellowed in three languages for them to turn back. A portly, heavy-faced man with close-cropped hair, he was a cartoon of a Prussian general, Merrill reflected, and the only man he had ever seen who appeared to strut while sitting down. The correspondents shouted that they had come to offer propaganda and publicity to Mustafa Kemal, to which the aide retorted, in pungent Turkish, that he gave not a damn for either one. Dejected, the three returned to Smyrna.

Passing through the Jewish quarter, they could see that the Italians had the neighborhood well in hand. As Kemal's original benefactors, they were in an enviably privileged position. Italian cavalry officers had met with their Turkish counterparts outside the city and were now accompanying Turkish patrols through the Armenian quarter, ostensibly to search out would-be assassins and troublemakers. The Italians had also taken upon themselves the protection of the Jewish population, since a large number of Jews had obtained Italian citizenship after the war, at a time when Italy was not averse to inflating the numbers of her subjects on Turkey's southern coast. They had organized and outfitted a Jewish militia whose members were now escorting Jews from isolated areas to the safety of the Beth Israel Temple in Salahane—a prosperous Jewish community at the city's edge—and were making themselves generally conspicuous to ensure that no unsuspecting Turk would mistake their protégés for native Christians.

Such noticeable precautions caused a resurgence of panic among the minorities. The railways ceased to operate as Armenian and Greek employees hurried home to their families. Native Smyrneans as well as refugees rushed to foreign buildings to ask for protection. Possessing the most institutions and the reputation for the most benevolence, the Americans were the most harassed.

Turkish patrols distributing leaflets printed in Turkish and Greek handed one to the Reverend Hartunian, an Armenian evangelical pastor, as he was returning to the American Collegiate Institute after a meeting with the Greek and Armenian archbishops. Earlier, he had left his wife and children in the safety of the school. Hartunian read: "Mustafa Kemal has given strict orders to the soldiers to harm no one. Those who disobey these orders will be punished by death. Let the people be assured of safety." Overjoyed, the Reverend offered the Lord a prayer of gratitude. He had much to be thankful for—he had survived six massacres in his lifetime, his family was intact, he had at last obtained a visa to take them to America, with passage reserved on a ship scheduled to leave for New York on September 12. His boundless faith in God required that he trust his fellow man.

At the College, his announcement that it was now safe for everyone to return home was greeted in stony silence by over a thousand Christians. The Reverend gathered his wife and children and left. No one else budged.

To Captain Hepburn's dismay, renewed assurances of safety were now having no effect at all on the Ottoman Christians, who were making it singularly difficult for the Navy to follow Admiral Bristol's orders. Captain Hepburn's instructions expressly forbade him to do anything that might give the impression of "a naval demonstration" and ordered him to establish friendly relations with the Turkish forces. He had approved leaving most of the sailor guards ashore since he was bound also to protect American installations and personnel, but he could not increase the number of guards without making their presence obtrusive and giving the wrong impression. On the other hand, a few dozen men in scattered positions were scarcely able to defend the buildings against an onslaught of refugees. "Let one try to force a way in and the whole crowd will push forward, as I have seen this afternoon wherever there appears to be a sign of foreign protection," he wrote Bristol. "I have asked the guards to keep indoors, out of sight, to avoid being an irresistible invitation to the refugees." Yet at the YMCA, the YWCA, and the American Collegiate Institute, they had somehow managed to get inside, and their presence now put America in the position of appearing to protect Turkey's enemies.

Hepburn hurried to the *Konak* to explain matters to General Murcelle Pasha, the ranking Turkish officer of the moment. Murcelle greeted him coolly, but became friendly upon learning that the Captain was American and not English, as he had mistakenly assumed. Hepburn explained that his armed guards were ashore only to protect American lives and property and said that he was anxious to withdraw them as soon as he could be assured of the safety of American buildings and personnel. He felt relieved at the General's understanding attitude, then reached the consulate only to learn that Murcelle was being superseded by another General and that he would have the explaining to do all over again.

The sight of refugee mobs plaguing the consulate gates renewed Hepburn's apprehensions. Some Greek priests had led their entire congregations before the building; those crowds were attracting others and the street was becoming impassable. The Captain sent an officer to Turkish headquarters to ask that the street be blocked off and was rewarded by a squad of Turkish soldiers who promptly drove the Greeks away at bayonet point. The Turkish officer in charge explained that patrols would soon be posted throughout the city to keep civilians in their houses. "The most effective measure that can be taken," Hepburn noted approvingly.

An American officer, his car somewhat the worse for half a dozen bullet holes, arrived out of breath and informed Hepburn that the American International College at Paradise had become a refugee camp and that snipers shooting at the refugees were hitting the buildings. Hepburn, preferring to believe that the snipers were Greek stragglers shooting in panic, was annoyed at the College president for having let the refugees in instead of clearing out with his faculty and coming down to the city, as Hepburn had advised.

There was more ominous news. Refugees escaping from nearby Alachati reported that in the Greek Cathedral a Turkish officer had torn the American flag off the coffin of Private George Dilboy, opened the coffin, and scattered the remains over the floor. A hero of Belleau Wood, Private Dilboy had been posthumously awarded the Congressional Medal of Honor; now his body, after long delay, had finally reached his parental village, at his father's request. True to their word to Admiral Bristol, the newsmen did not report the incident.

It was small comfort to Hepburn that his English colleagues were in a less enviable position. Turkish patrols had refused to let Admiral Brock land and he had been forced ignominiously back to his battleship. Reports from the suburbs had it that Turkish forces were reacting to the English flag as a bull might have reacted to the Turkish. There were even rumors that *chettes* running amok in Boudja and Bournabat had murdered an elderly English doctor and a Dutch couple. Hepburn was inclined to discount these as figments of overstimulated imaginations; but with the approaching dusk there were signs that the jitters were rubbing off on some of the longtime residents. "Funny thing," he noted in his diary that evening, "the terror is in the air and quite palpable when it begins to grow."

Sooner or later the refugees had to be dispersed, and Hepburn could see no alternative but for the Turks to allow them to return to their homes in the interior. He resolved to take the matter up with the proper authority as soon as Kemal and his entourage arrived. First, he had to find out how one was supposed to congratulate a victor still technically declared an outlaw. Horton, he hoped, would know the protocol.

But the American Consul was beset with troubles of his own and no manual of diplomatic etiquette could help him. He had scarcely slept since the early part of the week, and his face was pinched with exhaustion and concern. The Captain discovered that Horton had been besieged, not only by American citizens but by some of his official colleagues as well, for all manner of advice, protection, and assistance.

To those who knew the man it was natural that others would turn to him in time of crisis. George Horton was something of an anomaly among foreign officials in Smyrna. Unlike the majority, who had arrived since the end of the war, he had worked in the area for thirty years and was thoroughly familiar with its history. At a time when Americans and Englishmen were notoriously inept at foreign languages, he spoke fluent French, Greek, German, Italian, and Turkish. Virtually every segment of the Smyrna population affirmed Horton's sensitivity to its point of view, and in reports that were models of clarity he had detailed the attitudes of these respective groups for Admiral Bristol and the experts at the State Department. Even Bristol conceded that the man's views on the Greco-Turkish question were "plainly fair and square."

Horton's appointment to the Foreign Service had been whimsical. A successful poet, literary critic, and author of two best-selling novels, as well as a journalist on the *Chicago Herald,* Horton had steeped himself in the classics and had mastered both ancient and modern Greek when fate wrested him from the midwest at the age of thirty-four. He had written a number of editorials for the *Herald* at election time supporting Grover Cleveland. These had pleased the new President and led to the unexpected offer of a consular post in Berlin. "I saw no connection between such editorials and the ability to fill a consular post intelligently, nor do I now," he wrote in 1927. He refused the job in Berlin, opted for one in Greece, and was appointed Consul to Athens in 1893. In 1909 he was transferred to Salonika, and in 1911 he was appointed United States Consul at Smyrna.

From the outset of the war until Turkey broke diplomatic relations with the United States in 1917, Horton had charge of all Allied interests in Smyrna. The governor-general of the city was then Rahmi Bey, a tall, shrewd, aristocratic despot with an insatiable appetite for good food, expensive liquor, and lavish gifts. The governor's tastes were duly indulged by Smyrna's leading citizens and ignored by the overbearing German officers who were descending on the area. "I cultivated Rahmi Bey," Horton wrote, "as he was my only source when any of my charges got into trouble, which was frequently. I soon discovered that the governor-general had no faith in the final victory of the German-Turkish arms, and that he was extremely anxious to keep an anchor to windward. He was playing a double game; of keeping in at the same time with the authorities in Constantinople and with the prominent British, French, and Italians at Smyrna." Even war had failed to budge these confirmed Smyrneans, although their countries were fighting against Turkey and they were therefore technically enemy aliens. They had some anxious moments when Rahmi Bey felt obliged to show his government that he was not so forbearing as he appeared. There were token arrests and deportations of leading Armenian and Greek citizens into the interior, and Horton was kept busy running about in search of Rahmi Bey, who at such times liked to make himself inaccessible.

Horton had a stack of letters from those days attesting to his having saved numbers of lives. During the Greek occupation he had received similar letters from grateful Turks testifying to his help in times of stress. But now he was in a kind of official limbo and there was little he could do to help his beleaguered friends. If American lives and property were in jeopardy, he could only refer matters to Captain Hepburn, whom he knew to be deprived, on Bristol's orders, of any effective means of protest.

"My position here at the present moment as a representative of the American government is extremely difficult," Horton wrote to the Department after the Turkish conquest. "The day before yesterday American citizen George Carathima, Captain Carathima of California, came here to sell his property and return to the United States where he had been for a long time established. He was attacked by Turkish soldiers, beaten, and thrown into prison. . . . I confess that I do not know what to do about an incident that occurs to me to be very serious and humiliating." It was worse than that for George Carathima, who as it happened never returned. ("No reason to impute bad faith on the part of the Turkish authorities," Bristol insisted: the man was probably alive somewhere. In 1925 the Admiral finally admitted that "Carathima was undoubtedly killed.")

Although he felt no great anxiety for American businessmen and missionaries, Horton was intensely uneasy about the fate of other naturalized citizens like Carathima. He had managed to evacuate those who could afford passage, but there remained well over a hundred who were too poor to pay their way. The conviction that many of these would be killed led him to collect them in the theater with their immediate relatives, such as mothers or children. Captain Hepburn had insisted on ejecting other relatives—a tragedy, Horton thought, since large families often lived together. It had not been easy to persuade the Navy that these people were in imminent danger, and he wondered what he was to do with them if the State Department did not soon answer his request that they be repatriated to the United States at government expense. The Navy might take them as far as Piraeus, but destitute Greece was scarcely in a position to care for indigent American citizens. Then there was the question of those thousands of Ottoman subjects who had nowhere at all to turn.

Hour after hour, all week long, they had been filing past his desk, identically harassed faces flushed with the conviction that he was their last hope of escape before the holocaust. He could understand their fears better than he could the dogged optimism of some remote authority.

Least of all could he understand how commerce could carry on inexorably in the face of human catastrophe. Already some of the businessmen who had volunteered trucks for distributing food to refugees were showing themselves more interested in moving tobacco to ships. Men and women were pleading vainly for passage while immense freighters sat idly at anchor awaiting merchandise. The Shipping Board representative—a Mr. Moore—considered it "a matter of considerable importance" to have the *Hog Island* deliver a load of tobacco on schedule to Alexandria. As a personal favor to Horton, the ship's captain had allowed him to smuggle aboard a number of potential victims, among them a wounded Greek soldier.

Since the first day of September, Horton's days and nights had been an endless round of conferences, interviews, and errands of mercy that were to become legendary among the Greeks. He had gathered hundreds of families at the Point and scoured the harbor to beg or buy their passage, often at his own expense. Thanks to his ingenuity scores of small fishing vessels sprouted the stars and stripes and maneuvered their way safely to the open sea. But he could not assure American workers that their native wards at American schools and orphanages were not in danger of being molested, or that the American Navy would protect them if they were in such danger. The orphanages were filled with Armenian children who had seen their parents killed not long before. They were being kept alive with American dollars and American care, but the United States would take no responsibility for them. Horton composed lengthy memoranda to the State Department explaining why it would profit America to offer asylum to some of the refugees. These were not the sort of people who would congregate in cities, he pleaded. Most of them were agriculturists, highly skilled in the cultivation of the finest grades of tobacco and grapes. They could be dispersed to areas where their skills were in demand. He despaired of a favorable reply; Congress had just arrested their immigration by passing the most stringent immigration laws in its history. Immigrants from Turkey were virtually barred.

The Consul's greatest personal anxiety was for his friend the Greek Archbishop Chrysostomos, a venerable figure beloved by his people and anathema to the Turks because of his outspoken devotion to the Greek cause. Horton had last seen the Archbishop on the eve of the Turkish occupation, when Chrysostomos called at the consulate to ask if something could be done to protect his people. The Consul could not bring himself to reply; he urged instead that the Archbishop accept the French offer of a marine escort to haven on one of their battleships. Chrysostomos refused. He was dressed in black and his face was pale and infinitely sad. "As he sat there in the consular office, the shadow of his approaching death lay upon his features," Horton said. "At least twice in my life I have seen that shadow upon a human visage and known that the person was soon to die."

All Saturday afternoon and into the evening the Turkish infantry followed the cavalry into Smyrna, in perfect order and discipline—and in a bewildering assortment of uniforms. Some of the men were outfitted in rough khaki, others in American army uniforms, complete to the buttons. ("It would be interesting to know where else, except Russia, these army uniforms could have come from," an intelligence officer later wrote Bristol. "It would seem a wise precaution to remove Army buttons from all uniform clothing sent to relieve the poor Russian Bolsheviki before it leaves the United States.") Other Turkish soldiers wore baggy trousers, crossed bandoliers, and carried an intimidating array of daggers. These troops were sometimes referred to as *chettes* (irregulars), although knowledgeable foreigners tended to discount the distinction between regular and irregular troops. Turkish leaders themselves admitted that the formerly rebellious outlaw bands had become fully integrated into Kemal's army by 1920, and had thereafter submitted to its discipline. According to a United States military intelligence report, in 1922 that discipline was "excellent and maintained by fear of superior officers, by brutality and example." The same report noted that morale was maintained "by the desire for loot."

Armenian and Greek shops were the first to be looted. Small bands of civilians initiated the action, keeping discreetly to side streets; then, discovering that the Italian and Turkish patrols were standing by offering no interference, soldiers, too, became emboldened, and were soon joined by their officers. They broke into elegant shops on the Rue Franque and walked away with their arms heaped with laces and satins, their pockets bulging with watches and jewels. "They proceed without interruption or qualms," wrote a French officer. "They work at their leisure, picking out the most valuable objects and discarding the rest. What have they to worry about? They are helped by the patrols who constitute the only police."

Looting soon turned to armed robbery. Lieutenant Merrill watched a band of soldiers hold up a civilian in the Armenian district and go through his pockets. "They paid no attention to the staff car, simply moved their victim aside to let us pass," he said. The houses, he noted, had their shutters tightly drawn.

Inside, families huddled together in darkened rooms trying to convince one another that they were being unreasonably fearful. In the Ashjian household Krikor's sons, Onnig and Stepan, were parading one logical argument after another to prove why the prevailing jitters were unjustified. Onnig, a lawyer in his early thirties, had managed a week before to overrule his father's plea that the younger members of the family leave for one of the Greek islands. Krikor himself had escaped two massacres in his lifetime and felt too old to run again.

Onnig was insisting that there was no danger whatever. He had been educated at the Turkish university in Constantinople, on his father's premise that Armenians in Turkey had to be prepared to work with Turks, and he had heard that a former classmate would soon be appointed civilian governor of Smyrna. His office colleagues assured him that the Turks had no quarrel with Armenians, and why should they have, Onnig asked, when even that reprobate of a self-styled Armenian general, Torcom, had received scant attention from the community when he had come to rally an Armenian legion? The old fool had spent his days at the fancy Kramer Hotel and had gone off with a handful of recruits and his bar bills unpaid. No, Kemal had no quarrel with the Armenians. Moreover, he had well-disciplined forces; he even had the *chettes* under control. And then, too, Onnig pointed out, there were all those Allied ships.

Mention of the ships never failed to break the tension for a little while; long enough for the women to scurry to the kitchen to bring out food, and for the smaller children to climb down from their parents' laps and chase each other around the room. Then someone would wonder aloud about the fate of a friend or relative in one of the suburbs, out of sight of the foreign ships, and the family would again close ranks and listen halfheartedly to the young men's arguments.

Krikor rose and moved to the shuttered window. Between two slats he could make out Zaven, the Armenian watchmaker across the street, fastening a Turkish flag over the doorway of his shop. Two Turkish soldiers moved into Krikor's line of vision. One reached out and tore off the flag while the other gave the watchmaker a resounding slap across the cheek. Then, as one soldier held his rifle to Zaven's chest, the second snapped the watch and chain from the shopkeeper's belt.

Suddenly the first soldier fired, tilting the rifle upward so that the shot blasted Zaven's chin and tore through his crown. The two soldiers sauntered out of sight as Zaven's faceless body slumped against the wall of his shop and slid into the street. He had not uttered a sound.

Behind him, Krikor could hear his son droning on about Kemal's good intentions.

"That's enough, Onnig," he said hoarsely. "Out there it has already begun."

The Reverend Hartunian, oblivious of any danger, left his wife and children at home and set out for the market place to buy some meat. He got no farther than the Collegiate Institute at the corner where a Turk stood before the building shouting to those inside, "Where is your God now? Let him come and save you!"

Hartunian turned back. "I still did not think to take my wife and children and return quickly to the American building," he recalled. "My wife was preparing lentil soup for supper. The table was set. I offered the blessing and we were about to sup. Suddenly there was a scream in the house next to ours. Our neighbors had been attacked. The *chettes* were threatening them with death unless they gave money. Our neighbors were pleading, saying 'We have none!' "

The Hartunians hid in the cellar until the pastor's wife insisted that they make a try for the school while the Turks were still occupied next door. Grabbing his passport, some money, and a red fez, the clergyman followed his wife and children out the door. The sailor guard at the school, taking them for Turks, refused to let them through the gate. "My God," thought the Reverend, "the American thinks us Turks and locks us out. The Turk thinks us Amercanized and massacres us. What are we to do?" The family began to shout: "Please open the door, quickly!" Luckily, Armenians inside overheard and made the sailors understand. The door was opened and they were taken in.

"At this hour, 11:30 P.M., everything is quiet, peaceful and dark along the quay," Hepburn was writing aboard the *Litchfield*. "It will be too much to expect that there will not be some serious affairs in certain sections of the city during the night, but knowing the conditions, I certainly must say that the Turks deserve a high mark for their efficiency, good discipline and high military standards displayed so far."

CHAPTER XI

Having received permission to loot, the soldiers thronged into the city with joyous hearts and there, seizing the possessors and their families, they made the wretched unbelievers weep.

> The Turkish historian
> Seaddedin, writing of the fall
> of Constantinople, 1453

Sunday noon was cloudless and brilliantly sunny as Mustafa Kemal left Nif in a convoy of five cars bedecked with olive branches. At the entrance to the city two long lines of cavalrymen drew their swords; sun flashing on steel, they galloped alongside his open touring car as it made its way through cheering throngs to the government house abandoned by the Greeks only days before. The clang of hoofbeats on marble reverberated against the stone of the archways as the horsemen passed under the closed bazaar, and accompanied the roar of the exultant crowd.

There were more cheers when the Conqueror appeared on the balcony of the *Konak,* a tall, imposing figure savoring his victory. He then retired to confer with General Noureddin, an officer well known both for his strength of command and his contempt for foreigners, into whose hands Kemal was bestowing control of Smyrna.

Kemal's next move held the Allies in suspense. Would he dare to move on the neutral zone they had demarked and occupied to protect Constantinople and their access to the Dardanelles? If he did, were they not bound to stop him as they had stopped the Greeks? The English thought it imperative that they do so. The French pretended to agree, but were ready to hedge. As for Kemal himself, this last military maneuver would prove a calculated bluff, meant to provide bargaining power. He had no need to take on the Allies, either singly or collectively, for what would be his as soon as a peace treaty was signed. He would give them their access to the Dardanelles; such a gift would guarantee their solicitude in the future. He would confine his nation's boundaries to an area acceptable to the West—so long as he could regain Eastern Thrace, and see all Turkey cleared of its remaining minorities. The motto "Turkey for the Turks" had already been determined. Soon Kemal would mount a campaign to purify the very language of every strain not essentially Turkish. The bulk of the Jewish population would eventually be driven out through discriminatory taxation and cultural pressures. In joining his nation to the twentieth century, Kemal was to complete the task begun by his predecessors—the final effacing of its unassimilable elements from the land.

By now the Conqueror's task was considerably lightened. The northeastern provinces were wiped clean of Armenians; so, in fact, was virtually every hamlet, village, and town throughout Anatolia. Less than two hundred thousand remained in Constantinople and Smyrna.

Although they were far greater in number, the Greeks posed less of a problem in disposal. As enemies whose compatriots had been defeated at war, they could be ejected from the country and— given the cooperation of the Western powers—Greece would be obliged to accept them. But the Armenian population had not been engaged in the war; there was no acceptable reason to evict them from their homes, no country to which they could be sent. Excited Turkish troops were already raising havoc in the city and, according to lugubrious tradition, it was against the more helpless Armenians that they unleashed the force of their hatred. To a Turk, it was inconceivable that an Armenian should fail to be a traitor: "No Armenian can be our friend after what we have done to them," Talaat had declared to Morgenthau. Kemal had now to decide whether to restrain his troops or give them license to dispose of the Armenians once and for all.

On Sunday night, the Italian consul, Count Senni, confided to the British vice-consul that Kemal was meeting with his aides to decide on the disposition of the Armenians. By Monday morning the Armenian quarter was surrounded by a cordon of Turkish soldiers. A public crier went through the streets inviting Turkish inhabitants to leave the area. By afternoon a new proclamation appeared: Anyone caught concealing an Armenian in his home would be brought before a court-martial.

In the Turkish quarter there were signs that the populace was being roused to action. The rumor spread that an Armenian general, Torcom, had organized a volunteer army in Smyrna during the recent war, and that his ferocious bands had preyed on the Turks of the surrounding area. An American visitor asked some Turks whether it would be safe to enter the Armenian district. It was by no means safe for the Armenians, they told him, and he would be wise to stay away.

It was only slightly more secure for some of the sentries, as two British marines posted at the oriental carpet factory were startled to discover when an Armenian with whom they were conversing fell dead at their feet in mid-sentence. "There was a shot from somewhere and it picked him out between my two men," said Sergeant-Major Fripp. The marine noted, too, that the same cavalry soldiers who rode into view in perfect formation disappeared behind a hill, left their horses, and walked back to join in the fun. He had seen from about seventy-five to one hundred soldiers of different kinds and categories, "with different kinds of uniforms, some clean and some dirty, some with armlets on," he said, "and they were breaking into buildings and throwing bundles out. They were putting the loot on wagons and carting it away. They simply gave us a cheer and off they went with it." In another part of town an American officer was observing that the shops were virtually cleaned out. "All the looting was most orderly," he wrote.

Shortly after noon General Noureddin sent for the Greek Metropolitan. The two had met during the first months of the Greek occupation, and as he approached the General in the latter's conference room at the *Konak* Chrysostomos extended his hand in greeting. Noureddin spat, declaring he would not touch that filthy hand. He pointed to a dossier lying open on his desk. On the basis of these sworn accusations, he said, a revolutionary tribunal in Angora had already condemned Chrysostomos to death. "There is nothing left but for the people to give their judgment," he shouted. "Now get out of my sight!"

The Patriarch was walking slowly down the steps of the *Konak* when the General appeared on the balcony and cried out to the waiting mob, "Treat him as he deserves!" The crowd fell upon Chrysostomos with guttural shrieks and dragged him down the street until they reached a barber shop where Ismael, the Jewish proprietor, was peering nervously from his doorway. Someone pushed the barber aside, grabbed a white sheet, and tied it around Chrysostomos's neck, shouting, "Give him a shave!"

They tore out the Patriarch's beard, gouged out his eyes with knives, cut off his ears, his nose, and his hands. A dozen French marines who had accompanied Chrysostomos to the government house were standing by, beside themselves. Several of the men jumped instinctively forward to intervene, but the officer in charge forbade them to move. "He had his hand on his gun, though he was trembling himself," one of the men said later, "so we dared not lift ours. They finished Chrysostomos there before our eyes."

The Archbishop's murder was reported to Admiral Dumesnil aboard the French flagship. He shrugged his shoulders: "He got what was coming to him," he said.

News that Turks were killing Armenians in the back streets poured into the consulates all afternoon. So did confirmation of an attack on Dr. Murphy, the retired army surgeon in Bournabat. Turks had broken into his home and beaten the old doctor with their muskets when he tried to protect a young servant from their assaults. The doctor died that night of his injuries.

In Boudja, a husband and wife, Dutch subjects, were murdered in the street in front of their home. A priest hurried to the suburb to recite prayers over the pair. As no coffins were to be found, husband and wife were buried directly in the earth that afternoon.

Bombs were meanwhile raining in on the walled courtyard of the Armenian Cathedral, where over a thousand local inhabitants had barricaded themselves for protection. Two girls dressed as nurses were sent out to seek help from one of the Western consulates, and priests set the Cathedral bells to pealing as a call for help. The girls never returned, but some Italian priests stopped at the gate and were asked "for the sake of humanity to intercede, wherever you can, to save the people." Turkish and Italian officers arrived, the gates were opened, and all the men who emerged were arrested and led away. The women and children were taken to the quay.

It was by now crowded with humanity, as those who had been

squatting there all week were joined by others escaping from their homes and unable to gain entrance to a foreign building. Every Armenian and Greek in Smyrna had become a refugee. Hundreds were heaped like potatoes on barges lying along the breakwater. Closer in, small boats dangerously overloaded with human cargo moved vainly from ship to ship, their passengers begging to be taken aboard.

"Some people were jumping into the water, but nobody was picking them up," Marika Tsakirides recalls. She was thirteen years old at the time, squeezed between her brother and mother in a rowboat with two other families. She remembers that people were swimming to the big ships and grabbing the tow lines. "I remember one big ship with an English flag. The sailors were shouting 'No! No! No! No!' I remember so well because it was the first time I heard 'No, No, No,' like that, in English. They were throwing water on the people and cutting the ropes."

Typhus was breaking out on shore. Jacquith wired the Near East Relief in Constantinople for doctors, nurses, medicine, food. The agency responded immediately by sending a medical team, composed of Dr. Wilfred Post and two nurses, and a load of medical supplies by U.S. destroyer. Hepburn estimated the number of destitute at well over three hundred thousand. "Entire population of seven hundred thousand faces starvation," Major Davis cabled Bristol.

In the streets of the Armenian quarter Turkish forces proceeded systematically at their task of flushing out the population. Groups of soldiers, assisted by civilians, moved from house to house, breaking down the hinges of iron doors with crowbars, relieving the men of their cash, the women of their jewels, then attacking their victims. Women and girls were raped, knifed, or pursued into the streets, where they fell prey to other gangs. A few managed to hide or to reach a foreign building, but these were already so overcrowded that few of the new arrivals were let in. Men were either murdered in their homes or lashed together at the wrists and led away to be killed at the edge of the city. One hundred at a time were murdered beside the *Konak*. The Reverend Dobson observed a group of two hundred kneeling on the road beside his home. At dusk Monday all two hundred were butchered, "by steel," wrote the chaplain, "to avoid rifle fire." By official order swords and daggers had replaced the noisier weapons on Monday evening.

Refugees crowded the entrance to the theater that served as

American sentry headquarters. "Pitiable objects," Lieutenant Commander Knauss, who was in charge of the guards, characterized them in his report for the day. "For two days they have been huddled in small heaps, never stirring except when one of their number approaches with a gourd for fresh water. If the Turks come through their faces express more than fear. They are terror-stricken, and as I feared a stampede would ensue in case of panic, I made all preparations for running down the iron screen promptly. It was fortunate that we had done so, for at 2:00 A.M. several Turks rode into them and grabbed a man, and there was scarcely time to drop the door before the frantic mob tried to find their way in. Today I have seen during my rounds over a hundred dead and four people killed in cold blood."

Lieutenant Merrill described the scene in slightly different terms for Admiral Bristol's benefit. "The refugees are in a blue funk," he wrote. "No one could imagine without seeing them 'under fire' what a chicken-livered lot the Christian minorities are."

CHAPTER XII

*Strange how you can foregt the time of day, but happen-
ings like this stay on your mind forever.*

MELVIN R. JOHNSON
Interview, March 20, 1967

Melvin Johnson was on guard at the Smyrna theater Monday afternoon when his C.O. came by on his rounds. "All right, Johnson,"
he said, "get on a clean pair of whites, you're going to the Young
Women's Christian Association."

"Yessir," said Johnson. "What for?"

"To relieve one of the men," Knauss said. "You haven't been
drinking, have you?"

Johnson thought he had better come out with the truth. He had
missed lunch and his head was whirling. "Certainly I've been
drinking," he said. He had just returned from an errand to the
British consulate, where the sailors had treated him generously to
their rum rations. He had ridden back on an abandoned horse. It
had seemed the sensible thing to do at the time, but the horse
hadn't been combed in a year and Johnson's whites were the color
of mud.

"Go back to the ship and take a bath," Knauss said, "and if you pass inspection they'll send you out as relief. But there'll be no drinking, you understand?"

"Yessir," said Johnson.

At the YWCA, located at the edge of the Armenian quarter, Johnson discovered that the sailors had had no sleep for twenty-six hours. Outside, the screams began at dusk and persisted without letup all night long. Inside, five hundred women moaned, children wailed, there was little to eat. It had been too much for one sailor.

"They were jammed in there so tight there wasn't an inch to move," Johnson recalled. "But then more of 'em would push up against the doors—crying—and, well, we weren't supposed to but we'd let 'em in."

That night there began a fearful pounding at the steel door, the main entrance to the building. "Like somebody breaking it down," Johnson said. "I hollered, 'Stand by! Man the machine gun!' That was a joke because none of us had ever fired one. 'O.K. now, point it at the door,' I says, and I tell one of the kids to go upstairs and look out the window and see what it is. We thought it was a bunch of Turk soldiers trying to come in, see. The kid comes down laughing. 'What's the joke?' I can't see nothing funny—all the women screaming and hollering. He says, 'You'll never guess what's trying to come in here.' It was a bunch of army mules, rubbing their backsides up against this steel door. To me, that was the funniest part of the landing force. Yeh. We were scared, you can believe it. And all the time those women, some of 'em giving birth from fright—you know, ahead of time. And not enough food. It was something pitiful."

Hoping to find a bakery, Johnson and another man slipped out the back door early the next morning. "That's when we saw the victims," Johnson said. "They were lying all over in the sun, swelling up with the heat. Two of 'em was women. We couldn't take but one look.

"We'd turned back when this Greek soldier comes staggering around the corner like he's drunk. Uniform all covered with blood. He's all in. Just staggering. They had these hitching posts along the streets there, and he falls up against one of 'em. Then this torpedoman—nice little fella—he says to me, 'It'd be an act of mercy to kill this guy right now because they're gonna get him when they come 'round that corner,' he says. They'd stopped to loot, we could hear 'em raking through some store or other. And I think we—we were on the verge of shooting him when he started

123

groaning. And I says to the torpedoman, 'No. Let's quit. He'll probably die when they come 'round the corner.' So we went back in
and bolted the doors. Oh, we were scared, I don't mind telling
you!"

In the heart of the Armenian quarter, sixteen-year-old Rose
Berberian cowered in the coal bin of a neighbor's cellar, her face
touching the coals. She scarcely dared breathe. Footsteps pounded
across the floor overhead. A man's voice, in Turkish, demanded
gold. There were long, agonized screams, followed by moans. Then
it all started again. Turning her face a fraction to one side she
discovered that her hands were covering her ears. She raised her
head and heard only silence. The sounds had been ringing in her
head. Then she remembered that the house was empty.

Rose's father had a barber shop in the suburb of Karatash. On
Friday, when both the horse-trolleys and the ferry boats had
stopped running, he had sent word that he would stay in his shop
until everything settled down, and asked the rest of the family to
seek refuge at a neighbor's. He was never heard from again. Monday night, the crew of the British battleship *Iron Duke* observed
the massacre at Karatash through their field glasses.

Next door to the Berberians lived an Italian family who had
been escorted to the Italian consulate on Friday night. But the
house beyond belonged to Mr. Aram, a wealthy Armenian merchant. He had once befriended Kemal's armies in the interior by
providing essential supplies, and in return he had been given an
official letter acknowledging this help and informing anyone concerned that Mr. Aram and members of his family were to be protected. Mrs. Berberian was therefore delighted to accept Mr. Aram's
invitation to join his household. She put her money, jewelry,
and important papers in a secret drawer at the back of a desk and
locked it, took a few clothes and a small amount of food, feeling
certain that their stay would be short, and with her two daughters
and son (Rose was the youngest) slipped over to Mr. Aram's house
on Saturday evening. It was crowded with other friends and relatives.

There was some shooting that night, but the assemblage put it
down to sniping between Turks and Greek soldiers who had been
left behind. Sunday was rather pleasant. The younger people joked
and played cards to pass the time, and Mr. Aram frequently read
his letter aloud to reassure everyone that there was nothing at all
to worry about even if the Turks should come. But beginning Sun-

day night, terrible sounds came from the streets nearby. Rose heard voices shouting, "Come out! Why are you hiding inside like mice? Come out or we will come in and kill you." Peering through the blinds, Mr. Aram reported that Turkish soldiers had brought wagons and were loading them with furniture and clothes. They were working along the street behind the garden, prying the hinges off the iron doors with crowbars and causing a terrible crash as each door fell. By morning they had reached the street in front of Mr. Aram's house.

"We were frightened, but Mr. Aram kept waving his letter and telling us to relax," Rose says. "He was a fat man, normally jolly and easygoing, but he was perspiring and pacing the floor and fingering his letter. He couldn't sit still. Once he was on the verge of running outside and offering it to a Turkish officer supervising a gang of looters across the street, but his brothers held him back."

After lunch the younger women retired to a bedroom to escape the tension for a little while. They were talking about school, Rose remembers, and about the fact that normally this would have been registration day at the Collegiate Institute, when they heard heavy footsteps pounding up the stairs. The door flew open and one of the intruders cried out, "Give us gold!" Mr. Aram had apparently become so unstrung that he had opened the door a crack and stuck his letter through to solicit protection. At that, one of the soldiers had cried out, "What's this?" flung the precious paper to the ground, and stormed in. It occurred to Rose later that the man probably couldn't read.

Rose was more outraged than frightened that first moment. "Where do you think we're to get gold?" she started to say, but had scarcely opened her mouth when one of them lunged for her. There were at least three vicious-looking men with daggers at their belts. She turned and ran to the terrace, prepared to climb to the one next door, but the dividing wall was too high for her to reach. Mr. Aram's fourteen-year-old daughter—a huge girl for her age— was behind her. Rose shouted, "Lift my feet, my *feet!*" and as the girl complied, Rose grasped the top of the wall and hurtled over it. Before she could turn to help her friend, Rose heard the girl scream as the soldiers caught her.

Rose had fallen to the terrace of still another neighbor, a pharmacist who had left the city. French windows were standing open and she ran into the house, searching desperately for a place to hide. The place had obviously been ransacked and it crossed her mind that this was a good sign; it meant the Turks had already been through this one. Then she realized that if they did return it would be to search her out, and she ran wildly, like a rat in a maze, in and out of rooms, from one floor to the other, until she found herself in the cellar.

She hid in the coal bin all day, dozing from time to time. Long after dark, hours after all was still, she found enough courage to creep upstairs and out onto the terrace. There was screaming in the distance, but next door it was silent as a tomb. "I had the feeling that I was the only Armenian alive on the street; that soon I would be the only one in the entire city," she recalls. In panic, she began to call her brother's name, her sister's, softly at first, then recklessly louder.

"Rose?" It was unmistakably her brother's voice, coming from the attic of still another house, the one belonging to the Italian family who had gone to the Italian consulate. Rose jumped down easily to Mr. Aram's terrace. But from there the house next door appeared inaccessible, until she saw that if she could climb the metal grape arbor and crawl along the top of it, she would be within arm's reach of the attic window. She inched along the arbor on her stomach until her brother reached out an arm and pulled her inside. Her mother and sister were there, too. While the marauders were distracted they had reached the attic, as Rose had just now, by crawling over the vines. Since this house was protected by an Italian flag, it had not been molested. For the moment, the Berberians were safe.

All during Monday, September 11, Captain Hepburn resisted pressure from Consul Horton to evacuate the naturalized Americans. Horton wanted them taken aboard the destroyers, but the Captain feared that the Turkish authorities might oppose such a move, in which case, he wrote Bristol, "the evacuation would soon be interrupted and our present satisfactory relations with the Turkish authorities would come to an end." Considering the possible effect of such a move on "the interests of those native born Americans who had large interests to protect," Hepburn refused. The American position was quite precarious enough, thanks to the refugees.

Lieutenant Merrill managed to arrange an interview with the new commander, General Noureddin. At four o'clock on Monday afternoon Hepburn presented himself at the *Konak*, along with Merrill, Davis, and Jacquith—the American relief officials from

Constantinople—and Dr. Wilfred Post, a missionary doctor who had served in Turkey for years and spoke the language fluently. Also in tow was Vice-Consul Barnes.

After congratulating the General on his military success and on the excellent appearance of his troops, Hepburn introduced Major Davis and Mr. Jacquith as Admiral Bristol's special relief emissaries, and suggested that the only solution was to get the refugees back to their homes in the devastated districts as soon as possible.

The General retorted that such a step was entirely out of the question. If the Americans could see what horrors the Greek army had committed on its retreat, he said, and if they could remember, as every Turk did, "the six thousand Moslems massacred during the Greek occupation of Smyrna," they would realize the impossibility of such a suggestion. "Take them away," he snapped. "Bring ships and take them out of the country. That is the only solution."

There followed a staccato of retorts between Dr. Post and the General that made Hepburn groan inwardly with regret at having brought the doctor along as interpreter. Like so many of the old Turkey hands, the man was more concerned about the minorities than about American interests. No one could follow the conversation, but the Captain overheard frequent mention of "Merzifon" and realized that this was a thoroughly undiplomatic reference to the place where Dr. Post had been working when the Turks were butchering the Armenians of that area. (As it happened, Noureddin had himself initiated the reference by expressing resentment that the Americans in charge of relief work in and around Merzifon had given larger sums of money to the Christians than to the Turks.) Hepburn broke in, hoping the doctor would transmit his next remarks accurately.

American institutions, he said, were being stampeded by panic-stricken refugees and were filled with them. American guards were still ashore. "But it is no part of our naval mission to protect these refugees now that the Turkish authorities are in possession of the town," he declared, "and I do not want you to construe our presence in that way." Hepburn added that he would be glad to remove the refugees from the buildings as soon as suitable places could be found for them and the necessary protection provided. Could such provisions be made?

The General appeared irritated. He resented the question, he said. In fact, he was being subjected to too many questions. Hepburn wondered how many the doctor had been interjecting.

By now Noureddin appeared to have had enough talk about refugees. A regiment of Turkish cavalry was prancing past the building and the old soldier moved to the window and lost himself in admiration. The crowds below were cheering. The General ushered his guests to the balcony as the cavalry cantered past in perfect formation, singing a weird Turkish air. He made a sweeping gesture. "Look at them!" he exclaimed. "Five hundred kilometers in twelve days and they fought all the way!"

That night Major Davis of the Red Cross cabled to Bristol: "Refugees must leave the country or be taken away. Safety of life not assured. Believe this is final decision of the Nationalist Government as solution of the race problem."

Still later, aboard the *Litchfield*, Hepburn was preparing to turn in when Merrill arrived with some startling news about George Horton. The Consul had confided to correspondent Constantine Brown that war between England and Turkey would break out in two days, and asked Brown not to minimize the Smyrna massacre in his dispatches, since England planned to offer the atrocities as part of the *causus belli*. Brown had immediately reported the conversation to Merrill, who had run forthwith to Captain Hepburn.

Hepburn was dumbfounded. Was the American Consul losing his wits? If he had such information, why had he reported it to a newspaperman instead of to him? As the situation was too delicate to report over the wires, the Captain alerted the *Lawrence* to set off for Constantinople Wednesday morning. Merrill would convey the news to Bristol in person.

Horton had indeed heard that war between Great Britain and Turkey was imminent; everyone in the diplomatic corps was aware of the possibility, as was every newspaper reader from New York to New Delhi. If Kemal attacked the neutral zone around the Dardanelles, England wanted it known that she, at any rate, was prepared to stand fast. Horton had considered this latest information, received from an aide at the British consulate, just another of those news items from "reliable sources" calculated for public consumption, and had thought little about it until late Monday afternoon.

Watching his nightmares materialize had by then drained the Consul of his last reserves. All day he had been besieged by half-crazed refugees, all with the same recital of looting, rape, and murder. He had seen men stabbed on the consulate steps, women and children herded away beneath his windows. Hepburn had sent for Turkish soldiers to drive the poor wretches from the street, and he had seen a soldier strike one gray-haired old woman such a violent blow across the back that she had fallen to her face on the cobblestones. When Horton had run downstairs another woman had come screaming toward him, her dress wet with fresh blood. "My boy! My boy!" she was sobbing. "She did not say what had happened to her boy, but the copious blood told its own story," he said later.

In the face of these horrors Horton had heard American officers repeatedly assuring the Turks that they were concerned only with their own citizens, and only the native-born Americans at that—the naval authorities now deemed it indiscreet even to make inquiries about naturalized citizens of Armenian and Greek descent. The horror was mounting, predictably enough, since to the Turks such an attitude was an open invitation to slaughter.

Horton had closed his eyes for a few moments in the wardroom of the *Litchfield* late Monday afternoon, while near him the two newsmen, Brown and Clayton, sat typing their stories. One of the men suddenly stopped writing, read over what he had written, and tore the sheet from the machine. "I can't send this stuff," he said as he crumbled the paper in his fist. "It'll queer me in Constantinople." His companion agreed. It was time, they told each other, to be moving on "to dig up some Greek atrocities." Their words had struck Horton like a hammer blow. After dinner he had gone to Brown's hotel to make as strong a case as he could for reporting the truth.

Still later he reported the newsmen's conversation for the benefit of the State Department. "It struck me as curious," he wrote, "that men in the presence of one of the most spectacular dramas of history should think it their duty to hurry away in order to find something that would offset it. . . . I don't know what the game is, nor who is back of it. I am convinced that these men sent off reports to their papers praising the conduct of the Turkish troops and their benevolent and efficient taking over of this city."

The Consul's suspicions were well-founded. News dispatches from Smyrna reported looting "by Greeks, Armenians and Turks before the entry of the Turkish forces," and emphasized the disciplined entry of the Turkish troops.

CHAPTER XIII

Cui bono? Who stands to gain?

Roman proverb

Captain Hepburn counted thirty-five bodies on his way to the consulate. He had been counting bodies all morning on his trips around the city, and although he was anxious to keep the record straight, he was having trouble distinguishing new bodies from old; the heat swelled them up so fast that hardly any looked fresh. Admiral Bristol had had enough of exaggerated rumors. He wanted no hearsay, no reports other than what his officers saw with their own eyes. He wanted an *exact* body count.

At the consulate the Captain learned that *chettes* had attacked the president of the American International College in Paradise and beaten him senseless. Jumping into his staff car, he headed for the campus, the four-mile ride taking longer than usual because of the bodies that had to be lifted out of the way.

Paradise, that "little corner of America," was an Eden of modern buildings, delightful gardens, and substantial faculty homes. Here, on and around the campus, lived the colony of

American teachers, among them the Birges, the Lawrences, the Harlows, and the Reeds. "Jake" Jacob, the YMCA director, and his assistant, Asa Jennings, had chosen to live there, too. The community had its own electric power plant, a private elementary school with an American teacher, and American playmates for their children.

The main Smyrna-Boudja road wound through Paradise and on into the East. The camel caravans that habitually passed beside the College gates had been replaced by Greek soldiers streaming by as they hurried toward Chesme, and at the tail end of the evacuation, on Saturday morning, the College had been caught in a crossfire between the remnants of a Greek regiment and the approaching Turks. Sailors posted at the compound watched from the roof of the main buildings as the three-inch shells exploded overhead.

Having disposed of the Greek soldiers, the Turks had turned their fire on the refugees crowding by the gates. In order to discourage them from begging entrance, the authorities had not raised the flag. Now an emergency was declared, the flag was raised, the gates were opened, and over a thousand men, women, and children poured onto the campus. Mrs. Jennings was keeping a diary: "They were not admitted at the gate beside our house as it would have directed the firing that way and over the campus," she wrote. "People were injured and killed, and later from our window we watched them buried. Asa going by auto into Smyrna —shots flying around the car all the way."

Outside the campus Turkish soldiers shot at anything that moved. Anna Birge and her three small children, the youngest a baby, crawled to the College on hands and knees from their house half a mile away, as bullets rang past their ears. Moments after they had left, Turks broke into the house, smeared the walls and paintings with jam, and hacked the furniture to pieces. They then turned on the school's community center, which stood at some distance from the main buildings.

Ignoring the advice of Chief Crocker, who was in charge of the sailor guards, President MacLachlan sallied forth confident that he could reason with the Turks. The Chief went with him while half a dozen sailors followed behind. They came upon some thirty to forty fierce-looking men sporting an imposing array of weapons strung across their chests and waists. Crocker, who could see that his group was outnumbered, motioned to his men to turn back.

The Turks fired on them as they walked away, but missed. They then attacked Crocker and MacLachlan, stripped the two of their clothes, and beat them with clubs and bayonets. The president lost consciousness but Crocker was able to parlay long enough to allow his men to seek help from a Turkish officer, who scattered the *chettes*. At Captain Hepburn's request, General Noureddin sent a Turkish guard of one hundred men to Paradise Tuesday evening to protect the American compound.

News that Turks were firing over the wall of the American Collegiate Institute and terrorizing the refugees gathered in the courtyard greeted Hepburn on his return from Paradise. The sailors were plainly in need of help, according to Knauss, their C.O. Among other scenes, they had witnessed a girl of fifteen being torn from her mother and father and dragged into an alley. "Her screams were plainly heard," Knauss said. "Then the Turks returned, and one of them wiped a bloody knife on the mother's forearm and led the couple away." Hepburn sent Knauss to the *Konak* to request a Turkish guard for the building.

At Turkish headquarters Knauss was politely misdirected to the Customs House, where officials were so hazy in their directions to the proper district command that Knauss insisted on a guide; he was reluctantly provided with an officer who made a great show of reprimanding looting soldiers by standing up in the touring car and shouting: "Stop it!" The pillagers gaped. The commander in charge of the Armenian district, when Knauss finally found him, insisted that the quarter was most quiet and orderly. Knauss countered that he had passed through that district a dozen times a day and that matters were going from bad to worse. The official agreed to provide a Captain and a squad of twelve soldiers to guard the Institute, after Knauss insisted that he was "interested only in the Americans within, and in the lives of the sailors guarding American property."

Knauss had driven scarcely fifty yards when the Turkish Captain seated beside him leaped out of the car, ran across the street to where a dozen Turkish soldiers were burdened with loot, and proceeded to make a show of thrashing them with his riding crop. That done, he confided that he had been marching steadily for sixteen days and asked Knauss to pinch his leg to see how hard it was. "As we passed through the streets he frequently blew a shrill whistle and all groups we passed were very orderly, especially one with a weeping woman," Knauss reported.

The Captain suggested that the sentries be posted in pairs, a bluejacket and a Turkish soldier together. Knauss told him that he could not post his men outside the buildings because they were "only there to protect American lives, within, from outlaws and robbers who might break in." Aware that the Turk wanted to enter the building, Knauss kept him talking on the stair until the refugees would have time to clear away from the corridors. "And when he remarked that it was cooler within than without, we entered, and while there were fifteen hundred refugees in that building, not a head was in sight in the hallway. I told him I would feed his men, who at that moment came up. I looked over the guard and showed him the Chief Petty Officer from whom they would take orders, and all seemed well."

But not for long. Driving back to the quay, Knauss came upon a French officer and two sailors backed against a building while a pair of Turkish soldiers covered them with rifles. The officer was talking fast, trying to make gestures with his hands and keep them up at the same time. Suddenly, Knauss noticed that the second soldier was pointing the rifle at him. With about twenty feet between them, Knauss stepped on the gas and shot for the gunman, causing him to jump to one side and slip on the curb. Looking back, he saw the man taking aim. He screeched around the corner and sped away. The dead, he noticed, were now being removed in trucks.

He had no sooner left the Institute when the Turkish soldiers ostensibly protecting the place began driving the sailors frantic by nosing around the entryways and trying to sneak inside the buildings. The Turks were friendly enough to the sailors; they tried to converse in sign language and showed them jewelry and watches they had looted, but the refugees were already frightened and the sight of Turkish guards was not calculated to reassure them.

Unable to walk in the courtyard, all fifteen hundred were now penned indoors. Food supplies were nearly exhausted. The sailors shared their rations with the inmates, and all but nursing mothers and the very ill were fed only once a day—mostly on grapes, bread, and olives. Eight babies had been born since Saturday; the staff moved their own beds to the cellar and installed mothers and infants there, to muffle the cries. Upstairs, no one slept. There was scarcely room to sit down.

Rumors whiffled through the rooms like wind before a tempest, although the staff had admonished late arrivals not to talk. "This day, there was a rumor that there would be an attack upon the College," the Reverend Hartunian wrote in his diary. "This night, there was another, that in a little while Turkish officials would enter the building and take all the men away for deportation. I, my son Albert, and about ten other Armenian young men hid in the attic of the building—a dark and dust-filled, narrow place, like that stable where in 1916 I had been imprisoned. . . . In great fear passed this night also."

In another attic down the street Rose Berberian and her family were parched with thirst. Although the pump made a fearful noise —they had tried to prime it once, and retreated upstairs in panic —by Tuesday evening it was clear that they would have to draw water or expire.

Unable to sleep, Rose and her mother went to the cellar to try once again. Slowly, haltingly, they worked the screeching pump until they were rewarded with a silent gush of water. They had filled some pitchers and were on their way upstairs when the door was flung open and the Italian landlord walked in, accompanied by an Italian marine, a Turkish officer, and a Turkish enlisted man. The women froze, jugs in hand.

"So!" cried the Turkish officer, turning to the landlord. "No one was in your house, eh?" The Italian protested his ignorance. He had evidently come to prove to them that no one was concealed in his house, and he indignantly insisted that he knew nothing about these people. They had broken in without his permission.

Rose explained that they had sought refuge in the house. "They came and killed our men and took away the other women," she said, "and we came here for safety."

The Turkish officer flew into a rage. "Who killed your men and took your women?"

"The Turkish soldiers," said Rose.

He gave her a resounding smack across the face. He slapped her mother's face even more viciously—Rose could see it beginning to swell. "You are a liar!" he screamed. "Put on your shoes. The police will teach you to tell lies about Turkish soldiers."

Rose clenched her fists to restrain an impulse to claw the man's face, and was instantly overcome with the realization that it was all over now. Her hands and legs began to shake as though she had palsy.

"What's the matter with you?" the Turk asked.

"I—I've been sick," she said, "and I have no shoes here, no

clothes. Please, let me go to my aunt's house—it is just down the street—to get some clothes before you take me to the police." She had no aunt down the street, but she had spoken unthinkingly, to gain time.

The officer turned to the enlisted man and ordered him to accompany the girl and return quickly.

"It was the first time I had stepped outside for four days," Rose recalls, "and when I saw the street, I was more terrified than before. Dead bodies, swollen, lay all about on the stoops and stairs of the houses and across the narrow streets. I had to step over them. If I had an aunt down the street she would surely have been killed by now; the officer knew that. If I walk into a building, I thought, this soldier will probably kill me. That is why they let me out."

Instinctively she had been walking toward the Collegiate Institute at the end of the street. The gate was locked, but there was a small trap window at one side with a bell below; visitors were supposed to ring the bell and someone would come to the window. Rose rang, an American sailor opened the window and peered through at her. She whispered, in English, "I am a student here. Please let me in—quickly!" He mumbled something about getting Miss Mills and shut the window. Rose closed her eyes and moaned. Behind her the soldier was shuffling his feet impatiently.

"Oh Miss Mills!" she wailed when the Acting Head finally arrived. "This man behind me—do you see this man? He is going to kill me. Please let me in! My mother is—"

"Where is your mother? Go bring your mother, dear," said Miss Mills gently.

"They are going to kill us!" she cried. "My mother is in a house down the street. If you send a sailor to get her she might be saved. You can't leave me outside. They are going to *kill* us, don't you understand?"

The soldier was getting suspicious. "What are you talking to these people about? Get your things and let's go." Rose continued to plead and in another moment the Turkish officer came up behind her, with her mother. He was obviously seething, but he took in the American flag and the American sailor and said smoothly, "Oh? So you wanted to come here? Why did you not tell me, I would have brought you myself. Take your mother and the hell with you both!" And he marched back—to find the others, Rose supposed.

135

"The Armenian quarter is a charnel house," a French officer noted on September 13: "In three days this rich quarter is entirely ravaged. The streets are heaped with mattresses, broken furniture, glass, torn paintings. Some young women and girls, especially pretty ones, have been taken away and put into a house that is guarded by Turkish sentries. They must submit to the whims of the patrols. One sees cadavers in front of the houses. They are swollen and some have exposed entrails. The smell is unbearable and swarms of flies cover them. Day and night I make a tour of this quarter, and women who are crazed join me in the street; their clothes torn, their hair flying wild, they attach themselves to me. They beg me to take them from this quarter. First there are four, then eight, then a dozen and the number of women grows. I am in uniform and just about the only one to circulate on foot. Where to take them? Everywhere is filled: the churches, the schools, the Alliance Française are overflowing. So I disengage myself and try to reassure them. There are no men in this quarter; all are dead, or hiding, or they have been taken away."

Lieutenant Commander Knauss recorded: "This has been the day of greatest slaughter yet in the Armenian quarter, and the Turkish attitude is changing toward Americans, as well as Europeans. A few days ago they were ostentatiously saluting the American flag. Now no attention is paid to it."

Correspondents Brown and Clayton, who had spent the day interviewing Mustafa Kemal, were typing up his comments for American consumption. "As you have seen," he said, "there have been no massacres or anything approaching serious disorders in Smyrna. Such pillaging and killing as have occurred are inevitable when an army enters a city after marching four hundred and fifty kilometers through their own land, burned and sacked, and having seen their parents and relatives slaughtered. It is difficult to contain them, but control them we will. You can say that order has been completely restored from today."

A report in the *New York Times*, datelined Italy, noted that in Smyrna, "Mustafa Kemal Pasha is asserted to be inexorably punishing any attempt to transgress his stern orders to respect life and property."

Vice-Consul Barnes estimated that seven out of ten houses in the Armenian quarter had been raided. Attuned to Bristol's semantic requirements, he concluded that there was "no massacre."

To everyone's surprise the Greek population remained relatively unmolested, although a number of Greeks reported as "dangerous elements" were thrown into prison, among them the father of a sixteen-year-old Smyrnean named Aristotle Onassis.* A well-to-do merchant and informal banker, Socrates Onassis had been blacklisted by the Turks for his involvement in a Greek compatriotic society during the Greek occupation. In nearby Kasaba the Turks hanged Socrates' brother Alexander in the public square for similar activities, while in Thyatira a sister perished in the town church with her husband and child and five hundred villagers when the Turks set it ablaze. In Smyrna proper, Greeks were being robbed and killed—but more or less indiscriminately, since there were too many to dispose of systematically ("There seemed to be a definite plan to clean out the Armenians and to deal with the Greeks at their leisure," Consul Horton testified later), and since the Turkish authorities, as they had hinted more than once, were counting on the foreigners to take the bulk of them away. But no one made a move to oblige. The Allies were unwilling to work together and even less willing to act alone.

The Italians, smugly aware of all that Kemal owed them, were safely in the victor's graces and prepared to hold tightly to this favored position. Admirals Dumesnil and Levavasseur, the ranking French officers, were busy ingratiating themselves at the *Konak* and at Kemal's suburban villa. Trying to guess the Conqueror's next move, they hoped to dissuade him from marching on the neutral zone where the French would be expected to join the British in stopping him. They made it clear that they had no interest in the refugee problem.

Back in Constantinople Admiral Colby Chester was once again on the scene, flanked by two middle-aged sons, all three Chesters

---

* Details of the Onassis saga vary from one published account to another, and Smyrna's most famous escapee has not proved anxious to clarify minor discrepancies. The accounts are unanimous in acknowledging the young Aristotle's talent for ingratiating himself with the right people at the crucial moment. Combining luck with charm, he was able to curry the favor of both a Turkish General and an American vice-consul (James Loder Park, described in Onassis biographies as John Parker) by digging up some sources of whiskey—of which American and Turkish headquarters were equally in sore need. (Kemal, who eventually died of cirrhosis of the liver, was no teetotaler.) Armed with Turkish and American safe-conduct passes, he was able to move freely about the city and eventually gain access to enough of his father's cash to buy his release. It is said that Onassis, senior, later berated his son for paying out too much, thus driving Aristotle from Athens to Argentina, where he made his first million.

137

convinced that a lifetime's dream was at last on the verge of fruition. Chester, senior, was by now in his mid-seventies, a white-haired, wiry old man of unflagging determination, who had never lost faith that in time the Levant would come to rest as his dominion. Indeed, Abdul Hamid's largesse offered quite an empire. It included 2,800 miles of railroad network stretching from the Black Sea to the Mediterranean and from Angora to Mesopotamia. His Ottoman-American Development Company (to be fully capitalized as soon as the Nationalists gave the word) would obtain, free for ninety-nine years, all the sand and gravel necessary for road-building, and the right-of-way from quarries. He could expropriate any privately owned land he needed, and any materials he might wish to import would be exempt from all customs duties and taxes. Chester had convinced himself that nothing would please the Turks more than to see him installed as their economic czar. The San Remo agreement notwithstanding, he was equally convinced that he had the blessing of the British. Having recognized that he would make an ideal bargaining weapon when the time came to negotiate the peace, Nationalist officials encouraged Chester, predictably causing a flurry of alarm in various capitals in the West.

The Chesters were meanwhile proving their devotion to the Turkish cause. The September 1922 issue of *Current History* featured an article by Admiral Colby M. Chester, U.S. Navy, Retired ("one of Theodore Roosevelt's closest friends and for years an observer of world affairs"), in which Chester declared that the Turks had been falsely maligned during the World War; that their policy toward minorities had been one of the utmost benevolence; that in fact, "the Armenians in 1915 were moved from the inhospitable regions where they were not welcome and could not actually prosper, to the most delightful and fertile parts of Syria . . . where the climate is as benign as in Florida and California whither New York millionaires journey every year for health and recreation. All this was done," wrote Chester, "at great expense of money and effort."

Bristol considered the family a trifle indiscreet for flying the American flag in celebration of the Turkish victory, but he was on the whole sympathetic to Chester's hopes and rather taken with the old man's bolder schemes, such as his plan to use navy ships, planes, and other supplies to equip and transport a survey expedition into "his" territory, with the Department of the Interior providing the experts.

Bristol was all the while preoccupied with nudging more sluggish businessmen into negotiating contracts with the Nationalists before the Europeans edged in. He sent for the local representative of the Baldwin Locomotive Works and suggested he get busy and make the proper contacts to see about rehabilitating the Anatolian railroads. The Admiral was surprised that the man hadn't thought of this himself: "I must admit I do not think Mr. Livingston is much of a live wire," he noted.

The Greek Ionian Bank was preparing to take over the Constantinople Branch of the Guaranty Trust Company, much to the Admiral's disgust. Suspecting that this venture would be a medium for obtaining private loans for Greece now that the Allies and the United States had reneged on theirs, he intended to see that American institutions refrained from patronizing this Ionian Bank. He vowed to transfer his personal account before the takeover on October 1.

Although determined to keep Greece financially destitute, the Admiral had no qualms about dumping impoverished Americans from Smyrna on Greek soil. After listening to Merrill's story he approved the evacuation from Smyrna of naturalized American citizens as far as Piraeus and ordered Horton to accompany the evacuees on the *Simpson*. Vice-Consul Barnes was to be left in Smyrna in charge of American interests.

Meanwhile Captain Hepburn had decided independently that the time for evacuation had come. On Wednesday morning Horton had drawn him aside and informed him that Sir Harry Lamb, the British consul, was in an inner office asking Horton to take charge of British interests. Anglo-Turkish relations were apparently at the breaking point and Sir Harry had reminded Horton that there were treaties in force between the two countries calling for such mutual help in a time of emergency. Hepburn insisted that Horton refuse, on the excuse that the United States had no official relations with the Kemalist government and that the American consulate might be closed at any moment.

To reinforce this argument, it struck Hepburn as a propitious moment to announce the evacuation of all naturalized American citizens who wanted to leave and of all American-born women and children. Native-born American men who had property interests, or were engaged in relief work, were urged to remain. To avoid antagonizing the Turks, Hepburn decided to seek their approval. They gave their permission with ostensible reluctance and strong expressions of regret that Americans should think it necessary to take such a step. Hepburn soothed Turkish officials by explaining that the only Americans who would be going were those "practically in the same status as the refugees in the streets" and that he had delayed the action "until order appeared fairly well established so as to avoid spreading mistrust among other foreigners." He assured the Turks that responsible American businessmen intended to remain and carry on.

By noon it was evident that the French and Italians, as well as the British, were already in the process of evacuating their nationals. As the Europeans assembled at evacuation points opposite their respective battleships, refugees swarmed toward these points begging to be taken along. A heavy guard was needed to prevent the small landing boats from being swamped.

The naturalized Americans were gathered in the theater, and the native-born were forewarned that a Navy flag atop the building would signal the evacuation of women and children. The flag was hoisted shortly after noon, and the *Simpson*, which had been moored a mile north at the Standard Oil docks, was ordered to get under way and anchor as close to the theater as possible. They were lowering the whale boats when word reached Captain Hepburn that the American Collegiate Institute was surrounded by flames.

CHAPTER XIV

Auxilium Deus ipse negavit. Even God refused his aid.

The Greek historian Christobulus,
referring to an adverse wind preceding
the fall of Constantinople

For several days there had been signs in the Armenian quarter
that the Turks were preparing a conflagration. "Today (Monday,
September 11) I saw with my own eyes the Turks taking bombs,
gunpowder, kerosene and everything necessary to start fires, in
wagon-fulls here and there through the streets," the Reverend
Hartunian had recorded in his diary. That same day Anita
Chakerian, a young teacher at the Institute, saw the Turkish
guards dragging into the building large sacks, which they deposited in various corners. They were bringing rice and potatoes,
the men said, because they knew the people were hungry and
would soon have nothing left to eat. The sacks were not to be
opened until the bread was exhausted. Such unexpected generosity led one of the sailors to investigate; the bags held gunpowder and dynamite. On Tuesday night, wagons bearing gasoline drums again moved through the deserted streets around
the College.

Just after midnight on Tuesday the wind shifted its direction away from the Moslem quarter and a gusty breeze began blowing toward the harbor. A rash of fires broke out within an hour.

At 1:00 A.M. on Wednesday, Mabel Kalfa, a Greek nurse at the Collegiate Institute, saw three fires in the neighborhood. At 4:00 A.M. fires in a small wooden hut adjoining the College wall and on a veranda near the school were put out by firemen. At noon on Wednesday a sailor beckoned Mabel Kalfa and Miss Mills to the window in the dining room. "Look there," he said. "The Turks are setting the fires!" The women could see three Turkish officers silhouetted in the window of a photographer's shop opposite the school. Moments after the men emerged, flames poured from the roof and the windows. "Like all the other buildings this was burning from the inside," said the nurse. The soldiers moved on to the Khan, a Turkish hotel with a series of shops beneath. Their departure signaled an explosion and another fire. Said Miss Mills: "I could plainly see the Turks carrying tins of petroleum into the houses, from which, in each instance, fire burst forth immediately afterward. There was not an Armenian in sight, the only persons visible being the Turkish soldiers of the regular army, in smart uniforms." Two stone houses with iron shutters were fired next, then the baker's shop. By three o'clock in the afternoon, one entire street was ablaze.

Because the wind was carrying sparks toward the school's laundry rooms, the sailors set some of the refugees to spreading rugs on the rooftops and organized a bucket brigade to wet them down. The Turkish guards ordered the refugees to come down. "I told them to stay where they were and not to be afraid," Nurse Kalfa reported. "But then a Turkish officer came and told them he would shoot them if they did not come down. He said it was forbidden to go on the roof. As our men were anxious to save the school, and as we had refugees in the laundry rooms, they did not listen to the officer. At that, he fired a shot into the air and we told them to come down."

The Smyrna fire brigade had been working steadily for fourteen hours by this time. A mixed company of Turks and Greeks (the Greek firemen had taken their families to the fire station for safety on Saturday), it was organized and supported by the London insurance firms which underwrote the properties in Smyrna. Fires were not unusual in that city but this, Sergeant Tchorbadjis soon decided, was an epidemic. Between midnight on

Tuesday and ten thirty Wednesday morning, he had already responded to six alarms, all in the Armenian quarter and each fire more devastating than the one before.

The ten thirty alarm on Suyane Street disclosed ten houses ablaze. These fires were barely under control when an alarm came from the Armenian church several streets away. Leaving some firemen at the church, Tchorbadjis hurried on alone toward some flames on Tchoukour Street. "I climbed to the roof and found bedding on fire," he testified later. "Then I went down into one of the rooms and saw a Turkish soldier, well armed. He was setting fire to the interior of a drawer. He looked rather fiercely at me when he saw me, but he left. I caught the strong smell of petroleum."

According to Sergeant Tchorbadjis there was no keeping up with the fires after that; they broke out so often and burned so fiercely that there was neither enough water nor enough manpower to contain them. Orders came from Fire Chief Grescovitch to try to keep the fire within the bounds of the Armenian quarter.

"In all the houses I went into I saw dead bodies," Tchorbadjis said. "In one house I followed a trail of blood that led me to a cupboard. My curiosity forced me to open this cupboard—and my hair stood on end. Inside was the naked body of a girl, with her breasts cut off. At another house there was a girl hanging from a lemon tree in the yard. There were plenty of armed soldiers going about. One of them went in where there was an Armenian family hiding and massacred the lot. When he came out his scimitar was dripping with blood. He cleaned it on his boots and leggings.

"On one of the roads I saw a man about forty-five or fifty years old. The Turks had blinded him and cut off his nose and left him on the streets. He was crying out, in Turkish, 'Isn't there anyone here Christian enough to shoot me so that I will not get burnt in the fire?'

"We had to evacuate, finally. The streets became too hot to work in and we wanted to get all our gear away before the station burned. At the end, we had to leave it behind."

Fireman Emmanuel Katsaros was hosing down the Armenian Club to halt the advance of flames from next door when two soldiers went into the building carrying tins of petroleum. Looking through the window, Katsaros noticed that they were emptying the liquid on the piano. He turned to a soldier who was guarding the door: "On the one hand we are trying to stop the fires, and on the other you are setting them," he said.

"You have your orders," said the soldier, "and we have ours. This is Armenian property. *Our* orders are to set fire to it."

It was four o'clock in the afternoon; fires were closing in on three sides of the Institute, and there was still no word from Navy headquarters. The buildings were arranged around a court-yard and as the fires encroached, refugees who had been sheltered in the laundry rooms at the most vulnerable point in the compound were added to the crush in the main building and told to wait for the signal to leave. They could smell the smoke and hear the explosions just beyond the school walls. There were over 2,000 refugees within the Institute by now.

"I stood all afternoon in front of the gate," Petty Officer James Webster wrote in a letter to his family. "I had to use the butt of my gun to keep the people away from the door, as the fire was getting closer all the time. But we knew that if we let them out, the Turks would kill them."

Realizing that evacuation was inevitable but that with only twelve sailors on hand a mass exodus of all the inmates would spell disaster, Miss Mills, after a conference with the Chief, in-structed her staff to weed out the "school family" from the bulk of refugees, so that the sailors might escort the smaller group to the quay ahead of the mob. But the sorting out, which had to be done discreetly to avoid a stampede, was complicated by the fact that the vast majority of teachers, servants, and students refused to be separated from their families. Instructed to gather at the rear gate, they brought their relatives with them and crowded behind Miss Mills and the sailors, accompanied by several hundred alert refugees who were keeping a close watch on the move-ments of the Americans and taking no chances on being left behind.

The shutters at one end had caught fire just as Ensign Gay-lord drove up to the rear gate in a truck, with orders from Cap-tain Hepburn that the sailors were to abandon the building and escort bona fide Americans only to the docks. Miss Mills refused to budge without her students and staff. Gaylord barked an order, three of the men lifted her to their shoulders, and carried her through the back door. "Girls, follow me!" she shouted. She was still struggling when they put her, along with several dozen stu-dents and employees, into the truck and drove away.

Petty Officer James Webster and six sailors remained. "We cannot be responsible for you once we open the doors," one of them announced. "We advise you all to leave together. Stay close together, as close as you can." Then he opened the gates to lead the way.

Webster had to push his way through the gate. They were miles from the waterfront and none of the sailors knew which way to turn. Some of the streets were on fire, burning rubble was blocking others. Turks were shooting into the crowd behind him. To keep from being stampeded, he had to stop every few moments and fire over the heads of his followers.

Anita Chakerian tried to follow, but the door was narrow and the crush at the exit overwhelmed her. She found herself being pushed and pulled in circles. She stumbled, lost a shoe, and would have been trampled but for two strong arms lifting her and carrying her out the door. It was one of the sailors. "To this day I still wonder who he was," she says. "God bless him for saving my life." Outside, he set her down and tried to force his way back. There were over a thousand refugees waiting behind the front entrance to the main building.

When the sailor guarding the front door was summoned to the rear gate on Ensign Gaylord's arrival, he had asked the Reverend Hartunian to take his place for a moment. The minister and his family, with the rest of the refugees massed behind, were still standing obediently behind the door. "*Badveli*, what is going to happen?" a friend asked.

"I don't know," said the Reverend, "but I feel God is about to do something."

Suddenly someone shouted, "The building has caught fire from one side!" Another man, returning from the rear of the building where he had gone to investigate, announced that the Americans and all the sailors had fled.

"We are betrayed!"

They poured out into the approaching dusk. The sky was lit up in a fearful orange glow, and across the road Turkish soldiers were standing with their rifles in hand. Hartunian started to turn back. "But where am I going? The building is on fire!" He went forward.

Mabel Kalfa, who had come around to the front entrance to find her mother, now found herself stumbling forward with the rest. "There were shots, and everyone turned back in a panic," she said. "Afterwards we came out again but we did not know where we were going."

Neither did Rose Berberian. Linking arms with her mother, trying to stay with the herd as the sailor had suggested, she found the winding streets a fiery labyrinth. Turks were still shooting into the crowd, killing some, wounding others, pulling the men aside. Flames rose up in sheets, walls crashed, cinders burned underfoot. After weaving about for several hours, Rose found that the group had come to the street running parallel to the quay, one short block from the water, and was standing before the French consulate. When Rose saw the Tricolor, and French marines guarding the building, she decided that this was the place to stop. Most of the school crowd moved on.

The street was mobbed with people begging entrance to the consulate, and the marines had linked hands to form a chain around the building. "I was in rags," Rose says, "no shoes, my dress torn, my face and arms black with dirt and dust. I had found two pairs of men's socks—white ones—in the attic of the Italian family and I was wearing these, one pair on top of the other. They were now black, too.

"Fortunately I spoke French fairly well; I had learned it at the Armenian school I attended before entering the Institute. I asked my mother to stay outside and wait for me and I walked up to a marine and began talking to him in French. 'For God's sake,' I said, 'Pour l'amour de Dieu, laissez-moi entrer. I am French. They killed my family. I have no papers, they were destroyed in the fire. My home is burned. Look at me; how can I have papers when I could not even save my shoes? I want to go back to my country. I do not want to stay in this place anymore.'

"One of the marines turned to the man beside him, 'Lift your hand and let her through.'

"But I was hardly inside when over the megaphone they were announcing that everyone had to leave at once. The fire was nearing the consulate. But now we could leave under the protection of the French soldiers! We were escorted to another building, this one on the waterfront. Immediately they set up tables there, and they said, 'Ladies first,' and people began to line up to obtain papers.

"I was not anxious to be near the head of the line. If I could hear the questions, I would have time to prepare my answers. So I listened: 'Name? Age? Nationality? Your passport?' That was

146

all. The answers came in halting, often badly accented French, yet the consuls were turning no one away.

"And so my turn came. 'Name?' 'Rose Berberian.' 'Age?' 'Sixteen.' 'Nationality?' 'French.' 'Your passport?' 'Burned. Our house burned. We lost everything. I have my mother with me.'

"'You speak French very well,' the man said, smiling. 'Where did you go to school?' And he handed me the paper authorizing our passage to a French battleship.

"It was the wildest scene imaginable on that quay. Women, men, children, weeping, crying. One lady, I remember, had gone mad and was dancing and singing. People were sobbing for their families. It was a scene of horror—all those suffering people!

"I began explaining to everyone near me. 'If any one of you speaks French, get on the line. They will give you a paper. Just say you are French.' I kept walking through the crowds telling this to everyone. Then, incredible as it seems, I heard my sister calling my name.

"She looked like something out of a bandbox. Dressed in her best clothes, her broad-brimmed straw hat with blue velvet ribbons. For a moment I felt sure that I too had gone insane, but she began talking and quickly explained: After my mother and I were taken away, she and my brother had escaped the attic by climbing back over the vines to Mr. Aram's house. Then, before the fires had reached our street, they took the chance and slipped over to our own house. There they changed into their finest clothes. The house had been looted—the desk with the money and our jewelry was gone—but they had not touched the wardrobes upstairs, so my brother wore his best suit, and my sister her Easter clothes. He took his cane and even put on his spats. Then she took his arm and they walked casually out the front door and down the street, arm in arm, talking French. In this way my brother escorted my sister to the quay. Since he was a strong swimmer, he decided to try for the nearest ship. Months later, when we were reunited in France, he told us that it was an English ship. When he reached it, the sailors had thrown hot water down on him and on others circling the ship begging to be taken aboard. So he had gone farther out, to an Italian ship. The Italians had pulled up everyone who managed to swim that far.

"I explained to my sister that I had a French pass, and I went back in the line to get one for her. The official was very obliging.

"When I returned to my mother and sister, a poor woman was

147

standing nearby with four small children. 'Please,' she said, 'I don't speak French. Please go once more and tell them that you have found your aunt and cousins. You will be saving our lives.'

"This time they laughed to see me coming. 'What? You again? And who have you found this time?'

" 'My aunt and four small cousins,' I said sheepishly. 'What can I do?' The Frenchman added their names to the pass.

"Motorboats had been coming to the quay and those with papers were being taken aboard. The French sailors were exceptionally good to us. They fed us, washed us, took care of the wounded and the sick among us. For three days we were on this ship. We discovered that those who could pay their way were being transferred to merchant ships. But we had no money, not a penny. I mentioned this to one of the sailors on the third day, and he said I must speak with the Captain.

"The Captain was a gentle man. He took all our names, including those of my aunt and cousins. 'Don't worry, my child,' he said, and he wrote a paper for all of us. We and other penniless passengers were authorized to go to Marseilles, where the Sisters of Charity had set up a camp to receive us."

Virtually everyone saved that evening owed his life to a sympathetic foreigner. Fifteen-year-old Charles Kassabian was following on the heels of one of the sailors. "I didn't take my eyes off him," he related recently, "even though it meant losing the rest of my family. My father had taken out a passport and a visa to bring us all to America. My older brothers were in America. The tickets were paid for, but we ran to the American school the day the Turks came in and there was no boat, nothing after that. And then when the fires started, my father, he had a few hundred dollars with him, he said to my mother, 'We'll divide this money in case we lose each other.' So my mother pinned this money in a handkerchief inside my shirt.

"So we're running out from the school and I lose them because I'm watching that sailor, and when he goes this way, I go this way. And there are thousands—if I say millions it won't make any difference because it's that crowded—and the streets are burning all over. Buildings burning. Every place burning. *Every place!* We come to the quay and I don't know how it happens but I see my family. In all that mess we find each other. We can't believe it. Boy, are we happy! But what are we going to do now? My mother is cold, shaking. I pick up a rug right off the ground there and I put it on her shoulders. Then I see this sailor again, and he's taking people to a little boat, and I run to him and try to make him understand. I say, 'Brother in America.' I say, 'Passport.' And maybe that makes the difference because he waves his hand, 'O.K., come on,' and all of us run to the boat. So pretty soon we're safe and alive on this big American ship.

"It's dark. September it gets dark already six thirty, seven. And these people are swimming out to the boats and they're turning the floodlights on them and pushing them back. From the English boats they're pouring water on them. We can't believe it but that's what happened. They didn't pick up the swimmers. They took moving pictures."

It had taken Petty Officer James Webster an hour to get to the docks. He had lost the greater part of his following along the way, but there were still thirty or forty people behind him. He left them at one end of the quay and pushed his way to headquarters to see about getting them on a boat that would take them off to one of the destroyers. The fire, blazing fiercely, was lapping its way to the quay, and Webster noticed that the Turks had guards at the end of the docks to prevent people from moving away. "It looked to me as though they wanted to burn them up," he wrote.

John Kingsley Birge spotted Anita Chakerian and a small contingent of students and teachers from the Institute huddled together at the north end of the quay. "Don't move," he told them. "I'll see what I can do." He managed to find a boat, piled the group in, and rowed to the *Simpson*. Recognizing him, Hepburn ordered his men to lower the ropes. "We think Mr. Birge told them we were U.S. citizens," Anita says, "because when the Captain realized his mistake, he tried to have us put off, but the Second Mate argued with the Captain, saying he would rather be hanged than let us girls off the boat to a sure death. The Captain kept saying he had no orders. Finally they hid us below decks until we were safely out of the harbor."

Holding hands, winding their way through the flaming streets, the Hartunians, too, found the quay at last. "What a hellish scene!" the Reverend wrote. "The quay was bulging with humanity from end to end. Exhausted! Defeated! Pale! Terrified! Hopeless! The sea on one side, the flames on the other. The fire had spread so rapidly and become so intense that it devoured all before it and advanced with a roar. In a little while the magnificent buildings on the quay would also go up. And what about the people then?"

Half-dead with exhaustion and terror, the family found a place to rest on the stones, while Albert, the eldest son, went off to investigate the possibility of rescue and returned with the news that the Americans were taking their citizens aboard a destroyer. At the embarkation point the Reverend discovered that the civilian in charge was Jacob, the YMCA director, who had visited him in Zeytun years before. Hartunian had entertained him and taken him around the area. "In this or that way I had cast my bread upon the waters," he thought. And so the Hartunians, too, were rescued. Because they had American visas, there was no problem about keeping them aboard.

Hepburn had been working feverishly all afternoon, directing the evacuation of citizens on the *Simpson*, by now loaded and ready to lift anchor the moment Consul Horton arrived. The Americans had been grouped in squads in the lobby of the theater, and as a pair of whaleboats drew up to the sea wall, officers rushed two squads at a time across the road and into the boats. A double file of guards posted from doorway to shoreline kept the desperate refugees from boring into the line. Despite the Captain's misgivings, the operation had gone off without a hitch.

There had been some nervous moments. Against everyone's better judgment, Anna Birge had insisted on bringing eight Greek and Armenian boys along from Paradise, hidden among the luggage. They were the younger "beneficiary" students at the College, scholarship boys who had been orphaned in earlier massacres and had been living at the school. For three years she had mothered them, and as the cars drove up to take the women and children away, she had called them together and offered them their choice of coming along in the truck, or staying behind. There was a risk either way; if they did not come, the Turks might deport them; if they did come, they might be shot. They must decide which risk to take. There was an outcry from the faculty; with all her good intentions, Mrs. Birge was proposing to endanger the entire convoy. But the sailors were willing and she was adamant. "Where's the baggage?" asked the driver.

"I have human baggage," said Mrs. Birge, and she turned to the boys. "Which of you is coming?"

"We were about twenty in number, and it seemed as if each one of us looked on the truck as a lifesaver for a moment, and then the picture changed in our weary imaginations into a funeral procession," one of the boys wrote later. "It was a question of life and death, and yet one that required an instant decision. Eight of us declared that we would take the risk and go.

"The men protested to the sailors, but Mrs. Birge won out. We were put on the truck with bags, suitcases, and blankets around and over us. The truck started for Smyrna. In a smaller car, just ahead, Mrs. Birge rode with her three boys and some other Americans.

"As we came to a turn in the road we looked down and saw Turkish soldiers looking up at us with their guns in hand. We expected to be fired on, as they blocked our road. The truck stopped. Everybody was terror-stricken, motionless and almost breathless. I uttered a few English words and tried to look as calm as I thought an American would. Then they cleared our way, and standing by the side of the truck began talking, pointing to a woman who had been shot through the legs and lay groaning by the roadside. Suddenly the engine started and we rushed past in safety. Among the many dead bodies, we saw men, women, and children shot to death, bodies drawn up into horribly strained postures, with expressions portraying the endurance of excruciating pain. A picture of our own fate, we thought."

Two Turkish officers, one a former student at the Boys College, stood at the door of the theater to insure that only Americans entered the building. The theater was guarded, as well, by sailors from the *Litchfield*. Recognizing the officer as a former student, Mrs. Birge walked up to him and said, in Turkish, "Something is going to happen here in a moment, and if you do anything to prevent it you will spend eternity in the hottest kind of hell." Rushing her own three boys into the theater, she found her husband and asked him to watch the children for a moment. "I want to see someone," she said.

Captain Hepburn blocked her way at the door. "Some of my family have not arrived," she told him and pushed her way out. To the sailors, who tried to urge her back, she explained, "Some of my sons are arriving." They stood her against the wall; gun shots were flying wild up and down the street.

The truck drew up and stopped. The boys jumped out. "Right through the door, boys," said Mrs. Birge, herding them together. Again the Captain blocked the way. "Only Americans," he insisted.

"These are my sons," said Mrs. Birge.

"Oh?" said the Captain. "And how long have they been your sons?"

"For three years," she said.

"That's quite a family to raise in three years. I'm sorry but I can take only American names."

"All right, then, take this," said Mrs. Birge: "H. M. Casparian Birge, Evangelides Birge . . ." Vice-Consul Barnes was calling on the assemblage to group themselves by families. "Only Americans will be taken aboard," he announced firmly. Mrs. Birge rushed from one family to another; would each of them adopt one boy as their own? Eight mothers agreed. An hour later, she gathered her sons together aboard the *Simpson*.

A car from headquarters stopped at the YWCA to collect the guards before they had time to evacuate their gear: "Hurry up, hurry up, get in, quick." Melvin Johnson never knew what happened to the refugees, the women and children they had been forced to leave behind; but some had evidently escaped, for on the docks he ran across an Armenian girl he had talked to a lot at the Y. She was a school teacher, "a very interesting young woman," he says. "She spoke good English. Her name was Liberty. That's how it got translated anyway. We called her Liberty. So I took her with me and slipped her aboard ship, and I got two blankets and stood guard over her all night, and I gave her ten dollars; that's all I had just then. She didn't want to take it. I said, 'Look. You're going to a strange country and you don't know a soul. There's bound to be an Armenian section in there but you'll need this anyway.' So she wrote me two or three letters from Greece, and I finally got one from Boston. Said she'd found her mother in Greece and she gave me the address, said if I ever hit Boston . . . Nyland the street was, but I lost the number.

"And now this is the funny part. We got out so quick I had to leave the gear behind, and for one solid year I had to write a report—what become of the rubber ponchos. Finally I got a chief yeoman to dictate me a letter. I said: 'I think you'll find 'em in the ashes in Smyrna, Turkey, if you look for 'em.' They stopped bothering me after that."

Great clouds of smoke were engulfing the consulate when an officer arrived to prod Horton to the ship. In ten more minutes they would be unable to get a car through. Horton, who had been signing safe-conduct passes up to the last available moment, took up his personal files, grabbed a roll of rugs that were still encased in their summer wrapping, and ran to the car with his wife and a

Greek servant. His priceless books, paintings, and classical objects, the collection of a lifetime, were left behind.

The spectacle along the waterfront haunted Melvin Johnson for the rest of his life. "When we left it was just getting dusk," he remembers. "As we were pulling out I'll never forget the screams. As far as we could go you could hear 'em screaming and hollering, and the fire was going on . . . most pitiful thing you ever saw in your life. In your life. Could never hear nothing like it any other place in the world, I don't think. And the city was set in a—a kind of a hill, and the fire was on back coming this way toward the ship. That was the only way the people could go, toward the waterfront. A lot of 'em were jumping in, committing suicide. It was a sight all right."

The *Simpson* lifted anchor at 7:45 P.M. Horton, too, was on deck, watching the flames bearing relentlessly down on a human wall nearly two miles long. Banks of smoke rose so high that days afterward travelers on the Sea of Marmara, one hundred and forty miles away, mistook the spectacle for an immense mountain range. The glow and flame of the burning city were plainly visible for fifty miles, according to passengers on the *Simpson*.

Among them was reporter John Clayton, whose latest dispatch was at that moment on Chicago newsstands: "After forty-eight hours of Turkish occupation the population has begun to realize there is not going to be any massacre. Remembering the horrors of the Greek occupation in 1919, when more than four thousand Moslems were butchered, the Christian population has been clamoring for protection." Clayton's article referred to a little looting and a few victims of private feuds ("Turks, Greeks, and Armenians"), but announced that "the discipline and order of the Turks was excellent."

But now Clayton was pounding a new epic on his portable typewriter, without mincing words: "Except for the squalid Turkish quarter, Smyrna has ceased to exist. The problem of the minorities is here solved for all time. No doubt remains as to the origin of the fire. . . . The torch was applied by Turkish regular soldiers." Clayton had a scoop. His story, sent from Athens at dawn, was the first to reach print. Constantine Brown's dispatch in the *Chicago Daily News* was to be no less frank: "A crime which will brand the Turks forever was committed yesterday when Turkish soldiery, after finishing pillaging, set this city on fire."

George Horton thought that only the destruction of Carthage by the Romans could compare to the finale of Smyrna in the extent of its horror, savagery, and human suffering. "As the destroyer moved away from the fearful scene and darkness descended, the flames, raging now over a vast area, grew brighter and brighter, presenting a scene of awful and sinister beauty," he wrote. "Yet there was no fleet of Christian battleships at Carthage looking on at a situation for which their governments were responsible." The Turks had plundered, slaughtered, and now burned the city "because they had been systematically led to believe that they would not be interfered with.

"One of the keenest impressions which I brought away with me from Smyrna was a feeling of shame that I belonged to the human race."

CHAPTER XV

The fire of Smyrna was put out today by our forces.
Official Turkish communiqué
Angora, September 14, 1922

With the *Simpson* under way, Hepburn was beset with pleas from
Jacob, Birge, and some of the other Americans to save several
hundred students and native staff of the institutions who had been
rounded up in the course of the afternoon and assembled in
front of the *Litchfield* with promises of rescue. The Captain
found himself weakening. Two merchant ships, the *Winona* and
Hog Island, had been loading figs and now stood in the inner
harbor waiting to load tobacco for shipment to New York; but
with the quay so tightly jammed it was hard to see how tobacco
could be gotten through even if it miraculously escaped the fire.
On condition that only bona fide protégés of American institutions
would be taken on, Hepburn requisitioned the *Winona* and
sent them aboard. Vice-Consul Barnes, who had seen Turkish soldiers
pouring gasoline liberally along the street in front of the consulate, was meanwhile working feverishly to save the consular
records. The building caught fire just as the last files were being

carried away. The French consulate was ablaze, and the English, and the Alliance Française. The Ashjian family, who had found refuge in this last, poured out with a crowd of over five hundred. On the roof of the Kramer Hotel, an Italian signalman was waving flags to a colleague aboard his battleship when the roof caved in and he disappeared in a shower of flames.

Like ants, the people kept swarming toward the sea as churches, schools, and orphanages disgorged their inhabitants. They came out of hospitals, some on litters, others bearing the infirm and aged on their backs. Karekin Bizdikian, carrying his fifteen-month-old son in one arm, led his pregnant wife from the Italian hospital. She was already in labor, and having to force her to her feet added to his nightmare. Half dragging, half carrying her, he reached the quay and pushed his way to the end near the Point, where the fires appeared less concentrated. Here his wife sank to the cobblestones while he tried to prevent her from being trampled in the crush.

The water was filled with bodies, he remembers. "The Turks were going through the crowd with swords, robbing people, snatching girls, doing what they pleased," he said recently. "The French, American, and British ships were not making a move to help these people. The Italians were shouting and gesturing for some of us to jump into the water so that their small boats could pick us up and transfer us to their larger ones, farther out. But so many people were jumping in that our chances looked to be zero. Some Turks came along while we were debating what to do and grabbed some of the men around me—why they overlooked me I do not know. My wife's pains became unbearable again, and so we decided that the only thing to do was to drown ourselves, quickly.

"A tragi-comic touch saved us: neither of us could bear to throw ourselves into the water with the baby. My wife would pass the baby to me and say, 'I can't—*you* take him,' and I would pass him back to her. This went on for a time and then some Greeks standing near us, watching this pantomime, began to berate us for our foolishness. Suddenly, even in the midst of all that horror and confusion, we felt silly and gave it up."

By now the fire had reached the quay itself. Flames licked the theater. The Americans had abandoned it an hour before so that all the guards, as well as the remaining American civilians, were present and accounted for on the *Litchfield*. Dr. Post, although he was near collapse from exhaustion, refused to leave the quay and had to be carried aboard. He had been ministering to the refugees almost singlehandedly all week. Soon the mooring lines burned and the ship started swinging on its anchor. All vessels moved back two hundred and fifty yards, yet even at that distance the heat was penetrating.

Captain Allan of the *Bavarian* was astonished at the number of well-to-do Britishers who scrambled aboard his ship wearing a fur coat over nothing at all. "Half the people arrived without clothes," he said. "The poorer people, the Maltese, had the most raiment." The more affluent residents had been less prepared for disaster.

No one would ever know how many had perished. Turkish soldiers blocked avenues of escape, and their victims had no choice but to take the path of the fire. At the height of the conflagration the Czech consul and his entourage were allowed to slip through the cordon of soldiers after identifying themselves. "Under the command of an officer the Turks were driving Armenians and Greeks back from the road that leads out toward Bournabat," the consul's son testified later. "They kept the people back with their bayonets. They were actually driving them toward the fire." Colonel Giordano, liaison officer of the Italian consulate, tried to drive a truckload of Greeks and Italians out of the fire zone and found the road blocked by a Turkish troop convoy. They allowed him to pass but turned others away. "They invoke martial law and forbid the population to escape," he said. "It is incredibly tragic."

On the bridge of the liner *Bavarian*, grown men wept as they watched the scene. A British businessmen could see "the unfortunate wretches thirteen or fourteen deep swaying in the sweltering heat. With the very parcels in their arms actually on fire, men, women, and children struggled to get free, throwing themselves where possible into the water, or swaying this way and that, more dead than alive." The density of the crowd for a time was such that the dead remained standing, supported by the living.

To Ed Fisher, a YMCA worker who clambered aboard the *Litchfield* at the last moment, the scene compared to Bulwer Lytton's *The Last Days of Pompeii*. "The lamentations of the women and the piercing cries of the children are still ringing in my ears," he recorded a few weeks later. He could see figures dipping blankets into the waters of the bay and wrapping them around their bodies. The harnesses of horses caught fire and the frenzied animals dashed among the crowds, trampling many to death. Fisher had succeeded in evacuating six hundred Armenian boys from their orphanage only hours before the fire ravaged their building. He had left them at the south end of the quay, giving them an American flag for whatever protection it could afford, and advising them to take turns, two at a time, holding it aloft.

On the *Iron Duke*, Major Arthur Maxwell of His Majesty's Royal Marines, watching through binoculars, distinguished figures pouring out buckets of liquid among the refugees. At first he took them to be firemen attempting to extinguish the flames, then he realized, to his horror, that every time they appeared there was a sudden burst of flames. "My God! They're trying to burn the refugees!" he exclaimed. The British consuls, standing by ashen-faced, concurred.

At the northern end of the quay, near the Point, Turks flung kerosene on a crowded raft attempting to push off from the shore and turned it into a blazing torch. Cries of *"Kaymaste! Kaymaste!"* —"We're burning!"—reached the French battleship *Jean Bart*, where Takouhie Dabanian, nineteen years old and a stunning blue-eyed blonde, stood watching on deck. Before the fire, and against her father's protests, she had set out from her home in the suburb of Cordelio, put her accomplished French to use, passed herself off as "Dabanoff," and without any trouble obtained a *laissez-passez* to the battleship. Now she was weeping for her family while the marines hovering around her debated as to how they might effect a rescue. The nature of the holocaust precluded words of comfort. On rowboats, barges, and improvised rafts of all sizes and descriptions human cargo floated from ship to ship, faces raised, arms outstretched in speechless supplication. Disastrously overcrowded, many of these vessels overturned.

Italian ships took up everyone fortunate enough to swim or float within their reach. The French ships continued to take off boatloads from the shore as their consular officials offered passes to anyone lucky enough to be able to say, in French, "I am French. I lost my papers in the fire." Until nearly midnight the British and American ships stood by, impotent.

But by 10:00 P.M. the crews were threatening to get out of hand. Until then the sailors had been busy. Now, with the last of their evacuees aboard the *Winona*, there was nothing to do but watch. The sounds, which were as devastating as the scene, made their inactivity all the more unendurable. Above the steady noise of the rising wind and the flames, the crash of tumbling buildings and the sharp retorts of rifle fire, came the continuous wail of the multitude. With exits to the city blocked off by Turkish troops, nearly half a million human beings packed in an area a mile and a half long and no more than one hundred feet wide were trapped between the fire and the sea.

Two cargo lighters moored at the Point end of the harbor seemed to nod accusingly as they rose and fell with the tide. Major Davis and Mark Prentiss approached Captain Hepburn to suggest that the lighters be towed to the quay wall so that a few souls, at least, might drift out and escape the flames. Hepburn had already considered this idea and rejected it. The only boat on hand to do the towing had a low-powered motor and a capacity for only twenty passengers. He felt sure that such a boat could never handle the lighter in such a stiff wind, while to send the boat in alone would invite swamping unless she carried a guard almost equal to her capacity. Now if they only had some power launches . . .

Davis glanced at the perimeter of the bay where the Allied battleships loomed immense and black in the glow of the fire. Might the Captain approach the French and British? Hepburn thought not. It was a delicate proposition at best; coming from him it would appear official. Suppose Davis himself made the approach, informally, in the name of humanity. They had a boat lowered within minutes.

As he knew Dumesnil quite well, Davis headed first for the French flagship, only to discover that the Admiral was still ashore directing the evacuation of his nationals. Moving on to the *Iron Duke*, he found the British Admiral steadfastly refusing the entreaties of his staff to lower the boats. Brock insisted that the British position was at stake. After having been turned back to his battleship by Turkish sentries, he had succeeded in getting ashore and obtaining Noureddin's apologies for the incident, but the only way he could convince the Turks that England was not their enemy was to give assurance of British neutrality in the present circumstances. Neutrality, he now insisted, did not permit rescuing Armenians and Greeks. It was past midnight when the Admiral's Chief of Staff finally persuaded him that it would be unconscionable to take no action.

"Away all boats!" Once the squadron signal was given there

was no stinting of effort, for every man was at his station and bristling to get under way. Davis had scarcely returned to the *Litchfield* when the first power launches came sweeping in, all pulling large rowboats, with crews and boat officers of every rank from captain to midshipman. As the loaded boats returned from shore they were invited to unload their refugees on the *Litchfield* until Hepburn judged that there were between four and five hundred aboard—as safe a deck load as the destroyer could hold. (As it turned out later, there were six hundred and seventy one.) Thereafter, the refugees were taken to vessels lying farther offshore.

Worked to exhaustion, the oarsmen pulled alongside the destroyer to recuperate from time to time while American sailors passed down coffee. Swimmers were plentiful as fire drove increasing numbers into the water. Sometimes rifle fire would pick off a man or woman struggling to reach a ship, but those who managed to reach one were now pulled aboard. By ten o'clock Thursday morning every available vessel was filled. About twenty thousand people had been saved.

A frail woman with wild eyes and hair streaming down her face knelt in the bottom of her small rowboat and begged to be taken aboard the liner *Sardegna* with her young son. She was told to try another ship. She had been rowing from one ship to another all night, she said, sobbing. She had seen her husband killed and her daughter torn away. She could go no farther. The woman stood and threw herself into the water. Sailors fished her out and found a place for mother and son on the deck. Others were not so fortunate, and as the sun climbed overhead the cries of the suppliants on the quay rose louder than before.

Lieutenant Merrill, returning from Constantinople on the *Edsall* an hour before sunrise, had found the scene "indescribable." "The entire city was ablaze and the harbor as light as day," he wrote. "Thousands of homeless were surging back and forth along the blistering quay, panic-stricken to the point of insanity. The shrieks of women and children were painful to hear. In a frenzy they would throw themselves into the water, and some of them would reach the ship. The crowds along the quay were so thick and tried so desperately to close in abreast of the men-of-war anchorage, that the masses in the stifling center had nowhere to go but into the sea. Fortunately, the quay well never got actually hot enough to roast these unfortunate people alive but the heat must have been terrific there to have been felt on the ship two hundred yards away. To add further to the confusion the packs belonging to these refugees, consisting mostly of carpets and clothing, caught, making a chain of bonfires the length of the street. Occasionally the pack on a horse's back would take fire and he would go charging through the crowd at breakneck speed, knocking right and left the Christian minorities; truly a 'fiery steed.' The U.S. headquarters at Smyrna theater appeared like a large ball of fire. So hot was it in the street in front of this building that the four automobiles and two trucks parked at the door were burnt to cinders. Some of us saw a grim humor in the sign over the arched door in black letters two feet high. It was the name of the last movie shown: 'Le Tango de la Mort.' "

Merrill was so moved by the sight of the charred Stars and Stripes flying over the building that his normally crisp prose was shaken as he thought of it. "And through all this heat and flame and tumbling of walls, by some queer chance our flag remained. Even now it flies over the scanty remains of the front wall. Black, 'tis true, but an inspiration to many and a ray of hope to homeless thousands." The ray of hope was faint indeed. Soon, many of those who arrived hopefully at Ellis Island would be turned away. Hepburn, having transferred the refugees from the *Litchfield* to the *Edsall*, sent them to Salonika, and the *Winona* to Piraeus, with misgivings as to their reception. Among the *Winona*'s two thousand passengers were at least six hundred Armenian orphans. The boys had been found late Thursday morning, prostrate with exhaustion but still holding bravely to the American flag.

All Greece was in mourning; flags were at half-mast, buildings were draped in black, restaurants played no music. News of the fire had reached Athens by telegraph, and the atmosphere on the streets and in cafés was charged and restless. At Piraeus crowds gathered at the docks, scanning the horizon impatiently for signs of ships bearing the victims from Smyrna.

The appearance of the *Simpson* on Thursday morning raised a wave of excitement, but the initial cheers turned sour when word spread that only American citizens had been brought out. Later in the day a Japanese ship arrived whose passengers praised the exceptional kindness of the captain and crew; they had thrown cargo overboard to make room for refugees. There was no other traffic from Smyrna all day.

When the *Winona* reached Piraeus in the small hours of Friday morning, its crew found the gratitude of the populace overwhelming. At Salonika, too, there was a grateful reception. Captain Powell of the *Edsall* was pleasantly startled when the Captain of the Port, who could speak a little English, went aboard the destroyer and in the name of the Greek people thanked America for her great kindness in helping their stricken countrymen. "It is not surprising that this is done by America," he said, "the best friend if not the only real friend the Greeks have." He had tears in his eyes, Powell said. Then, and later, impoverished Greece accepted every refugee from Turkey, regardless of his origin.

In Piraeus Horton tried vainly to induce the Captain of the *Winona* to return to Smyrna for another cargo of human beings, but the Captain had on board a cargo of dried figs that was overdue in New York. He felt it would be useless to return, in any case. "By the time I get there," he said, "all the thousands standing on the quay will be dead of thirst and hunger."

The U.S.S. *Lawrence*, with Standard Oil Company officials from Constantinople on board, reached Smyrna late Thursday morning, moved directly to the Company plant, which had been spared, and took up her post at the Standard Oil docks. Sailors were once again landed to protect the enclave. From her deck, the crew watched the Turkish cavalry chasing down refugees and killing them along the beach. The work was still going on at nightfall.

On the battleship *Jean Bart* several marines had evolved a plan to save Takouhie Dabanian's family. The chief signalman had thought it up. "I'm the one who gives the signals," he had told her. "If we can get your relatives to [Vice-Consul] Guiffré's house, I'll signal to have them brought to the ship." Although the suburb of Cordelio was not burning, no one voiced the obvious possibility that the Dabanians might already have perished. The men advised her to tell an officer that her family lived only a block from the dock.

"I did as they suggested and the officer let two men come with me," she says now. "We found that the women of my family had escaped next door to the home of a neighbor who had foreign protection. The men were hiding in the cellar of my sister's house —it was the only house in the neighborhood with a cellar. In two minutes we gathered them all together and began walking to the Vice-Consul's house, but it was a tremendous distance.

"Now everyone along the way who noticed that we had French

marines with us, began to join the line. 'I'll be your servant,' a woman would say, and she would take my sister's baby. 'Let me carry this,' another would insist, and grab my brother's bag. One man came up to us and said, 'If you don't take me, I'll swear you are not French.' There were perhaps two dozen of us when we reached Guiffré's house. The marines let everyone who wanted to, join the line."

Thursday afternoon Lieutenant Merrill took a party of three men to a nearby suburb, "to rescue a friend's victrola and two pointer pups promised me." He noticed several burnt-out areas on the quay where people could assemble as they were driven from place to place by the fires. These relatively "safe" areas were, however, infested with Turkish soldiers, who were continually robbing the refugees of whatever they had left, and snatching away the younger women. The British vice-consul discovered during the afternoon that of about nine hundred refugees collected on the destroyer *Serapis*, there were not more than a dozen women between the ages of fifteen and thirty-five.

E. O. Jacob went ashore with other members of the relief committee and found that although the storehouse containing the main supply of flour was intact, the bakeries were destroyed. The Navy distributed flour and water among the refugees, "leaving it to their ingenuity to devise some method of baking." Fires were still burning fiercely along the waterfront, but the wind had shifted enough by Thursday afternoon to blow the flames inland.

As the afternoon progressed it became evident that the Turks were systematically hunting down Armenians. Vice-Consuls Park and Barnes, while making their way back to the *Litchfield*, witnessed five separate groups of Turks, armed with bloodied clubs, circulating among the refugees on the quay and searching out their victims. They saw one of these groups fall on a man and club him to death. "The proceeding was brutal beyond belief," Barnes said. "We were within ten feet of the assailants when the last blow was struck, and I doubt there was a bone unbroken left in the body when it was dropped over the edge of the quay and kicked into the sea." Noticing the look of horror clouding the Americans' faces, one of the Turks politely explained that the victim was an Armenian and shrugged his shoulders, as if to say, "What else was there for us to do?"

"While walking from this scene to the point on the quay where the *Litchfield* was moored, a walk of not more than five minutes,

I witnessed the shooting of three Armenians," Barnes reported. "Uniformed soldiers and officers, and boys of twelve were taking part in the killings as heartily as their elders." Captain Hepburn noted: "All reports indicate that every able-bodied Armenian man is being hunted down and killed wherever found."

The Captain was now convinced that the remaining refugees would have to be removed from Turkey at once if any were to survive. "Although my instructions forbade any joint action with foreign naval forces, I felt sure that they did not contemplate inaction in the face of a purely humanitarian emergency without parallel in history and which in my opinion could be met in no other way." Again he asked Major Davis, as Red Cross representative, to sound out Admirals Dumesnil and Brock—this time about calling a conference of senior naval officers and consuls, in order to formulate some kind of combined action.

Davis returned dejected. The word, from both the French and British, was a polite No. Neither of the Admirals wished to participate in such a conference.

CHAPTER XVI

To: *Admiral Mark L. Bristol*

Am convinced Turks burned Smyrna except Turkish section conforming with definite plan to solve Christian minority problem by forcing allies to evacuate Christian minorities. Believe they will now prepare for attack on Constantinople.

MERRILL
Smyrna, September 14, 1922

To: *The Secretary of the Navy*

That the Christians could have set fire to their own homes before leaving them is highly probable especially in view of the fact that when they evacuated the interior they set fire to their own villages before they left them. . . .

ADMIRAL MARK L. BRISTOL
March 27, 1924

When Captain Hepburn arose on Friday, September 15, he could see that the fires were beginning to burn themselves out; there was, in fact, virtually nothing left to ignite. There had been a resounding explosion directly in front of the *Litchfield*'s anchorage at midnight, and he saw now that what had been the Passport Control Office and the Custom House were smoking shells. Three-quarters of the city, including the Greek, Armenian, and European sections, was a similar mass of smouldering rubble. Only the Turkish quarter to the east, and the area around the railway depot at the Point and around the Standard Oil Company enclave to the north, remained intact.

As far as the refugees were concerned, Hepburn thought the situation was no longer pressing. "During the preceding forty-eight hours evacuations were carried on as a matter of an emergency of such gravity that ordinary considerations of policy had to be relegated to the background," he explained to Bristol. "The

Turkish authorities themselves, by their noninterference with these operations, have tacitly acquiesced in this view of the matter." Now that it was "no longer a case of imminent personal danger to the refugees on shore," it was not too soon, Hepburn decided, to mend his fences with the Turks, "in order that our future relations with the authorities, involving not only relief work but the property of our nationals, should not be jeopardized."

Taking along Barnes and Davis, as well as Archbell—a tobacco executive who had far-flung Turkish connections and could be counted on to be a far more ingratiating interpreter than Dr. Post —Hepburn called first on Abdul Halik Bey, the *vali*, to offer his condolences on the demise of the city. The Governor-General was wearing a grieved expression. The Turks had been so proud to have preserved Smyrna intact throughout all the devastation caused by the Greeks, he said, but the Armenians and Greeks had defeated them in the end.

The group was next ushered into the presence of Kiazim Pasha, the military commandant. The General, being something of a ham, enacted sentiments identical to those of the *vali* but with gestures that were decidedly more dramatic. He heaved his shoulders and stretched out his hands when Archbell translated Hepburn's sympathy. "We have lost the war!" he cried. "The Armenians have defeated us!"

From the attractive suburb of Bordova, where Kemal and his retinue had retired as guests of Lady Latife (whom Kemal would later marry and still later divorce), the Conqueror was less perturbed about the devastation of Smyrna. It was "a disagreeable incident," he told Admiral Dumesnil, but essentially "an episode of secondary importance."

In the course of the day the number of refugees in sight was considerably diminished. Jacob and Fisher, ashore on relief committee business, as well as Merrill and Rhodes on their way to Paradise, saw troops driving large detachments of civilians into the interior. All were convinced that the deported refugees were doomed. Still, the crowd in the streets was thick enough to impede passage as the two naval officers proceeded along the quay wall toward their car. Merrill was feeling some disgust toward the refugees; whenever he caught the eye of a female she would break into tears. "This steady weep business makes me ill," he said. "It looks so practiced."

166

At Paradise the officers found President MacLachlan well enough to make the trip to Smyrna—although he was on crutches, thanks to a broken tendon incurred while being clubbed to his knees. Rhodes persuaded the MacLachlans to leave after conveying Hepburn's orders that all but four of the sailor guards be withdrawn immediately, the rest to be withdrawn during the next few days. This news caused a flurry among the staff; with the guard withdrawn, and the buildings full of refugees, there was a greater likelihood that the College would meet the fate of her sister institutions. Such a prospect was intolerable to MacLachlan, who had spent his lifetime building the place up. The dean, Cass Arthur Reed, was more immediately concerned about his twelve remaining beneficiary students; he had promised to see them safely aboard a ship at the first opportunity.

Hovannes Simonian (later Bishop Elisha Simonian, Primate of the Western Diocese of the Armenian Church in America) carried President MacLachlan's bags to the waiting car. As the oldest of the beneficiary students, he had been acting as interpreter for Chief Crocker, who had told him repeatedly not to worry, that when the time came to leave he could depend on the U.S. Navy. Now a brisk nudge from the Chief and a few words from Reed told him that the moment was at hand, and Simonian climbed excitedly into the back seat. He was ostensibly going to help Dr. MacLachlan—in just this way a few Armenians had slipped through as family servants during the evacuation of the dependents. After the car was away, Dean Reed and Kingsley Birge, with a willing hand from the sailors, piled the rest of the boys on the truck and set off for the dock.

Hepburn, having just returned from the *Konak*, was preparing to board his launch when the truck drove up loaded with Armenian students instead of the sailor guard. The Captain was furious. He had given specific orders to bring only Americans from Paradise. Lieutenant Commander Rhodes, when called to account, insisted that he had delivered the message correctly; the College authorities had simply ignored them. "They counted upon my not being able to withstand the pressure if they actually brought the boys to the ship," Hepburn concluded. He sent them back to Paradise in the same truck.

Simonian had meanwhile boarded the *Litchfield* without difficulty and was gratefully counting his blessings. He had seen the others turned back, but unable to fathom the reason, he was comforting himself with the thought that they were being taken to another ship. It was afternoon when MacLachlan ordered him off as well.

"I couldn't believe it," His Grace recalled not long before his death. "I asked him if he realized what this meant. Here I was, safe on the ship, and he was prescribing my death sentence. We had been told that men over seventeen were soon to be deported. He knew this; it was apparently all the more reason for my going back. By allowing myself to be saved, I was somehow endangering the College. There was a pitiless logic involved that I very frankly was unable to comprehend.

"Crocker had to take me back in the launch. I felt too heartsick to look him in the face. I had a few moments of reprieve when the Turks refused to let us land and sent us back to the destroyer. But again, 'no'; MacLachlan and the Captain would not allow me to come aboard; they said I would be taken to the Standard Oil Company depot. I was taken there, but only to be put into a car and driven back to Paradise."

Merrill was meanwhile experiencing frustrations of his own. After returning from Paradise, he had taken Constantine Brown to meet Kiazim Pasha, introduced him as the only journalist in town, and suggested he be given the truth about the origin of the fire. Kiazim obliged by informing them that the police had arrested twenty-two Armenians "who had confessed belonged to a society of six hundred who had planned and executed the burning of Smyrna." Brown asked if he might see the captives. The General consented immediately, going so far as to send an officer to search for them, but so far as Merrill could see, Kiazim's firebugs were proving hard to locate.

After a time he had given up and driven back to Paradise with Reed, who gave him a trying afternoon. The man was for some reason in a nervous state. He fumed up and down the quay that he had given his car to someone and couldn't remember who it was. When he finally borrowed another, he couldn't do anything right, even by accident. "He took off his hat to privates, ran down generals, and stampeded cavalry right and left," Merrill complained. Nonetheless, matters improved when they drove to Boudja to check on Raymond Moreman and his Greek orphans. The orphanage was a gracious mansion, set in an immense grove of pine trees. Manicured grounds and an enormous fountain encircled by a driveway made the place seem as remote as Nirvana. Moreman, however, turned out to be a virtual prisoner in this attractive prison, for the Turks had not allowed him outside its ten-foot walls in six days. Merrill found fifty refugees on the grounds ("eating up everything but the pine trees") and turned them over to the Turkish commandant. For his part, the Turk promised that Moreman would be allowed to come and go, and to show his good faith he bought a round of raki.

The afternoon ended less happily for Fisher and Jacob when a Turkish soldier held them up a block from the quay. He relieved them of £350, told them to run, and fired a shot that sent them racing around the corner and into the arms of a Turkish officer leading a squadron. Excitedly, they poured forth their complaint, then pointed the direction in which the man had fled. "He can't have gone very far," Jacob said.

"Did he leave you anything at all?" asked the officer.

Yes, they had about £50 left.

"Hand it over!" was the sympathetic reply.

By midday Admiral Pepe of the Italian navy, with his inside track on Turkish policy, was alarmed enough to call a conference of Allied and American officials. The warning from Turkish headquarters could not have been more explicit: If the refugees were not removed by October 1, they would all be deported into the interior. Pepe, who did not have to be told what deportation meant, called the meeting for five o'clock Friday afternoon, aboard his yacht *Galileo*.

Present were Davis, Hepburn, and the British, French, and Italian consuls. Brock and Dumesnil were conspicuously absent, but had sent deputies. All in attendance agreed that the diminishing visibility of the refugees meant that they were already being deported in large numbers. All but the French representative agreed that immediate action was essential to save the rest.

It was decided that the first step should be an audience of senior naval officers with Mustafa Kemal to ask whether he would object to their taking joint action to help the refugees. Admiral Dumesnil's Chief of Staff demurred. In the Admiral's absence, he could not bind him to be a member of such a delegation. As the Admiral was at that moment meeting with Kemal and intended to discuss the refugees, the problem might already be settled. If not, the group would have to meet again. That dissolved the conference. "There will be no refugee problem to worry about by the time we get through conferring," Admiral Pepe remarked as he saw Hepburn off.

Prospects of "immediate action" appeared even more discouraging the next day when Hepburn finally succeeded in tracking Dumesnil down on the *Edgar Quinet*. The French Admiral was obviously preoccupied with more pressing matters. Although he did not tell Hepburn, he was in fact preparing to sail for Constantinople within the hour to confer with General Pelle about Kemal's persistent threat to move on Constantinople. If Kemal was not bluffing, his intransigence, on the one hand, and the British determination to stop him, on the other, placed the French in a ticklish position. Least of all could they contemplate two years of help to the Nationalists going down the drain.

Faced with Hepburn's request for his assistance in a joint rescue scheme, Dumesnil placed a premium upon delay. He was opposed to approaching Kemal just now. The Turks would interpret a joint appeal as "an ultimatum." It was a touchy moment to bother Kemal about Greeks and Armenians. In Dumesnil's opinion, more conferences and investigations were in order before anything could be done. Besides, he did not see the refugee situation as particularly urgent. He considered the deportations a "voluntary movement." Knowing that only the larger towns and villages along the railroad lines had been destroyed, many refugees were simply returning to their homes. The problem would eventually resolve itself.

Hepburn decided to leave for Constantinople immediately and lay the problem before Bristol. He sailed on Saturday afternoon, taking with him Fisher and five hundred and twenty inmates of an Armenian orphanage supported by American patronage—having obtained the permission of the Turkish authorities and assurances from Jacquith that the Near East Relief would pay for their future support. "I have been reluctant to violate our policy of taking off nobody except Americans until the general question of free evacuation had been settled," he explained to Bristol. "But some of the older girls had already been carried off by Turkish soldiers."

CHAPTER XVII

*The strange thing was, he said, how they screamed every
night at midnight. I do not know why they screamed at
that time. We were in the harbor and they were all on
the pier and at midnight they started screaming. We used
to turn the searchlight on them to quiet them.*

ERNEST HEMINGWAY
In Our Time

Saturday . . . Sunday . . . Monday . . .

The odor of burned flesh hovered over the remains of Smyrna.
Observing strict neutrality, the ships continued to stand idly at
anchor, awaiting orders from Constantinople. Each evening, at
dusk, a haunting sound would begin to rise and fall along the
waterfront, "like the sound of wind moaning through branches,"
minor in key and mournfully melodic. It was the refugees, praying
for ships. And when the night grew black enough for the Turks
to begin their nightly orgy, the destroyers would sweep their search-
lights over the quay in an effort to inhibit rape and slaughter, and
turn up their phonographs on deck to drown out the screams with
strains of "Humoresque" or the swelling tones of Caruso singing
from *Pagliacci*. On the battleships the navy bands obliged with
nightly concerts lasting far into the morning, with few intermis-
sions. Naval amenities suffered occasional lapses. An Admiral,
invited to dine with a colleague, had to apologize for arriving late

—a woman's body had become entangled in the propeller of his launch.

Kemal's ultimatum was by now plain enough, if it had not been plain all week. On Saturday, September 16, an official proclamation declaring Greek and Armenian men between the ages of eighteen and forty-five prisoners of war, and inviting all others to leave before October 1, was posted in conspicuous places and scattered by airplane over the quay. Commander Harry Powell of the *Edsall* reported to Bristol: "The Turks say, 'If these people are sent back into the country they will be killed.' They say, 'If you want to do something for the refugees, get ships in and carry them out.'"

Powell had approached officials in Salonika about sending Greek ships to evacuate the refugees, and had conveyed the information to Bristol that the Greeks were willing, provided someone could obtain the necessary guarantees from the Turks. On Monday, he cabled Bristol from Smyrna: "Italian Admiral conferred with Kemal, who said he would not take responsibility to allow Greek ships into the harbor."

After bribing the appropriate persons and offering the flour, Jacob arranged with the military bakery to supply bread for his group to distribute among the refugees. His errands of mercy took him some distance into the interior, for tens of thousands who had moved back from the quay—it was by now a reeking sewer—were continually being rounded up and marched to military barracks ten and twenty miles distant. Here the men were separated, bound together, and led away, and the rest thrust out again "prey to both soldiers and civilian rabble." Jacob found over eight thousand old men, women, and children in the barracks at Baldjova. "There is almost no water, and they have had no food for five days. We gave them over thirty sacks of flour, promised bread for tomorrow and arranged to repair the pumps," Jacob wrote on Monday. A Greek lady who was in the camp for several days remembers that the bread, when it finally came, smelled of gasoline. "We could not eat it," she says. "The Turks grabbed girls. On the way to the camp they grabbed girls and in the camp they came and took more."

The Ashjians were among a group of five to ten thousand huddled in a courtyard when the soldiers came and began driving them with whips toward the village of Mersinli. "On the way a soldier tore off my cousin Onnig's vest," Krikor's niece recalls. "Of course that was where he kept his money. Another aimed a revolver at my father's chest and emptied his pockets. In this way the crowd was robbed, pushed, flogged, and driven to the Halkapounar railroad station. Near here was a camp where we spent the night. There was hardly room to stand.

"We dozed, leaning on each other, and in the morning I heard a horrible commotion and saw that they were beginning to take the men from the women. They took all those who looked over fourteen and under sixty. They put the women and children to one side and selected the most attractive ones. Then Turkish officers came and chose those that pleased them and took these girls away. They took the men away too. Many weeks later, in Mitilini, we learned from a young man who escaped—I don't remember how— that they took our men some distance and killed them with machine guns.

"The Turks pointed toward the interior and began pushing us in that direction, but of course we were afraid to go that way and at the first opportunity we began again to try to find our way toward the sea. We walked all that day—hungry, thirsty, our feet torn and bleeding—until late at night we reached the Greek cemetery. Here we tried to sleep on the stones. Before the sun rose we once again started toward the quay. We were panting by the roadside when I saw Mr. Birge, one of the teachers of the Boys College, whom I knew well. I ran to him, begging him to find a way for us to escape. He promised to do so, asking us to stay where we were, and true to his word, he returned in half an hour and led us to the home of the wealthy Elmassian family. It was one of the few mansions left standing near the Point, and here the relief people sheltered us as we waited for ships."

One small freighter maneuvered her way into the harbor over the weekend and took off, without incident, all the refugees she could hold without sinking. She was a homely little "tramp" with a number of odd characteristics. Her name, the *Dotch,* sounded like a hybrid; she flew the flag of the defunct Russian aristocracy; her captain spoke English with a Greek accent and addressed his crew in a volley of Greek. She carried food supplies and two American passengers from Constantinople, and had sailed either unnoticed or unheeded through a formidable array of warships in the Sea of Marmara, past the British fleet lined along the eastern coastline of the Dardanelles, past Chanak, where Kemal's legions would soon be facing British forces across barbed wire that delimited the neutral zone. Esther P. Lovejoy, an attractive lady doctor, was one of the two passengers. The other was a gangling movie producer whom the doctor knew only as "Shorty." Both were Samaritans of one sort or another. Dr. Lovejoy, who had served in France during the war and more recently had been tending Armenians starving in the Russian Caucasus, interrupted a respite in Europe when word reached her of the Smyrna fire. "Shorty" had left Hollywood some time before, to document the Near Eastern scene with the hope of raising funds to help the victims.

Dr. Lovejoy had visited Smyrna before the war; now the ruined city reminded her of the trees she had seen in Belleau Wood, "with all the branches shot away save one stark limb." Near the Point, where jetties created a small whirlpool in a triangular segment of the bay, the water was clogged with the bloated carcasses of animals and humans exuding putrescent gases. American businessmen held their noses as they ducked into their new consulate, located among a line of buildings at this end that had been spared and appeared to Dr. Lovejoy to stand "like tombstones to the memory of the city." One man—a representative of the Baldwin Locomotive Works—confided to the doctor, as they stood on the deck of the *Edsall* one evening, that he had a weak stomach and had to get away from this scene. "Besides," he told her, "my job is to sell locomotives."

Two live wires, Archbell and Griswold, found it a propitious moment to organize a partnership as shipping agents. They engaged the necessary Turkish carriers and were busy hunting down freighters to ship out three thousand tons of tobacco that had escaped the flames. The American manager of a large export firm had fled aboard the *Litchfield* in a state of nervous collapse, after having witnessed a particularly grisly murder. He declared that he had resigned and would never set foot in the country again, but a more stalwart member of the firm had arrived in time to discover twelve hundred bales of tobacco intact and was shipping them out on Monday. At the new consulate, which was serving the businessmen as both home and office, Vice-Consul Barnes found himself "considerably inconvenienced" by the relief workers, who were attracting a less profitable clientele. They had a building nearby, but instead of using it as an office they had filled it up with a lot of refugees. Complaints to Bristol resulted in an order to "get these people out of the Consulate."

While no longer opposed to cooperating in a mass evacuation, Bristol and the Department of State were determined to avoid taking the initiative. There was not only a matter of transport involved, but also the problem of sustaining the refugees once they had been taken away. There was, moreover, the danger of setting a precedent; the whole of Eastern Thrace would have to be cleared of its Christians if, as it appeared, Kemal was to have it back. Noting an inclination among the European Powers to leave the charity to "rich Uncle Sam," after they had created the mess, the United States was not about to be trapped into assuming the burden.

Bristol and Allen Dulles, at the Near East desk, were determined, moreover, to discourage the notion that the conquering Turks had deliberately burned Smyrna. Foresight required that the disaster be minimized and the Turkish hand played down, not merely to accommodate the Turks, but in anticipation of insurance claims for the loss of American property. (The insurers, as it happened, were British.) In encouraging American business ventures in Turkey, Bristol had not seen fit to warn against war risk—indeed such a risk was not the best advertisement for investors—and so most claims were now valid only if the fire was deemed an accident. Tobacco losses alone ran into the millions.

Having spent Sunday afternoon with Hepburn, Jacquith, and L. I. Thomas, a director of Standard Oil, Bristol put his conclusions on record:

"In accordance with the observations that these gentlemen made personally in Smyrna, the general impression of each one was that whole thing was a horrible affair. Yet, as I listened to the different discussions of the situation from the time the Turkish troops entered Smyrna until two days after the big fire that practically destroyed nine-tenths of the city, I was getting a true picture of what had been more or less hazy from the telegrams and dispatches received on the same subject. It appeared to come clear to me that the burning of the city was an accident so far as the great loss of property was concerned."

Bristol took pains to convince the men that what they had seen was not necessarily the true picture. Thomas in particular had been so affected as to rashly declare that while he had been (in Bristol's words) "very decidedly pro-Turk before he had seen these things, now he had no use for them at all."

"Mr. Thomas has not had the interest in studying the characteristics of the races in this part of the world that I have had," Bristol explained. "Thus his statements, like the statements of many others, of horror at what they see gives anybody who hears them a wrong impression of the situation in this part of the world."

He was also forced to restrain Jacquith, who was condemning steamers like the *Hog Island* for loading with tobacco while refusing to take refugees. ("Such loose talk," he said, "will be a big boomerang.") And he kept reminding himself, during succeeding days, that men returning from Smyrna tended to be "a little hysterical" in their estimates of the number of people killed or burned. "When one's emotions are all calmed, the actual destruction of life will not prove to be great," he wrote confidently. He was more forthright in his talks with Turkish officials: "In an interview with Hamid Bey this morning (Sept. 21, 1922) I told him that my information was to the effect that not only were the men being evacuated, but that all the refugees, including women and children, were being driven back into the interior by the soldiers."

Harry Powell, who was now in command in Smyrna, felt that the situation had become serious enough to demand the evacuation of the Boudja orphans to Salonika on Monday, along with the younger students at Paradise and the native women on the College staff. They were taken away on the *Simpson* Monday evening. It had been an excruciating day for Powell. The Americans discovered that the entire military government had changed hands without notice; the new crowd had never heard of the relief committee, and so the job of cultivating relations, greasing palms, and obtaining permission to distribute food had to begin again.

There had been a near-incident that afternoon when Powell's sentries weakened and allowed two Greek priests to rush into the consulate for asylum while being chased down by Turkish cavalry. These cavalry charges were in fact unnerving the sailors. "I— I could hardly take it," said Melvin Johnson during a recent interview. He had been escorting a tobacco executive into the interior of the city (it was the last time Powell was to permit such an adventure) and he remembered marveling at the businessman's cool. "They'd horseback the victims right down," he said. "They'd stand up in the stirrups to have enough pressure on the bayonets, and they'd come *down* on 'em. Right through their shoulders and head and anything else. You see my hair is grey? I think that caused it. I still think about it nights."

"It's good for him to talk about it. Maybe now he'll get it off his mind," said his wife. Johnson offered the name of a shipmate who would corroborate his testimony. "You go find him. He'll tell you that what I'm telling you is the truth."

The friend, when found, was willing enough to talk, but his wife was decidedly uneasy.

"I'm still being paid by the Navy," he explained in an undertone when her back was turned. "Back in those days they were a lot stricter than they are today in military life. We weren't allowed to tell anything. But now I *know*—"

"Watch it, Daddy!" his wife broke in.

The old sailor winked. "Our purpose was to protect American property and American citizens only. We had nothing whatsoever to do with any of the rest of it." He added hurriedly that there was a lot of killing all right, and offered that he'd seen some things that would—"

"Careful, Daddy!" said his wife.

CHAPTER XVIII

*You remember the harbor. There were plenty of nice
things floating around in it. That was the only time in my
life I got so I dreamed about things.*

ERNEST HEMINGWAY
In Our Time

Tuesday . . . Wednesday . . . Thursday . . .

Still no ships. In ten days Kemal's ultimatum would expire.
"After that, deportation to Asia Minor, months of weary trekking,
a perfectly planned program of long drawn-out extermination,"
Jacob wrote. Tuesday morning he had met M. Carnier, a French
official of the Turkish Public Debt Administration, just back from
Phocia, "a town where the Turks have never been molested in spite
of previous Turkish excesses. He reports that he witnessed the
whole of its Christian population being deported into the interior.
He himself has been robbed of his last penny by Turkish soldier
escorts sent with him for his 'protection.' "

Observers agreed that license to rob and rape, loot and scourge
were part of a scheme to reward the victorious Turkish troops.
Hepburn thought that "if they wanted to, the Turks could establish
order in two hours." It was supposed to be traditional with Moslem
armies to be allowed a certain period of license after a victory, and

authorities hinted that an attempt to suppress this privilege would cause a revolt, but Hepburn doubted this. "My observation on the discipline of the Turkish troops in Smyrna leads me to disbelieve that any revolt would have followed stern repressive measures," he told Bristol.

Not only were repressive measures lacking, but officers were themselves setting the example. On Monday, when the sated forces were withdrawn, a fresh batch of soldiers and officers repeated the pattern with renewed energy. Each evening the dead would be gathered in a burnt-out area behind the new consulate, piled in trucks, and driven inland to be burned. "The odor of burning flesh is easily recognizable," wrote Lieutenant Commander Knauss.

A handful of American civilians trying to fight the nightmare with bread and bandages wondered which would give out first— their nerves or their supplies. "I have seen men, women, and children whipped, robbed, shot, stabbed, and drowned in the sea," wrote Asa Jennings, "and while I helped save some it seemed like nothing as compared with the great need. It seemed as though the awful, agonizing, hopeless shrieks for help would forever haunt me."

Jennings had in fact saved quite a few, and was soon to effect a rescue of unprecedented proportions, although judging by appearances he was the last man in Smyrna to qualify for the role of hero. A frail, unprepossessing man of about forty-five, he had given up the pulpit (he was an ordained Methodist minister from upstate New York) and taken up administrative work in various posts overseas with the YMCA. He appeared to be an insignificant little man, barely five feet tall in shoes, and seemingly doomed to second place. But he had scarcely arrived in Smyrna with his wife and two boys late in August, to take up the job of Boys' Work Secretary, when Jacob and Fisher had gone off on vacation, leaving him momentarily in charge.

By the time the others returned, early in September, Jennings had accepted a Greek merchant's offer of his house at #490 on the quay, stocked it with provisions left by the Greeks, and begun using it as a supply depot to feed refugees. When the nature of the Turkish occupation became clear, Jennings hoisted the American flag on this house and proceeded to fill it with refugees, ignoring Hepburn's disapproval. After the fire, again without an "aye" or "nay" from naval or civilian officials, Jennings had moved fast to take charge of still another house on that sparse row by the Point and turned the first, which had survived intact, into an emergency hospital where sailors and relief workers could gather pregnant women, as well as children who had lost their parents ("many of them massacred in the presence of their children," according to Jennings). The navy patrols had also discovered that it was often possible to rescue young women "from a fate worse than death" by approaching the Turkish soldiers and officers who were leading them away and claiming the girls as their friends. These needy, too, they brought to Jennings, until the two houses held well over one thousand occupants. Jennings called them his "concentration camps."

Powell characterized Jennings' activities as "irresponsible," in his reports to Bristol, but he did little to discourage them beyond insisting that Jennings haul down the American flag ("It might prove embarrassing if the Turks decide to enter") and ordering the eviction of men of military age, lest their presence jeopardize the women. He also asked Jennings to live aboard the *Edsall*, but the little man was becoming rather more used to giving orders than taking them, and Powell, less scrupulous than Captain Hepburn about the refinements of "strict neutrality," appeared perfectly willing to close his eyes to minor transgressions. Under Powell's command Jennings found the Navy crowd "exceedingly kind in every way. In my attempts to save people from drowning and many other of my activities the Navy simply let me go. I was not even restricted in giving orders."

When Jennings boarded the *Edsall* for occasional visits, his orders were in fact gratefully accepted. He discovered this to be the case late one afternoon, when a cry for help drove him to look over the rail and he saw a swimmer in distress. Turning to some sailors, Jennings shouted for them to drop a line. The men moved fast and hauled aboard a small boy. He was naked, and shivering with fright as well as with cold. Jennings wrapped him in a pair of Navy trousers and, at the sailors' suggestion, hid him behind a boat. There the child promptly fell asleep.

Moments later another figure was seen swimming toward the destroyer. The ship's lights made the swimmer a target for the Turkish sentries and the sailors turned them off. The figure, obviously exhausted and still some distance from the ship, was struggling to stay afloat. The men watched in pained silence. "For pity's sake why don't you lower a boat?" Jennings asked.

The men were apologetic. They were aching to lower a boat, they explained, but they could not do so without orders, and no officer could give such an order without entering it on the ship's log, where it would stand as barefaced evidence of his breach of neutrality. "Well, *I'll* give the order then," Jennings said. *"Push off that boat!"* The men obeyed, rowed out to the floundering swimmer, and returned with a young girl. Just as they deposited her, unconscious, at Jennings's feet, an officer strode by, took in the situation, turned on his heels, and walked quickly away.

Wrapped in blankets, the girl soon revived. "She looked at us with a wild expression in her eyes, seeing all those men standing about her," Jennings recounted. "Finally, she realized she was with friends who would protect her, and such a look of joy and thankfulness came over her face as I shall never forget. Then thoughts of what she had been through must have gripped her, for she began to cry, calling out some name in her grief. We were helpless, for we could not understand a word of what she was saying. I then thought of the little fellow I had sequestered behind the boat and hurried back to my stowaway to see if he could help us with his few words of English." Jennings woke the boy and hand in hand they approached the group encircling the girl. As they came closer, the ring parted. "Suddenly," Jennings said, "I felt the boy's grip tighten in mine, the little fellow bounded from my side and threw himself on the girl. Then from her lips there burst the name she had been moaning before in grief. He was her brother, and there on the deck of that ship we had reunited them."

Despite such heartening episodes, Jennings was in despair as each passing day brought no sign of further progress in evacuating the people. A devout man, he had been praying. "Everyone was praying for ships. I, too, prayed for ships." Always one to help his prayers along with a little action, Jennings this time had no idea what else he could do. "I'm sure I was no more anxious for ships than others on the committee, and for that reason I did nothing toward trying to secure ships, as that task was not assigned to me nor was I asked to assist." But on the morning of September 20 Jennings awoke with a determination to do something. He was seized, as he said later, "with an uncontrollable urge" to save at least the people in his charge.

Acting on his impulse, Jennings rushed to the *Edsall,* borrowed Powell's launch, and with the Commander's blessing to "go and do your darndest," set out to comb the harbor. He first approached the

French steamer *Pierre Loti*. No luck. He then moved on to a large Italian cargo liner, the *Constantinapoli*. To save time, he stood up in his motorboat and shouted.

Did the Captain have refugees aboard?

"No." An immense, ocean-going liner stood empty!

Would the Captain take refugees?

The Captain was sorry. He had sailing orders to take cargo to Constantinople. He had no orders to take refugees. Jennings persisted. "Can the Italian consul here change your orders?"

The Captain looked doubtful.

"Has he the *authority* to change your orders?"

Well, yes, the Captain admitted he had.

Jennings scrambled aboard. "Good. I'll pay you 5,000 lire to take 2,000 refugees to Mitilini. I'll pay you 1,000 lire extra for your trouble."

Jennings worked all afternoon and night to prepare for the sailing. He had to obtain permission from the Turkish authorities, as well as from the Italian consul. The next morning, he discovered that the Turks had stationed two rows of soldiers from the front door of the house where all the refugees had been gathered, to the wharf where the ship was moored. "Although we had made it plain that no man of military age could hope to leave, some had tried in various ways to disguise themselves," he wrote. "It was heartbreaking to see the grief of loved ones when these ruses were discovered and soldiers pulled the men back from the ships. But there was nothing else to be done. It was either play the game as the Turks said, or not play it at all."

Jennings was exhausted when the ship finally drew away that afternoon. As the engines churned and the bow split the waters, refugees swarmed around him on the deck. "They kissed my hands and my clothing, and many actually grabbed me and fell at my feet and kissed my shoes. This was too much for me." He fought his way to his cabin, fell on his berth, and wept uncontrollably.

Eight hours later, when the *Constantinapoli* reached Mitilini, Jennings was seized with still another impulse. In the harbor, even under the shroud of darkness, he could see ships, twenty big, beautiful, empty transports, standing row on row—the bulk of the fleet that had evacuated the Greek army.

Before the ship had pulled away from Smyrna, Powell had informed Jennings that Admiral Pepe had finally obtained permission from Kemal for Greek ships to enter Smyrna harbor. Powell had also handed him two cables from Davis: one ordered him to land the refugees in Mitilini under the aegis of the Red Cross; the other authorized him to act as he saw fit "in any subsequent emergency." Using the second of his cables, Jennings now approached General Frankos, Commandant of the South Army and commander of the ships in Mitilini harbor, and asked if they might be sent to Smyrna. The General was willing to lend six ships provided he could have a written guarantee that they would be protected and permitted to return.

After delivering his refugees to the governor-general of the island, who offered to take as many more as he could feed, Jennings boarded the destroyer and headed back to Smyrna, making the trip in less than three hours. There, he grabbed a written statement from Powell and returned immediately to General Frankos at Mitilini.

Frankos read Powell's document and hedged. The Americans were offering to "escort the ships in and out of the harbor," but the statement said nothing about protection in case the Turks attacked. The Turks had no navy, the General pointed out, and they might well seize the ships and set out to capture Chios, or even Mitilini. "He was not convinced that the Turks had given permission and demanded further proof," Jennings said later. "I could appreciate his position and reasons for caution but I realized something had to be done right away, so I told him that I personally would accompany the ships in and out of the harbor." This was not exactly enough for the General.

Outside, through the gray, early-morning mist, a familiar-looking warship loomed in the harbor. It looked to Jennings like an American battleship, and yet he knew that there were no American battleships around these waters. He asked someone what it was, and was told that it was the Greek ship *Kilkis*. "Then I remembered. Somewhere, sometime before the war, I had read that the United States government had sold the Greeks the old battleship *Mississippi*. And there she was, with a different flag and a different name, lying at anchor right out there in the harbor. Somehow I had the strange confidence that through her I could get help."

Jennings found the Captain of the *Kilkis* eager to cooperate. Together, they worded a message to the authorities in Athens, which the Captain sent over the ship's wireless in code. It read: "In the name of humanity, send twenty ships now idle here to evacuate starving Greek refugees from Smyrna without delay." It was signed "Asa Jennings, American citizen."

Within minutes there was a query: Who the devil was Asa Jennings?

"I identified myself as Chairman of the American Relief Committee in Mitilini," said Jennings. "I didn't bother to explain that I held the position solely by virtue of the fact that I was the only American there."

The next message took longer in coming. It stated that the Prime Minister had called a cabinet meeting, and asked what protection Mr. Jennings could offer the Greek ships. Jennings replied that American destroyers would accompany them in and out of the harbor. Another question: "Will American destroyers protect ships if the Turks attempt to seize them?"

That was the ticklish point. By what authority could Jennings assure the Greek cabinet that America would back Greece to the limit, if necessary resisting a Turkish attack by force of arms? He gambled on an evasion: "No time to discuss details of exactly how ships will be protected. Stated guarantees should be entirely satisfactory."

But the Greek cabinet, at that moment so shaky that it was only four days from toppling, found Jennings's guarantees somewhat slender. At four o'clock on the afternoon of Saturday, September 23, with the negotiations hopelessly deadlocked, Jennings grew desperate. "I threw caution to the winds," he said. "I staked everything on this one. I told them that if I did not receive a favorable reply by six o'clock that evening I would wire openly, without code, so that the message could be picked up by any wireless station in the vicinity, that the Turkish authorities had given their permission, that the American Navy had guaranteed protection, and that the Greek government would not permit Greek ships to save Greek and Armenian refugees awaiting certain death, or worse."

It was not quite six o'clock when the reply came: "All ships in Aegean placed under your command to remove refugees from Smyrna." Jennings had been made Admiral of the entire Greek fleet.

The Captain of the *Kilkis* was asking his new chief for orders, but Jennings was for a moment too stunned to reply. ("All I knew about ships was to be sick on them.") He rallied quickly, convened a meeting of the transport captains aboard the *Kilkis*, and discovered that ten of the ships could be made ready to leave by midnight. Next Jennings remembered that an Admiral was supposed to have a flagship. ("Who ever heard of an Admiral without one?") He chose the *Propondis,* mainly because her Captain spoke a little English. "He was tickled to death to think his ship had been selected," said Jennings. "Whether he realized this meant he was to head the procession into the Turkish harbor, I don't know— I didn't stop to press details on him. At twelve o'clock I was ready, and, ordering the Greek flag run down, an American flag flown in its stead and a signal flag that meant 'follow me' run up aft, I mounted the bridge and ordered full steam ahead."

Midway to Smyrna the flotilla was met by the *Lawrence.* It drew alongside and the Captain asked Jennings if he would not prefer to ride the rest of the way on the destroyer. In truth, Jennings was feeling ill, but he looked back, "saw my nine ships following in good order, and, remembering my promise to the Greek cabinet that I would go with the first ship, declined with thanks and remained on the bridge."

The convoy moved on. Dawn shredded the night, revealing billows of thick black clouds over their destination. The odor of smoke, which had been discernible all the way to Mitilini, grew stronger as the sun rose behind Mount Pagus. Jennings was to remember that moment to the end of his life.

"Directly in front of us, gaunt brick-and-stone skeletons of once-fine buildings pushed themselves up from the charred debris that covered the ground. It was the most desolate, fearsome sight I ever saw. And at the water's edge, stretching for miles, was what looked like a lifeless black border. Yet I knew that it was a border not of death but of living sufferers waiting, hoping, praying for ships—ships—ships! As we approached and the shore spread out before us, it seemed as if every face on that quay was turned toward us, and every arm outstretched to bring us in. Indeed I thought that the whole shore was moving out to grasp us. The air was filled with the cries of those thousands, cries of such transcendent joy that the sound pierced to the very marrow of my bones."

CHAPTER XIX

*Following a ten days' siege the Ottoman Sultan Celebi
Mehmet I conquered the city, which remained in the hands
of the Ottomans till 1919 when it was occupied by the
enemy only to be saved by the armies of Ataturk in 1922.*
Capsule history of Izmir
from a recent Turkish
tourist brochure.

On September 24 the curtain rose on the final act of the Smyrna
tragedy, when the Greek fleet with Admiral Jennings at the helm
rescued fifteen thousand old men, women, and children from the
hell the city had become in two interminable weeks. On September
26 Jennings returned with seventeen ships and carried off forty-
three thousand more exiles to Mitilini. A cargo fleet under British
charter joined in the rescue on the third day. By October 1
one hundred and eighty thousand refugees had been taken from
Smyrna, the last ship pulling out exactly six hours before the
expiration of the deadline.

American and Allied commanders now prevailed on the Turks to
extend the time limit another eight days so that British and Greek
ships might evacuate nearby ports. Another sixty thousand persons
were thus plucked from the shores of Urla, Chesme, and Ayvalik,
where they had been gathered for two weeks. This brought the
grand total evacuated to nearly a quarter of a million refugees.

During this operation a revolutionary (antiroyalist) government took over Mitilini; until a similar coup toppled the royalist regime in Athens five days later, Jennings was working under two governments. The new rulers sanctioned the enterprise "without hesitation," despite Bristol's precautionary cable to the U.S. Navy in Athens: Should Greek authorities inquire, Bristol wanted it understood that the navy role was "confined purely to using good offices with Turkish authorities in permitting Greek ships into the harbor." He made it clear that "we have not, repeat NOT, promised naval protection of any sort nor have naval authorities given any assurance of assistance or care of refugees after evacuation."

The magnitude of the operation and its completion within the prescribed time limits enabled the American and British navies to cover themselves with glory. The American sailors, no less than the British, deserved to be praised as much for being "guilty of many unauthorized acts of humanity," as Dr. Lovejoy later expressed it, as for helping to expedite the evacuations. Yet it was difficult, if not impossible, to publicize their humanitarian acts without turning public opinion at home against American policy in Turkey. Certain American churchmen were already badgering the State Department to take a stand on behalf of the minorities, or at the very least to exert strong diplomatic pressures. Secretary of State Hughes responded to these protests by asking Bristol to impress upon Kemalist officials in Constantinople the fact that their minority policy was making it exceedingly difficult to change American public opinion toward Turkey. In reply to the clamor at home, he insisted that the government, "keenly alive to every humanitarian interest . . . has not failed to take every appropriate action" within limits beyond which the Executive branch could not go without approval from Congress. This did not quiet certain church leaders, who were advocating force, if necessary, to save the half-million Christians of Constantinople.

That city was now in turmoil. Steamship offices were mobbed with prospective customers offering enormous sums for space on louse-ridden freighters. "Every Greek is wearing a fez trying to camouflage himself as a Turk," wrote the *Chicago Tribune* correspondent. Tourists could pick up bargains in anything from amber beads to oriental rugs, as Greek and Armenian merchants unloaded their wares in desperate haste to accumulate foreign currency. The Grande Rue de Pera offered some unusual sights. One man, jogging along with five coffins strapped to his back, explained to an astonished reporter that he was searching for the likely location of a massacre; another man was seen staggering toward the docks carrying a red-hot kitchen stove, "the smoke curving gracefully from the chimney." Belly dancers were alarmed because three "American" jazz bands—whose members were Greek—had already pulled out. Enterprising Turkish barbers were getting bargains in nickel-plated chairs from "American" dentists who held Greek passports. "There is plenty of good business opportunity for hustling young Turks anxious to get along, in replacing the fleeing Greeks as barbers, fruiterers, tattooers, and cocaine salesmen, but most of the Turks are too busy keeping their *nargilehs* bubbling and watching the street cars go by," wrote the *Tribune* reporter. "They think what fools they all are to be so scared."

Foreigners took a less sanguine view. Bristol himself was alarmed that the Turks were arming their civilians and thought that the greatest massacre of all time was likely to follow a Turkish occupation of Constantinople. A director of the Board of Missions wrote to his home office that Americans were leaving the city in droves. In Washington the Near East desk became concerned enough to send a long memorandum to Secretary Hughes suggesting that it might be time to take a firm stand on the protection of minorities as well as the freedom of the Straits. Hughes hastened to acknowledge the "forcible representation of the matter" but did not yield to the suggestion because of "other considerations which cannot be ignored."

On September 24, somewhat after the fact, since the evacuation was already getting under way, Bristol and the other High Commissioners were finally agreeing in Constantinople that their navies might work together in Smyrna. Rumbold, who had called the others together, opened the meeting by expressing the concern of his Foreign Office for the plight of the refugees. He did not explain that London had had its share of concerns that week, having discovered that first the French, then the Italian forces were withdrawing from Chanak, leaving the British alone to protect the Dardanelles. Curzon had rushed to Paris and once more become so unnerved as to rush from the conference room in tears. The cabinet had been further stunned to discover that it could not rely on help from the Dominions. Under the circumstances it seemed laudable that the British Board of Trade was speeding fifteen ships to help evacuate the Anatolian refugees. His Government, Rumbold said, was also appropriating £50,000 "on condition that each of the other countries contribute a like amount." In an undertone to Bristol, Rumbold confided that he didn't expect anything from the French and Italians. "We [meaning England and America] will probably have to put up all the money," he said.

The Admiral bristled. He had before this thought of Rumbold impertinent, and he was now thoroughly annoyed at what he considered "this attempt to give the impression that he was initiating all this relief." He countered testily that the Americans had been offering relief all along, and added that "likewise, before this, I had directed our destroyers at Smyrna to evacuate as many refugees as possible." (On September 20 Bristol had sent Powell the necessary orders for U.S. naval assistance in loading Greek ships.) He was less disgusted with General Pelle of France and Marquis Garroni of Italy, who did not appear eager to participate in the operations at all: "They felt that there were enough ships provided already for the refugees, so they wouldn't send any."

More pleasant news from Smyrna greeted Bristol later that day. John Clayton had returned to the city and been granted an interview with Kemal in which he had asked the Turkish leader about the Mesopotamian oil rights. "Your Excellency," Clayton had said, "those who have studied the oil question in its bearing on international politics realize that Great Britain must have access to large petroleum deposits or cease to be a world power of the first importance. Therefore, to my mind, the problem of the petroleum fields in Mesopotamia is certainly of greater importance than Constantinople, and is possibly of as much importance as the Straits. Would you express the attitude of the Turkish Nationalist government toward the British claims to the Mesopotamian oil?"

Kemal's reply was decidedly heartening to the American position. "All the territories in question," he said, "are in the province of Mosul, which is part of the territory of the Nationalist Pact. The great majority of this territory is Turkish. I do not think the possession of this territory is necessary for the exploitation of the oil fields in that region. For instance, there is nothing against American exploitation of oil fields in Turkey, as America has no political ambitions in our country. If England would follow a similar attitude it would be a most reasonable one from their point of view."

Bristol's biggest headache of the moment was the press. Eyewitnesses arriving at foreign ports were already giving out spectacular news stories to reporters, and it seemed inevitable that after the mass exodus there would be a barrage of uncontrollable publicity. On September 22 the Admiral had cabled the State Department urging the release of an official account to offset "exaggerated and alarming reports appearing in American newspapers regarding Smyrna fires." He offered a sample which the State Department was pleased to use:

American officers who have been eyewitnesses of all events occurring, Smyrna, from time of the occupation of that city by Nationalists up to present, report killings which occurred at that city were ones for the most part by individuals or small bands of rowdies or soldiers, and that nothing in the nature of a massacre had occurred. During the fire some people were drowned by attempting to swim to vessels in harbor or by falling off the quay wall, but this number was small. When mass of people were gathered on quay to escape fire, they were guarded by Turkish troops but were at no time prevented by such troops from leaving the quay if they so desired. It is impossible to estimate the number of deaths due to killings, fire, and execution, but the total probably does not exceed 2,000.

Bristol's tone suited the policymakers. In the current issue of *Foreign Affairs* Elihu Root was pleading for "restraint of expression," noting that "nations are even more sensitive to insult than individuals."

Coincidentally, feature articles appearing in the *New York Times* by Mark Prentiss, the foreign trade specialist in Smyrna as Bristol's "special relief representative," began to show a marked shift in point of view. Although Prentiss did not appear to be an especially sensitive man ("High hat," said the sailor who drove him around. "He didn't seem to think much of enlisted personnel"), he was initially shaken by what he saw: "I have seen terrible sights until my senses are numb, but the sight of two hundred thousand people, mostly women and little children, penned up and burning and those escaping being driven to a bare, devastated country for starvation, is past all comprehension, but these facts exist." In this first article, dated September 18, Prentiss did not equivocate about the fire:

---

* Bristol's figure has gone down as the historical verdict to date. George Horton estimated over 100,000 lost at Smyrna. His estimate makes more sense because of the roughly 400,000 Ottoman Christians (native Smyrneans plus refugees) in Smyrna during the days immediately preceding the fire, there were at least 190,000 unaccounted for by October 1.

Many of us personally saw—and are ready to affirm the statement—Turkish soldiers often directed by officers throwing petroleum in the streets and houses. Vice-Consul Barnes watched a Turkish officer leisurely fire the Custom House and the Passport Bureau while at least fifty Turkish soldiers stood by. Major Davis saw Turkish soldiers throwing oil in many houses. The Navy patrol reported seeing a complete horseshoe of fires started by the Turks around the American school.

Prentiss's article went on to describe "one of the most tragic sights of all": four thousand refugees lying on barges near the breakwater, slowly dying of hunger and thirst as British sailors supplying them with water and Americans providing them with food "were forbidden all contact with them."

A few days later, however, Prentiss's vision and his assertions split company. The result was a decidedly schizoid tone in his article of September 20, in which details about "the indescribable torture and agony on the waterfront" were juxtaposed with such statements as the following:

The burning of Smyrna will rank as the world's greatest tragedy, and it is likely historians will divide the responsibility. The Greek action in arming civilians, together with prolonged and extensive sniping, exasperated the Turks beyond their officers' control. The officers exerted an effort to maintain order and establish a record for peaceful occupation.

By September 27 Prentiss had found a steady voice. "MARK PRENTISS PRAISES TURKS' PART IN POLICING THRONG OF 200,000 PERSONS IN NEED," rang out the *New York Times* headline. The minorities, Prentiss's article suggested, were literally scaring themselves to death. The man who had joined the Near East Relief to be of service to the victims was now being chauffeured about the city in the company of a Turkish major. "The fuzz told us where to go and where not to go," said the sailor who was doing the driving. "I was too busy to notice where we went. I had to keep getting out to pull stiffs out of the way."

Other reports, most of which did not reach the newspapers, belie Prentiss's unqualified praise of the policing. "15,000 taken off today in stifling heat and dust amid indescribable crushing, confusion, robberies, and beatings by Turkish soldiers," E. O. Jacob recorded in his diary. Commander Powell concurred: "Brutality and robbery at the gates and in the [railroad] yard was rather the rule than the exception."

Powell cited Esther Lovejoy as the heroine of that last fateful week. She was the only American woman on the scene and one of three doctors—the others were Dr. Post and a British Navy surgeon—who constituted a medical team. From early morning until late at night they were on the piers treating the ill, delivering babies, helping to move the injured. Later Dr. Lovejoy was to relate her experiences in detail, in an autobiographical volume titled *Certain Samaritans.* She considered it her duty to record her observations in Smyrna *"with special care,"* she noted in a letter, "because my confidence in history has been so shaken by the misinformation circulated regarding the finish of the Christian minorities in Turkey." Dr. Lovejoy found the powers of language insufficient to the task of description: "Pain, anguish, despair and that dumb endurance beyond despair cannot be expressed in words."

The Turkish authorities had at the end relented and allowed Jennings's ships to dock at the piers by the railroad depot near the Point. Two spiked iron fences with narrow gates separated the quay from the railroad yards; from there the piers extended a long distance to deep water. Across these piers, at intervals of two hundred yards, the Turks had improvised three more fences with openings only three feet wide. In order to reach the ships, women, children, and old men, with any worldly possessions they had managed to retain—bedding, clothing, a jug of water and perhaps a loaf of bread, cooking pots: items that in some cases would make the difference between death and survival through a harsh winter—had to file through a double line of Turkish soldiers and pass scrutiny at each of five heavily guarded gates.

The crush at these gates provided the least of their trials, for by now the refugees were numb to discomfort. It was here that the remaining men were torn away, and this last wrench, by a bullet or the stab of a bayonet if resistance was offered, and sometimes for no reason at all, provided the supreme test of endurance for their wives, children, and aged parents. Sometimes the men would be arrested at the first gate; more often they would manage to bribe their way past the first and the second, only to be captured at one of the last three. Soldiers would beat the men back with the butts of their rifles and lash the women forward with canes and straps, all the while shouting *"Haide!"*—"Begone!" "I shall never forget those women with their children clinging to their skirts as they moved backward, step by step, gazing for the last time upon the faces of their husbands and sons," wrote Dr. Lovejoy. She described the scene as "the most cruel, cowardly, and unsportsmanlike spectacle that ever passed under the eyes of heaven."

A few were saved by a whim, or a kind Turk. In his darkest hour Karekin Bizdikian had stumbled on a Turkish friend. "He dared not hide me, he had to turn me over to an officer," Bizdikian says. "But he took my wife and son to the house of an Armenian, who had been killed. The new baby was born there. Later, he took them to the pier. The new baby died in Greece of malnutrition. I never saw him."

Powell marveled at the "two sides of the Turkish nature," apparently unable to conceive that such duality could be a universal trait. He saw one of the harbor police carrying a child up and down the dock until he found the mother. "This same man would show himself to be quite a brute immediately afterwards, in his treatment of cripples or women," he wrote.

Americans, too, showed a second side. Dr. Lovejoy and Captain Rhodes of the *Litchfield* happened to be on hand one afternoon just as a young man was being arrested at the last barrier. He had paid for his life through the first four gates, and now his sisters were making a futile effort to buy him a last reprieve. The girls were beautiful and, like so many of the victims, spoke perfect English. They turned to the American officer and seized his hands. "Look at him," they said. "He is our brother. You can save his life. For God's sake say the word. He is sick!"

Rhodes had steeled himself against this sort of onslaught—he had forced himself to become "hard boiled" he had told Dr. Lovejoy—and at first he tried to shake the girls off. Then he caught the dark, pleading eyes and his reserve melted. "Yes, of course he's sick." He turned to the Turkish officer. "Anybody can see this boy's sick!" The Turk bowed and smiled, "Of course!" A few words to the guards and the boy passed through the last barrier as on a cloud.

Now a woman with a family of small children, whose husband had just been taken, seized the doctor's hand. "It was against the rules to interfere in any way," Dr. Lovejoy wrote, "but I looked toward the Turkish officer and indicated *that* prisoner. This officer was in a gracious mood. Without the slightest hesitation he set the man free. He did not need an excuse. This was merely a personal favor to an American woman. A small favor. Christian life was cheap that day on the Smyrna pier.

"Two men were saved, but what about the other prisoners? They

193

were all taken sick at once and were displaying the evidence of their ailments. As a matter of fact, they *were* sick. Human beings cannot suffer as they had suffered for two weeks and remain in health. But the gifts of life were over for that group of prisoners, and in a few minutes they were marched away."

Shorty, the American film producer, played his part one day after two young refugees who had been cooking for the relief committee confided why they could not leave with the other refugees. Their brother and a friend were hidden in the attic and they were feeding them every day. The next morning Shorty and a new relief worker with a cork hat pulled over his eyes could be seen carrying a litter aboard a refugee ship. Shorty returned alone. The cooks left soon after. The meal at Jennings's house was a disaster that night, but while some Americans grumbled, Shorty beamed over the makeshift supper.

Aware that the Turks considered attractive girls a part of their loot, the sailors made special efforts to protect them. A husky young sailor at Jennings's camp had taken to standing in front of a pretty girl who sat in a niche by a window. He was overwrought when orders came returning him to his ship. "She is my girl," he told the doctor. "I got her that place near the window, and the blanket and pillow. I've kept her there and brought her food for nearly two weeks, and I don't want no Turk to get her now. Give me the God's truth. Promise me you'll watch her and get her aboard a ship!" Another sailor, smarting under a reprimand for helping young girls instead of old people, thought the priorities misguided. "What do you think about it, lady?" he appealed to Dr. Lovejoy. "I think we ought to get the girls aboard the ships first. The Turks don't want the old people."

Flagrant robberies took place just before the first gate, and again between the first and the second. "Systematic robberies, by soldiers on and off duty," Powell reported. "Posting my enlisted men at the gates had little or no effect in stopping the robbing or the brutality. Posting an officer at the gates had little more. I called it to the attention of the liaison officer, a captain, and asked that he report it to higher authorities. I also informed the Captain of the Port, under whom were the Harbor Police, and as a final recourse I called on Noureddin Pasha and reported it to him. It did not seem to interest him to any great degree."

Standing by one morning with an American businessman, as the robberies proceeded under their eyes, Dr. Lovejoy wondered why her companion was continually making excuses for the Turks. "If the Turkish officers were here, this would be stopped," the man said finally. Just then, a dazzlingly uniformed officer strode by and, after the American had complained to him, moved along the line of soldiers scolding and threatening offenders with his cane. The act was unconvincing to the doctor. She did not hear the officer's words, but by the results guessed at their gist—"Don't rob anybody in my presence; wait until I face the other way"—for the moment his back was turned, the enlisted men went right on with their extortion. The doctor kept her eye on the officer and saw him pass down the line with his menacing cane, then stop before an apparently promising victim, an old man, whom he promptly led aside and robbed—"incidentally giving an impressive demonstration of a thorough job to his subordinates." The businessman had seen the performance, too. "Dr. Lovejoy, please be careful what you say about all this in the United States," he pleaded. "Remember, we have to live here."

"*Haide! Haide!*" The American and British sailors picked up the chant: "*Haide,* git!" They were trying to keep the evacuees moving. But "walking the plank" was not easy. Many of the women and children had lost their shoes, broken glass littered the roadway of the piers, and children's bare feet slipped through the wide gaps between the boards.

Families were separated in the crush. Dr. Lovejoy saw an old grandmother, "naked from her waist to her feet and apparently unconscious of this fact," running in circles calling piteously for her children. The soldiers might call a halt at a gate after only one or two members of a family had passed through. They would hold frantic mothers back with their guns while the children were hustled up a gangplank. Since several ships were loading at one time, each destined for a different port, it was pure chance whether or not a mother would later find her children on her assigned ship or at its destination. Seeking desperately to keep their families together, some women tried to scale the seven-foot fence and were more often than not clubbed down. Others lost their bundles or were pushed off the pier into the shallow water floating with carrion. Here they would stand, holding their children out of the water, until a kind sailor would notice them and lift them out.

On Friday, September 29, a strange Levantine craft with painted oars and pale red sail wove its way through this infested water, stirring up its nauseating odors, and landed at the north end of the quay. It was the Moslem Thanksgiving and the picturesque crew had brought twelve rams as a sacrificial offering. The ceremony, chillingly symbolic to many of the observers, involved some ritual chanting around the sheep, after which the officiants cut the throats of all twelve animals, wiped their knives and hands on the victims' wool, threw the carcasses into the caïque, and rowed away. The sacrificial blood remained on the stones of the quay.

Dr. Lovejoy left that night. The *Litchfield* was returning to Constantinople and the doctor was hitching a ride so that she could rush to the United States and raise funds for the American Women's Hospitals—the only agency preparing to set up medical facilities at the throbbing Greek ports, where pestilential diseases were already beginning to break out.

At the pier by the American launches, a young boy passed her suitcase to the sailor. "Listen!" she heard the sailor whisper, "Take this suitcase aboard the ship for the lady and don't come back. You hear? *Don't come back!*"

The vice-consuls and several other Americans were gathered in the wardroom when the Captain suddenly turned and asked the doctor about the boy who had come aboard with her suitcase. Until then the conversation had been turned on the evil Russians, and the doctor had found herself marveling that men could focus their antipathy on Russians with the sounds of Smyrna ringing in their ears. Now she wished they would revert to the discussion, but the Captain was insistent. What happened to that boy? Dr. Lovejoy murmured that she did not know the boy.

He was promptly fetched and questioned. "He was small in stature, looked very young, not more than twenty, and spoke English well," she wrote. "He was pale and trembling, for it was a case of life or death to him, although but a light, unimportant matter to those used to this sort of thing from the other end of the game. Mr. Jacob identified the boy as one of those who had been helping the relief workers on the quay. Therefore he knew that in saving others he may have lost the chance to save himself.

"He was a brave boy. Not a word did the Captain get out of him about his friend the sailor who sent him aboard. I had not noticed particularly, but standing before his judge in the bright light of the cabin, his thin, blanched face contrasted strikingly with the older, harder faces of that company and strangely suggested the 'Judgment' upon which his religion was founded.

"There was no fault in this boy except that he was an **Orthodox** Christian. My plea for him was of necessity denied. In the beginning the Captain might have closed his eyes, but having called attention to the case he was bound by the rules and as helpless as Pilate.

"The Captain of the *Litchfield* was an efficient officer. Wherever he appeared during the evacuation order was maintained. Day after day I met him on the quay and pier. He seemed like a man with a kind heart, and a strong defence reaction against this weakness within himself. In the performance of their duties such men are apt to lean backward from their humane impulses.

"The boy was sent ashore—two of them, for another had meanwhile reached the ship. This seemed very cruel, but orders are orders and neutrality is neutrality."

The muezzin was chanting his evening prayers when the *Litchfield* set out that night. The refugee ships, too, were pulling away. There was only one day to go before *giaour* Smyrna would be cleared.

The remnants of the Ashjian family wept softly aboard their ship. Two sons were gone, and Krikor—sixty-seven years old and stricken with acute asthma—had almost made it. Well beyond the last gate, the thrash of a rifle butt had felled him within twenty feet of the gangplank.

The family of Marika Tsakirides, intact, found it impossible to rejoice amid so much sorrow. "Very few people were so lucky," she says now. "Almost everyone lost someone. 'A mother lost a child; a child lost a mother.' It has become—how do you say? A saying. A refrain. In Greek the words sound beautiful:

> '*E Mana hani to pedi,*
> *ke to pedi ten Mana.*'

That is what happened in that time."

CHAPTER XX

In a never-ending, staggering march the Christian popu-
lation of Eastern Thrace is jamming the roads to Mace-
donia. The main column crossing the Maritza river at
Adrianople is twenty miles long. Twenty miles of carts
drawn by cows, bullocks and muddy-flanked water buffalo,
with exhausted, staggering men, women and children,
blankets over their heads, walking blindly along in the
rain beside their worldly goods.

ERNEST HEMINGWAY
The *Toronto Daily Star*
October 20, 1922

For a day or two in mid-September 1922, the Smyrna fire captured
the lead headlines in American newspapers. The evacuation of
Smyrna was not so featured. The Hall-Mills murder case (the
killing of a Protestant clergyman and his attractive choir singer,
in apparently titillating circumstances), the opening of the
World Series, and Mrs. Harding's health vied for first place
with conjectures about renewed warfare in the Near East. Headlines proclaimed Kemal's intent to pursue the Greek army into
Thrace, the British government's determination to prevent his
crossing the Dardanelles, and British labor leaders' warnings that
the British public would not tolerate another war. One day the
French were said to be joining the British in a move to stop Kemal;
on the next day it appeared certain they would do no such thing.
The Soviet Union made aggressive noises against England but
denied any intention of fighting. It was rumored that Kemal would
go to any lengths to have his way. It was counterrumored that he

would not be so rash as to venture across the Straits with the British fleet flagrantly displaying no less than three battleships, three cruisers, two aircraft carriers, and a destroyer flotilla carrying a battalion of Royal Marines. The *Chicago Tribune* consulted a phrenologist and reported with obvious relief that neither Kemal's courage (as evidenced by the breadth of his jaw) nor his ambition (width of skull from base to tip of chin) was a match for "the extraordinary protuberances above his ears," which denoted an abundant supply of caution.

The lumps on his skull notwithstanding, Kemal kept the Allies in considerable suspense during the last weeks of September. Their more perceptive officials, however, found clues to his real intentions in the generous interviews he held with certain select foreign correspondents. Kemal was lately avoiding talk of Constantinople, dwelling instead on the terms of the National Pact with special emphasis on an immediate return of Eastern Thrace, leading those close to the scene to conclude that the Turkish chief would settle for a diplomatic victory in preference to a military gamble.

His strategy seemed less obvious in certain London quarters where Kemal's shrewdness was being underestimated in the face of all the evidence. Lloyd George had so insulated himself from the realities that the antiroyalist revolution in Greece and Venizelos's appointment as Ambassador to Great Britain were making him hopeful of a Greek victory at the conference table, if not on the battlefields of Thrace. Churchill, who had opposed Lloyd George's policy all along, was by now outraged enough at Kemal's highhanded challenge to British honor to issue a belligerent communiqué in the name of the cabinet. As he recorded in a cooler moment, he hoped that his country might "escape without utter shame from the consequences of lamentable and divided policies." Kemal had no such need to save face; he was simply stacking his hand for the negotiations to come. Invited to a conference with the Allies, he took his time in answering the note, while the official world held its breath.

Kemal had enough insight to understand the British position, just as General Harington understood Kemal's well enough to pocket a bellicose ultimatum to the Turkish chief from London. It had arrived at a moment when Kemal's troops, face-to-face with the British, were obviously under orders to avoid provocation. They grimaced amicably at Harington's men, offered cigarettes, even pointed their guns backward to disclaim hostile intentions. The British reciprocated, to the point of helping the Turks put up some barbed wire that a Turkish general had ordered strung along his lines. And Harington, in a singular gesture for a military commander poised on the brink of war, gave an interview to the Turkish newspapers in which he expressed his regret that the state of war between England and Turkey had thus far prevented him from making more Turkish friends, although he had a good many, whom he cherished.

Key newsmen were once again serving to promote the Turkish viewpoint. John Clayton, after a respite in Athens and Constantinople, was back in Smyrna on September 23, the day Jennings's first ships drew into harbor. Censorship prevented Clayton from elaborating on this spectacle (although he later wrote some moving accounts of the plight of the Greeks in Eastern Thrace); instead he derided the Greek army's retreat through Anatolia as "one of the blackest spots in the whole history of Western civilization." He was rewarded, the next day, by an interview with Fethi Bey, Kemal's Minister of the Interior, and drew another scoop when the Minister declared that the entire Christian population of Anatolia was to be expelled. "No Greek can live in Anatolia among the Turkish population after this retreat," Fethi Bey declared. "There is only one solution—exchange the Christian populations for Moslem minorities in other parts of the world." Clayton asked if he could consider this suggestion as official. "You may," replied the Minister. Clayton noted that Americans found this "the happiest solution." In an interview with Mark Prentiss on September 27 Fethi Bey specifically offered "to freely exchange all the Christian population in Asia Minor for the Moslems of Western Thrace." Prentiss forwarded his scoop to Bristol.

That perennial, "unofficial" French emissary, M. Franklin-Bouillon ("Boiling Frankie" to the British), who had negotiated the secret deal between Kemal and the French and whose name spelled bad news for the minorities, appeared in Smyrna at the end of September. Within days Kemal had agreed to confer with the Allies, providing he would be guaranteed Eastern Thrace. He appointed as his government's representative to the conference Ismet Pasha, a trusted associate who had the added advantage of being deaf.

The conference opened at Mudanya, a mudhole on the Sea of Marmara, on October 3, 1922. The first session was underway before the Greek delegates arrived; since "space was limited," they were not invited to the conference table. Neither, presumably, were Ward Price of the *Daily Mail* and M. Franklin-Bouillon, both of whom were conspicuous in the Turkish camp. Franklin-Bouillon flitted between the Turks and the French, "urging the former to resistance and the latter to surrender." Harington called him "a perfect curse." Rumbold said that "his policy was pernicious."

The conference ended, after a number of histrionic scenes, with the Turks gaining Eastern Thrace and the British just enough concessions—a few neutral zones around the Dardanelles, a temporary Allied contingent in Eastern Thrace—to hold up their heads, although Lloyd George lost his, politically speaking. His Near East policy was defunct, his labor support had bolted, and his opponents found this an auspicious moment to trounce him.

As a result of the Smyrna debacle, a number of Greek officials were soon to lose their lives at the hands of infuriated Venizelists. Among those executed was poor, insane Hadjianestis—he is said to have walked bravely to his death. King Constantine fled Athens in time to avoid the possibility of a similar fate, and at Constantinople the Turkish Sultan was hurriedly smuggled aboard a British ship in the dead of night and taken to Malta to insure his safety.

The Greek army, which had been massing in Eastern Thrace in hopes of being allowed a last stand against the Turks, was ordered to leave forthwith. Turkish gendarmes were allowed to enter the area immediately. Their number did not prove too great an issue at Mudanya: "We closed on eight thousand well knowing that they would not abide by any number laid down," Harington recorded. Discussion about the Christians remaining in Turkey was postponed, but Kemal made his position unmistakable in a rousing speech before his Grand National Assembly in Angora on October 4: "We must clear our enemies from every part of our nation. But we may not need war to accomplish this. If they will make the enemy leave Thrace, we will not be forced to resort to military operations." "The enemy," as far as the Turks were concerned, was not restricted to men in uniform.

The Christians of Eastern Thrace, many of them recent settlers, were not waiting for the diplomatic niceties to be completed. The terms of the Mudanya agreement had scarcely been announced when they could be seen trudging in interminable files westward across the plains of the Thracian peninsula toward the Greek frontier, an area of eleven thousand square miles that the Allies had previously determined belonged to Greece. The Bulgarian frontier was closed to the Greeks, although open to Armenians. The exodus was for the most part on foot. The railway, a French concession, was inadequate and its authorities offered little assistance to the refugees, while complaining that foot traffic along the railway lines was interfering with service on the plush Orient Express.

The new refugees were mostly Greek peasants. In the two years that the territory had belonged to Greece they had transformed the barren wastelands; the wheat crops that year had been unprecedented. They left their vineyards, their orchards and their fields, their crops newly harvested. They drove their cattle before them. On carts, wheelbarrows, wagons, donkeys, oxen, and on their backs, they carried their possessions. Hemingway described "an old man marching bent under a young pig, a scythe and a gun, with a chicken tied to his scythe." Small children stumbled under enormous loads. Pregnant women tramped through the mud rather than impede the pace of the oxen. It was a medieval tableau, the exodus to Smyrna all over again; but a larger one this time— longer lines, greater distances—and in the season that turned the primitive pathways to rivers of mud. The Turks had never built roads; the Greeks had not had time to build them.

"A husband spreads a blanket over a woman in labor in one of the carts to keep off the driving rain," wrote Ernest Hemingway. "She is the only person making a sound. Her little daughter looks at her in horror and begins to cry. And the procession keeps moving. . . . No matter how long it takes this letter to reach Toronto, when you read it in the *Star* you may be sure that the same ghastly, shambling procession of people being driven from their homes is filing in unbroken line along the muddy road to Macedonia." There was no Near East Relief along the line of march, no medical facilities, only the Greek cavalry cantering alongside, spattering the bent figures with mud and, soon after Mudanya, Turkish gendarmes who took away the livestock, saying that it was against regulations to remove the animals from Turkey. Admiral Bristol was incensed that the refugees should try to remove their cattle. He promised to see that the Allies would do everything in their power "to restore stock to Eastern Thrace where it belongs." The Admiral's attentiveness was already beginning to pay off. A message from Vice-Consul Barnes in Smyrna informed him that the Turkish authorities were "facilitating in a marked manner

American commercial activities whereas such facilities are not being granted to other foreigners."

In the end most of the refugees had to abandon their household possessions as well as their livestock. Children fell by the wayside. The cold nights took their toll. The specter of famine haunted the line of march and waited at its destination. Bandits swarmed after the travelers. The Allied contingent on hand for thirty days turned up only at concentration points, such as seaports. The French officers, especially, manifested little sympathy. Why the devil were these people in such a hurry, they wanted to know. Reporters questioning scores of refugees received identical answers:

"Where are you going?"

"Don't know."

"How are you going to live?"

"Don't know."

"What are you afraid of?"

"Smyrna," they would say, and they would draw their hands across their throats. Constantine Brown, who was following the exodus, had apparently forgotten Smyrna. He thought the stampede was aggravated by the people's gullibility; they were being told "exaggerated tales" about Smyrna by refugees who had escaped to Thrace, and these tales were actually being believed, he wrote.

"Whither shall I lead four hundred thousand exiles?" cried the Greek governor of Eastern Thrace. Through an ironic coincidence his first name was Xenophon.

In fact there was nowhere to lead them but to Greece, her ports and islands already teeming with refugees from Anatolia. The Allies were at best indifferent to the problem. Dr. Fridtjof Nansen, the renowned explorer (he would soon devise and lend his name to the stateless passport), was delegated by the League of Nations to study ways and means of helping the refugees, but when he tried to purchase some of the abandoned grain from the Turks he encountered opposition from the Italian authorities and no help from the French. Bristol had already cabled the State Department that the Greek government should be made to "handle all relief work in her own country and our relief organizations not be drawn into operations in Greece." He urged American relief "for the Turks left behind." The State Department was "inclined to agree."

In Athens people slept on the streets, in a royal villa, in the ruins of the Parthenon, in the theaters. Every velvet-lined box in the National Opera housed a family; other refugees slept in the orchestra and on the stairs. Makeshift camps sprawled for miles along the beaches. Abandoned automobile tires were cut up for sandals. Pots, pans, even sewing needles became collector's items. With the approach of winter pneumonia, tuberculosis, malaria, and trachoma reached epidemic proportions. Virtually every refugee was ill. These conditions halted the small tourist trade on which Greece was by now almost totally dependent for revenue. Cruise ships were boycotting Greek ports.

By December pestilential diseases among the boatloads of refugees arriving from the Pontus—that region of Turkey bordering the Black Sea—were so virulent that the Greek government was forced to call a halt to emigration from that area. Ship after ship, crammed to the gunwales with human freight, rolled at anchor in the stormy seas, flashing out essentially the same distress signal: 4,000 [5,000 . . . 6,000] REFUGEES. NO WATER. NO FOOD. SMALL-POX AND TYPHUS FEVER ABOARD.

The Greek government addressed a plea to the United States High Commission in Constantinople, requesting that further human shipments from Turkey be stopped "until it is possible to thin out refugees." There were now nearly one million, unhoused, and epidemics were raging. There was still no sympathy from official U.S. quarters: Should the Greek government persist in barring refugees, and should these begin congregating in Constantinople and ports on the Black Sea, Turkish officials could "very properly" deport them into the interior to prevent epidemics—"and results of such deportations are already too well known to merit comment." At that reaction from the United States High Commission, the Greek cabinet met again and decided to revoke its ban. Jennings's ships were now assigned to the Black Sea service. The "Admiral" himself was for the moment on the Greek mainland helping with the care and feeding of incoming passengers.

As there was no censorship over news reports from Greece, poignant accounts of imminent starvation drove the American Red Cross to release, in December, an emergency appropriation of three million dollars for six months. Dr. Nansen had suggested that a supervisory commission, under the League of Nations, coordinate relief work in Greece, but upon learning that the American Red Cross would not work under either Nansen or the League, the Greek authorities felt compelled to turn down Nansen's plan.

The Red Cross and the Near East Relief—both semiofficial agencies of the United States government—had pitched in during the Smyrna debacle; E. O. Jacob estimated that his committee had distributed 254,000 food rations and 3,600 tins of milk supplied by these agencies between September 11 and September 28. Now the Near East Relief announced that it had discontinued working with adults and would henceforth concentrate on caring for its orphans. Congress voted an appropriation of $200,000 to help destitute American citizens stranded in Greece and passed a temporary bill to admit refugees who were blood relatives of United States citizens.

The unsung heroines after the evacuation were a group of American women—among them Dr. Esther P. Lovejoy—who constituted the physicians and nurses of the American Women's Hospitals, a service organized in 1917 to work with the sick in countries ravaged by war. There was a feminist protest involved in the group's origin, for both the Red Cross and the armed forces refused to admit women physicians—and these ladies were not to be left out. Once the group was organized, the Red Cross agreed to sponsor AWH facilities, which were run entirely by women doctors. Over one thousand of them had signed up. They continued to offer their services after the men returned from the wars, saving countless lives in Serbia, Soviet Armenia, and Greece.

As the organization's "chief beggar," Dr. Lovejoy had hurried to the States at the end of September to prepare for the deluge in Greece. She traveled in steerage, having calculated how many quarts of milk the saved dollars would buy, and having discovered that in any event first-class passengers were not in an especially philanthropic frame of mind. She was back in Greece by late October, working with her colleagues and the beleaguered Greek government to set up dispensaries and hospitals on the dumping grounds of the Christian population of Turkey.

Until the Red Cross came through with a six months' allotment of a thousand calories of food per refugee, the American Women's Hospitals, together with the Greeks, carried the entire burden of their care and feeding. In January 1923 the women opened a quarantine station on barren little Makronissi Island, where the Pontus refugees could be carefully examined before being dispersed. Soon afterward, Dr. Lovejoy had to run home again to raise more money. Lacking the influential contacts of the Red Cross and the Near East Relief, the group's activities were never well publicized. A year later, in 1924, when the work was still going on in Greece, *The National Geographic* ran photographs of AWH facilities on the Greek islands but failed to mention the name of the organization that was maintaining them. "We have never been rich enough to maintain a publicity department," Dr. Lovejoy noted. "This service is best known by those who have been sick and in distress, and unfortunately, few such people write for newspapers and periodicals."

There was little help for the victims forthcoming from Europe. The International Red Cross set up a relief mission to Anatolia and Thrace, but it did not obtain permission from the Angora government to penetrate those areas until long after most of the Christian population had left. England was eager to find a solution but could "not give any assurances as regards voluntary societies in Europe" and made it clear that as far as the British government was concerned there could be no question of further help. The French attitude was summed up in a cable from the American chargé d'affaires in Greece to the Secretary of State on May 17, 1923: "My French colleague is indifferent in his comments." The French magnanimously offered to take a "trial shipment" of one or two hundred single adult refugees as farm laborers during the harvest season, if they could hand-pick these "from a sanitary and moral standpoint." The Italian government was reliably reported to be offering no assistance whatever.

In March 1923 the American Red Cross gave notice that it was withdrawing from its emergency work in Greece, making it plain, however, that a state of emergency continued and Greece could not be expected to handle the problem alone. The Greek cabinet thereupon accepted Nansen's plan for a Refugee Settlement Commission under League of Nations auspices. Although the Department of State refused to appoint a representative, or even to pass along names from one of its relief agencies, the League appointed an American, former ambassador Henry Morgenthau, as chairman.

One of Morgenthau's first acts was to send a heartrending cable to the Red Cross, asking it to continue its emergency work through the winter:

Highest appreciation constantly expressed here for recent Red Cross assistance. Greeks implore for its renewal to prevent wholesale starvation this winter. Refugees still unplaced. Our Commission prevented by its organic statutes from expending its funds for temporary relief. Greek government financially unable to cope with entire situation, hence this emergency. . . . Greek government has drawn heavily on her resources in permanently settling quarter of a million refugees. More than seven hundred thousand penniless sparsely dressed refugees are still inhumanely huddled in theaters, churches, schools, camps. Our Commission hopeful of accomplishing its task if some noble charity will keep refugees alive until spring.

Forwarding this cable to Allen Dulles, the Red Cross noted dryly: "We have sent him a simple acknowledgement by post." On December 29 the Red Cross formally refused its help, now giving as its opinion that "the situation does not indicate an emergency character."

With the assistance of the League of Nations, the Refugee Commission eventually managed to float a refugee loan at the not especially charitable interest rate of 8.71 per cent. "A loan bearing such interest naturally proved entirely successful," wrote a student of the period, "the sum required of the public being covered five and a half times at Athens, nearly twenty times in London, and entirely subscribed by Speyer and Company in New York."

After a five-year delay, the Great Powers had finally gathered at Lausanne, at the end of November 1922, to settle their peace terms with Turkey. There on the fragrant shores of Lake Lehman, in the Chateau d'Ouchy (a pile of stone "so ugly," said Hemingway, "as to make the Odd Fellows Hall of Petoskey, Michigan look like the Parthenon"), the delegates unanimously adopted a plan for the compulsory exchange of populations between Greece and Turkey. Dr. Fridtjof Nansen proposed the exchange and the Greeks accepted it, because it would force a return of any surviving deportees and because of the desperate need, in Greece, for the lands retained by Moslems. The Turks called it "a painful necessity, but logical." No other solution was in fact considered at Lausanne.

With commerce in mind, the Western Powers supported Greek demands that the Greeks of Constantinople be exempted from the exchange in return for the exemption of Moslems in Western Thrace. Having agreed to this bargain, the Turks were able to exert blackmail by threatening "to take measures" against the Greeks in Constantinople whenever they were thwarted in any of the particulars.

With most of the Turkish Christians already in Greece, the "exchange" actually applied to about 250,000 still remaining in Turkey, and approximately 350,000 Moslems destined to move from Greece. Although this transfer had been advertised for May 1923, the Mixed Commission appointed at Lausanne to supervise the movement did not even meet until late in October. This not only caused a delay in settling the hordes already in Greece, but it brought about a further disaster: since the Moslems there had not bothered to cultivate their fields that spring and summer, there was no harvest in the dead of winter, when the Greek refugees moved in. When the exchange finally got under way, the Turks proceeded to violate all the terms of the agreement. In the scattered areas of Turkey (mainly near Constantinople and the Black Sea) where Greeks remained to be exchanged, Turkish authorities either issued orders for their immediate departure, or prevented the departure of those employed on public works where their services were needed. Persons about to leave were not permitted to go to court to collect their debts. If they left their homes momentarily untended, the authorities seized their properties and then invoked a "law of abandoned property" which they claimed exempted them from paying compensation. Despite the availability of vast regions where incoming Moslems might be settled, the Turks chose to place them in villages and even, in some cases, in the homes of Greeks who were still there.

"The inability of the Commission to take a courageous attitude appeared very early," wrote Stephen Ladas, author of a definitive study of the exchange. The neutral member of the Commission refrained from taking a stand against Turkish violations, thereby encouraging the Greeks to take retaliatory steps and the Turks to even greater defiance.

Nearly two million people were involved in the migrations. 390,000 Moslems left Greece for Turkey, "in an orderly manner and all under the auspices of the Mixed Commission created under the provisions of the Convention at Lausanne." In all, 1,250,000 Greeks and 100,000 Armenians poured into Greece, only one-fifth of them after these benign conditions were established. They constituted an increase of one-third again over Greece's pre-war population. Although Armenians were not supposed to be included in the exchange, Greece accepted them without discrimination and instructed the Committee in charge of returning civil prisoners to bring them in and "treat them with the same considerations as Greeks."

The refugee problem in Greece was compounded because so many heads of families—potential breadwinners—captured at Smyrna were being forcibly detained in Turkey. The Greek government had already begged the State Department to intercede for the return of these men, but Allen Dulles had studiously ignored the request. Under Article 4 of the Exchange Convention all able-bodied men detained in Turkey were supposed to be returned as soon as the treaty was signed. It was signed in July 1923, but when the Mixed Commission finally met in October the men were yet to be released. Most had of course perished. Those who survived were finally set free in January 1924.

Among the survivors were Karekin Bizdikian, whose wife had given birth during the fire; Stepan Ashjian, whose father had been slain within yards of the ship that was to take him from Smyrna; and Hovannes Simonian, who would one day become the Armenian Bishop of California. Their stories are remarkably similar. From Smyrna they were marched—at different times and in different groups—to Magnesia, some fifty miles inland. Along the way the soldier-guards took their money, their shoes, their jackets, their trousers, and, if it struck their fancy, their underwear. Simonian soon learned that if he tore his clothes to shreds they were less likely to be removed. Sometimes the guards would rob their charges at knife point, then sell their clothes to the peasants gathered at the entrances of all the towns and villages on their route. These congregations of civilians greeted the prisoners with clubs, knives, daggers, and guns. Sometimes they fell upon the men at random; at other times they were more selective. It seemed that they had each vowed to kill thus and so many Greeks or Armenians. "You must emphasize that the Turks were even more vengeful toward the Armenians," Bizdikian remarked during his interview. "This is one of those mysteries. We cannot know why this was so, but it was so."

"They would lunge at a man, crying 'Here is an Armenian!'" said Ashjian. "Sometimes they would make a man talk Turkish and judge him by his accent, although the method was not foolproof. Sometimes a dark-skinned Greek was killed because his murderer assumed he was an Armenian." All three of these men were fair-skinned. All three learned to keep moving—for the guards bayoneted anyone who lagged—but to move at a carefully modulated pace, keeping toward the end of the file, since the villagers seemed to exhaust their energies on the first portion of the line, and those at the end were more likely to be spared.

The prisoners who reached Magnesia—at most one in three, all informants agreed—were put into a compound. Since its sheltered area was too small to accommodate the lot, most slept in the open.

The nights were wet and cold, and those who appeared ill were likely to be killed. Each morning they were taken to the town square, where the peasants from the neighboring villages came to select slave labor. Only those chosen for work were fed, the extent and quality of the rations depending on the generosity of that day's host.

Ashjian was a frail man. He was unused to physical exertion, and the long march had so depleted him that his chances for selection appeared dim. "In nearly a week I had eaten no more than a few pieces of bread that a generous companion brought back from his day's work," he related, "and finally one morning I knew I couldn't last much longer, so I begged to be taken with a road gang. At the job I could hardly lift the spade. The guard— he was something like an overseer—became so annoyed that he began to lash at me with his whip. Of course it only took one lash to knock me down.

"Very luckily for me, the road we were working on was in front of the office of the Red Crescent, and the director of this office happened to be watching from his window. The next thing I knew he had opened the window and was asking the guard to bring him 'that *giaour*.' When I fell inside, he asked me why I was not working harder, and looked pleased when I told him that I had never lifted a spade in my life; I had always worked in an office."

The executive was even more pleased to discover that Ashjian was fluent in German, French, and English, since he had a stack of letters that he had not been able to read, or answer. He took Ashjian on, ostensibly as his servant but in reality as his secretary, gave him some clean clothes, and fed him well. "But every night I would step back into my rags and go back to the compound to sleep," he recalled. "This arrangement went on for over a year. I took care of all his correspondence and he took care of me. He was a good man. After a time he let me write a note to my sister in New York. I signed it "Etienne" and simply let her know that I was alive. I couldn't remember her address very well—I put 'Fifth Avenue' when it was some other street—and I had to leave off the "ian" at the end of her name so as to get the thing out of Magnesia, but it reached her just the same. You have such wonderful mail service in the United States—at least you did in 1923.

"Then one day my boss turned to me and said, 'Stepan, I'm going to do something for you that might be my downfall, but my conscience will trouble me if I don't act as it dictates. I'm going to give you a Greek name, make up some papers for you, and send you to Athens with the next group of prisoners so that you can get out of this hell of a country and join your family. And God help me!' "

In Athens, Ashjian obtained a Nansen passport and was admitted to Lebanon. From there he emigrated to France. By 1924, even with a sister in the United States he would have needed an act of Congress to admit him to America. He married a French-woman and remained in France, but as he was too old to serve in World War II and is childless, he was never able to obtain French citizenship. He still retains his Nansen passport.

Bizdikian was kept at Magnesia for only a few days and was then driven inland to Ushak, a center for Greek military prisoners. He had long since assumed the Greek name "Karalambos," so he was put into the barracks with the Greek soldiers who were also being used as slave labor. He, too, was finally sent to Athens, in January 1924, after having survived innumerable adventures and a typhus epidemic that wiped out three-fourths of his companions and their Turkish guards. In Greece he was reunited with his wife and firstborn son, built up a business, and had five more children.

As a student of the American International College, Hovannes Simonian was repatriated somewhat sooner than the others, thanks to pressure on the students' behalf from Admiral Bristol. He was able to reach the United States under the sponsorship of a former teacher, Dr. S. Ralph Harlow, who had already adopted Simonian's sister and taken her to the States. Harlow, a brother of the Anna Birge who had so dauntlessly saved her "sons" during the fire, was incredulous when Simonian explained that he had been virtually handed over to his captors after he was safely aboard an American destroyer. In pungent terms he let the College know what he thought of such treatment.

Simonian was a student at the Hartford Theological Seminary when, one day in 1925, he was surprised to receive an indignant letter from an official of his former College berating him for disseminating "half truths" and "allegations" that he had been forced off the ship at Smyrna with President MacLachlan's encouragement. Lest Simonian should feel impelled to repeat his story, the College official had thoughtfully enclosed the "whole truth"—a somewhat garbled but rather pleasant version of his adventures, written in the first person and expressing Simonian's repeated and profound gratitude toward the College.

CHAPTER XXI

In the size of the lie, there is always contained a certain factor of credibility, since the great masses of the people will more easily fall victim to a great lie than to a small one.

ADOLF HITLER
Mein Kampf

For several years after the Smyrna debacle, American interests in Turkey conducted an intensive campaign to revise public opinion at home. This was no small task, for in the course of massive fund appeals the American Protestant leadership had created a certain amount of antipathy toward Turkey and sympathy for her minorities. Yet the Lausanne Treaty constituted a victory for Turkey on the question of the Christian population and a triumph of political and economic considerations for the West. Not the least of these was the matter of oil. According to Standard Oil Company historians, "there were many issues of importance at Lausanne but oil usurped the center of the stage."

In varying degrees every Western nation involved had to defend this order of priorities. But the greater the discrepancy between a nation's professed and actual motives, the greater its need to justify its policies. Political scientists might wave "morality" aside as irrelevant to the national interest, American historians might proclaim the triumph of American diplomacy; but spokesmen for America had been denouncing the ignominious motives of her rivals too loudly and for too long to let the nature of her triumph speak for itself. In 1924 the Near East desk at the State Department was still busily enlisting cooperative writers to its cause.

Although not technically a party to the treaty, the United States had sent three "observers" to Lausanne: Admiral Mark L. Bristol, Joseph C. Grew (he was later to be U.S. Ambassador to Japan until the attack on Pearl Harbor), and Richard Washburn Child, a magazine writer turned diplomat who, according to Harold Nicolson, was "typically American" in his conviction "that the whole Lausanne Conference was a plot on the part of the old diplomacy to deprive American company promoters of oil concessions." Child injected his advocacy of the "open door" into the proceedings with monotonous regularity. On one occasion, after an eloquent discourse of Curzon's, Child's remarks were so grossly irrelevant as to cause the more seasoned diplomats to gape at each other, Nicolson records, "in bewildered embarrassment." With single-minded insight, Child attributed their reaction to guilt: "I could see that my statement had given discouragement and doubt to several secret plans around the Conference table."

The United States had publicly committed itself to upholding the Capitulations—in order to protect its schools, religious institutions, and businessmen in Turkey—and to securing measures for the protection of minorities left in Constantinople. On these issues Ismet Pasha, once again his country's delegate, showed that he was prepared to conduct a siege that would outlast the limited patience of Western diplomats. Even Curzon's rapierlike wit was blunted, on occasion, against Ismet Pasha's impenetrable stubbornness on the question of Turkish sovereignty. But the English statesman won points for obstinacy too: When the first session broke up, England had obtained the freedom of the Straits—much to Soviet Russia's consternation.

On April 7, 1923, a few days before the conference was to resume, Angora dropped a bombshell with the announcement that it had granted Admiral Chester his coveted concessions. There was a shrill outcry from France, who for all her groundwork now found herself, along with Italy and Russia, with nothing much to show. Chester's exploitation rights covered the same area promised to France in Franklin-Bouillon's 1921 negotiations with Kemal. The nod to Chester was a transparent Turkish move to soften the

United States position on the Capitulations, but the Department of State, oddly enough, was not especially pleased about Chester's triumph. The British, whose Turkish Petroleum Company's claims in Mosul were now ostensibly threatened, appeared singularly unconcerned.

While upholding the "open door" (translated "equal rights to all comers") and professing to support all American claims, including Chester's, the State Department was under the distinct impression that Chester had no chance at all. Behind the scenes, Secretary of State Hughes (a former Standard Oil Company executive who would return to his job after serving his country) had been working hard on behalf of the firm for several years. By the autumn of 1922 the British had begun to perceive that "it was better to give the Americans a share in the Turkish Petroleum Company than to run the risk of letting them loose to compete for concessions. . . ."

In order to utilize State Department support for penetration into Mosul without risking criticism from rival companies, Standard Oil had reluctantly combined forces with such select American firms as Sinclair, Texas, and Gulf. "I believe it will be necessary to take some other interest with us, and a part of whom, at least, should be outside the subsidiaries," wrote Standard Oil director Sadler to Standard Oil president Teagle in September 1921. "I also think we should select the associates carefully and keep the list as small as possible." Under the circumstances none of the principals had to be concerned that such a joint corporate venture was in violation of the antitrust laws or that the "open door" was as tightly closed as they could wish.

Mesopotamia's oil-rich lands were all this time under British military occupation. In a canny move, the British had installed Feisal as ruler of the area in August 1921, when the French ousted him from Syria. With British encouragement, Feisal was now claiming this land—Iraq—as independent of Turkey. Curzon won another round at Lausanne when Turkey agreed to submit the dispute to the League of Nations.

It quickly became obvious that, minus Mosul, Chester's concessions would be as desirable as the turkey's neck; without the oil, and with the working population gone, a railroad network into the interior of Turkey was a far less appetizing investment. Searching avidly for capital, Chester was soon driven outside the United States. At this point the State Department, which had remained cool all along, announced sanctimoniously that it could no longer support him, since his chief backers were British. Chester's prospects thereafter went downhill. In time his more respectable backers split and his tactics assumed a desperate air; unsavory promoters reared their heads, known gamblers came into the picture, there was at least one attempt at blackmail, and one of his agents was arrested in Anatolia as a British spy. In December 1923 Angora announced that because Chester had not exercised his option, his grant was canceled by default.

Standard Oil and its invited participants, now allied with Britain's Turkish Petroleum, fared better. In 1924 the League of Nations gave Britain a formal mandate over Iraq, and in 1926 the country was awarded its independence over an area including Mosul, with the British to retain military bases in the country. Not long afterward the terms of American participation in the oil venture were settled and there remained only the problem of what percentage the one individual shareholder—Calouste Gulbenkian—was to receive. The shrewd Armenian, who had originally brought the various interests together to form the Turkish Petroleum Company in return for a fifteen per cent share in the project, had never relinquished his personal claim despite manifold attempts to squeeze him out. In the end, he settled for five per cent of all the oil in Iraq.

To State Department contentions that the Iraqi scheme was not in violation of the "open door," Gulbenkian snorted "eyewash." At the behest of American representatives, all references to oil claims were deleted from the final draft of the Lausanne Treaty.

In order to re-establish formal relations with Turkey, the State Department had to sell the treaty to Congress; but although inroads had been made on public opinion, a segment of the public was putting up strong resistance to what it considered a sellout of the Christian minorities. Led by some eminent educators, Wilsonian diplomats, leaders of the Episcopal Church (it happened to have no missions in Turkey), and several southern and midwestern legislators—the Bible Belt having been so thoroughly sold on Armenians as Christian martyrs that it was not buying any other view—this faction also included relief workers, teachers, and virtually the entire staff of the American Collegiate Institute. At least one missionary had been fired. On his return from Smyrna, a week before the fire, S. Ralph Harlow of the International College faculty had given an interview to the *New York Times* in which he denounced American policy and predicted that it would lead to disaster for the minorities in Turkey. He continued to speak out after the Smyrna debacle. "They told me to shut up," he said later. "MacLachlan and Reed demanded my resignation and said that I 'endangered the College.' I resigned. I have been made to feel that I ought to keep still, but justice seemed to me greater than buildings and institutions." In a more recent interview, Dr. Harlow—now Professor Emeritus of Religion, Smith College—remembered this experience as the most disillusioning of his life. "The missionaries were a disgrace," he said.

Prominent leaders of the Near East Relief and the Board of Commissioners for Foreign Missions took a very different view of the treaty. "We believe in America for the Americans, why not Turkey for the Turks?" George A. Plimpton (one of the charter members of the Armenian Atrocities Committee and later a director of the Near East Relief) asked rhetorically in 1923, after expressing his admiration to Turkey for trouncing the Greeks and dictating terms to the Allies. Plimpton expressed his concern that the loss of the Greeks (and presumably of the unmentioned Armenians) had "cost great suffering and involved great financial sacrifice to Turkey [in the sense that she had lost her merchants and major taxpayers]. Whether it was right or wrong is not for us to decide," added this trustee of Union Theological Seminary.

Having publicized these sentiments in a letter to the *New York Times,* Plimpton also printed them in *The Treaty With Turkey,* an instructive compilation of "statements, resolutions, and reports in favor of the ratification of the Lausanne Treaty," brought out jointly by some significantly interested individuals, the foremost being members of the American Board of Commissioners for Foreign Missions and the United States Chamber of Commerce. The burden of their combined effort was to praise Turkey, to dismiss and at the same time justify its actions against the minorities, and to demonstrate that if the Turks were in any way antagonized—as by rejection of the treaty—both American business and American philanthropy would suffer.

Such luminaries as Secretary Hughes, Herbert Hoover, Admiral Bristol, and Richard Washburn Child contributed to the volume. Playing to the current panic over an "international communist conspiracy," Hughes declared that "Turkey is not endeavoring to undermine our institutions, to penetrate our labor organizations by pernicious propaganda, and to foment disorder and conspiracies against our domestic peace in the interest of a world revolution." Secretary Barton of the Board of Missions, on the other hand, feared that Turkey might go communist. He argued that American schools in Turkey were now more necessary than ever, in order to make the Turks "look westward" rather than north. Bristol wrote that rejection of the treaty would "incur the ill will of Turkish officials and expose American institutions to unfavorable treatment." Trade concessions, according to Herbert Hoover, would not be granted to U.S. nationals unless Congress signed the treaty. Child compared Kemal's revolution to George Washington's.

Missionary arguments were no less pointed. "Millions of dollars [in philanthropic investment] will be endangered, if not sacrificed, if the treaty is rejected," wrote a representative of the National Council of Congregational Churches. Missionary doctors were being denied permission to practice in Turkey, he acknowledged, but "this permission will be granted as soon as the treaty is ratified." Missionary leaders were gratified to note that henceforth their clients would be exclusively Moslem. There was no need to feel concerned about the Christians: "Every adult in Turkey is free to worship as he chooses—the Mohammedans in their mosques, the Christians, where there are any, in their churches." As far as medical services were concerned, a missionary doctor observed that "There are no Christian patients applying. The Turks are beginning to realize that we are in Turkey primarily to serve the people." Unless the treaty was ratified this incipient good will would be jeopardized.

Choosing to overlook the fact that it was the missionary leadership that had prevented President Wilson from declaring war on Turkey in 1917, the various writers harped on his failure as a lost chance: "The right time to express indignation at barbarities was in 1917 when we were at war with Turkey's associates. President Wilson restrained Congress from declaring war, and we thereby lost our chance to influence the peace settlement in our own right." According to the General Secretary of the YMCA, excesses of the Turks had been "grossly exaggerated." "To try to insert into the treaty a clause regarding the present minorities in Turkey would be very similar to foreign powers having insisted after our revolution on inserting a clause to the effect that we protect the American Indians living in the thirteen colonies," he wrote, not doubting for a moment that such an idea was preposterous. Admiral Bristol, on the other hand, deemed it essential to have a clause "to protect corporations and individuals from the retroactive application of new and possibly excessive taxes."

After a time the arguments became not only strained but absent-minded. All the fuss over Armenians was nonsense, one writer declared, because "it is a fact that there were no wholesale massacres against Armenians until they lent themselves to Russia's schemes." But another writer argued that the Allies owed no debt to the Armenians because "military services which were alleged as a ground of obligation toward the Turkish Armenians were performed almost entirely by the Armenians of Russia." The volume ended on a reassuring note: "It's no use to talk of atrocities; when it comes to atrocities all these people are all the same." Historian Edward Mead Earle went one step further by surveying how dreadfully everyone had behaved toward everyone else throughout history.

This onslaught (representing newspapers and magazine ranging from *New Republic* to *Asia*) met with an impassioned rebuttal in such journals as *The Literary Digest* and the *New York Times' Current History*, both of which maintained a stalwart objectivity by printing the two viewpoints side by side. The debate went on long after Congress had rejected the treaty and the Department of State had side-stepped the problem by negotiating a Treaty of Amity and Commerce with the Turkish government. To prove its amity the United States gave up the Capitulations and allowed its institutions to fall under Turkish law, which required hiring Turkish nationals as teachers and forbade proselytizing. The Turks reciprocated by offering American archeologists the same rights as Turkish archeologists—of which there happened to be none.

Until 1927, when diplomatic relations with Turkey were fully restored, a flood of articles and books continued to review the Smyrna catastrophe. "The destruction of Smyrna by fire was the work of the Greeks," wrote a Mr. Abdullah Hamdi in *Current History*. Hamdi, a resident of New York, cited a Turkish newspaper as his source of information. George Horton presented his account in considerable detail, and at some cost to his career, in *The Blight of Asia*. "The torch was applied to that ill-fated city and it was all systematically burned by the soldiers of Mustafa Kemal," Horton concluded, adding that the Allied and American warships "impotently watching" the Miltonic scene provided "the saddest and most significant feature of the whole picture." In many quarters the book was considered "unbecoming."

No one publication raised quite as much concern at the State Department as Edward Hale Bierstadt's *The Great Betrayal.* The author (he had been executive secretary of the emergency committee that pushed a special refugee bill through Congress after the fire) charged that the State Department's policy of "American economic imperialism" and Bristol's excessively restrictive orders had contributed to the Smyrna disaster. Even before its publication, in 1924, installments of Bierstadt's book appearing in *The Christian Herald* provoked such a blast of angry letters to the Near East desk that Allen Dulles, unable to officially refute the charges head-on, was driven to seek personal testimonials. One zealous volunteer, a Mr. William T. Ellis, who identified himself as "a patriot and writer for *The Christian Herald*," had in fact to be restrained. "If it happened that Mr. Bierstadt's charges against the United States were true," Ellis had written in the draft of a rebuttal submitted to Dulles for approval, "we merit straightway the fate of Sodom and Gomorrah." Dulles thought Ellis should alter his tone and suggested some changes in phraseology, "so that it won't appear that American officials dumped the refugees on Greek territory."

Dulles leaned more heavily on the word of some of the relief officials present at the Smyrna proceedings. He urged them to write letters to editors, taking issue with Bierstadt's book. Mark Prentiss, among others, was exceedingly helpful, but the Department's most valuable witness turned out to be Asa Jennings.

Jennings had already taken a large step forward in the international world when, on Admiral Bristol's recommendation, he was appointed a member of the International Commission on the exchange of Greek and Turkish prisoners. After Bierstadt's book was published, Jennings wrote the Secretary of State defending Bristol's "spirit of swift succor" at Smyrna and told the Department that it could make any use it wanted of his letter. A copy was promptly enclosed in the Department's reply to each disgruntled citizen who had written in.

In the course of time, and again at Bristol's suggestion, Jennings returned to Smyrna in charge of YMCA clubs—which he wanted to rename "Turkish-Armenian clubs" since the word "Christian" had such offensive overtones. When the YMCA demurred, Jennings founded a new organization devoted to social service: "The American Friends of Turkey," financed by a Cincinnati clothing manufacturer known as Arthur "Golden Rule" Nash. During frequent lecture trips in the United States Jennings modestly dismissed his naval experience, and in subsequent presentations (in one instance by the aforementioned William Ellis) that story underwent a decided shift in tone. The Turks were scarcely mentioned, the Greek government had behaved rather cravenly about its ships; there had been suffering, yes, but "*c'est la guerre.*"

The epilogue of the Smyrna drama was played out in London at the High Court of Justice, during the first weeks of December 1924. The American Tobacco Company was bringing suit against the Guardian Assurance Company, Ltd. Maintaining that the fire was a result of "hostile and warlike operations," the insurance company had invoked its exemption clause and refused to pay. The claim was for over $600,000, and it was understood that the outcome of the trial would govern other claims totaling $100,-000,000.

A cast of familiar characters paraded to the witness stand before Mr. Justice Rowlatt. Spunky little Major Cherefeddin Bey described how he had been struck with a hand grenade as he led his cavalry regiment down the quay on September 9 two years before, but the Armenian culprit in his original story had now become "a uniformed, armed Greek soldier who threw the bomb." Beyond this incident the Major had seen no disorder at Smyrna because, he said, "nothing took place."

A Colonel Mouharren Bey admitted that feeling ran high against the Armenians because "we used to read reports in our newspapers of their behavior which led us to believe they were not friendly to us." Yes, the army had distributed proclamations referring to "the injustice and cowardice of the Greeks who nevertheless proved to be the most cruel enemy unlike any nation in the history of the human race," but the Colonel swore that his troops were well disciplined and denied that his patrols had participated in any looting, rape, or murder. "The patrols would never do such a thing," he said.

The Colonel was recalled to the stand after a witness for the plaintiff unwittingly revealed that a cordon of Turkish soldiers had held the victims in the fire zone. "Did you want to prevent the people going anywhere?" asked Mr. A. T. Miller, representing the Guardian Assurance Company.

"Yes, we prevent them."

"Going where?"

"We prevent them to be not escape from there only to stay

there." Mr. Justice Rowlatt thought this wasn't much of a translation.

Miller tried again with another interpreter. "Why did you have the cordon on the quay? Did you want them burnt?"

"No, only to keep them by the boats."

During his cross-examination of Mr. Chester Griswold (of Griswold and Brunswick, fig merchants), Mr. Miller again confirmed the presence of Turkish cordons around the city. Did Mr. Griswold think it right that the people should thus be prevented from escaping the fire?

Mr. Griswold thought it was done for their own good. The roads leading from town were in bad neighborhoods: "A good many bad characters live around there," he said.

Did Mr. Griswold mean to say that the cordon was placed there by the Turks "to prevent the people from falling into bad hands?"

"I presume that," said Mr. Griswold.

Griswold testified to having carried an American flag on his car, and to having placed American sailor guards at the bakeries —not to protect the bakers, who were Greek, but simply to keep them from selling bread. He had driven around town a good deal before and after the fire, in his capacity as secretary of the relief committee. The town was quiet and he had seen no violence.

Under cross-examination Griswold admitted that his Turkish business partner was the mayor of Smyrna and that he was also a friend and associate of a man named Archbell, a director of the American Tobacco Company—the plaintiff in the case.

Mr. René Guichet, chief engineer of the French railway company with offices at the edge of the Armenian quarter, had seen nothing unusual before the fire except a little pillaging and heard nothing except a few "joy firings"; but he had to concede that there was essentially little difference in the sound of a gun being fired in joy or in anger. The Armenian population had not been molested so far as he knew because they were at first "closed in," and later "they had left." Again, he was forced to admit that it was not easy to tell the difference between people shut indoors and people absent, but he had an intuitive feeling of the way it had been.

Witnesses of every nationality, including an English business associate of the enterprising Mr. Archbell (this one in the garage and agricultural machinery business) supported the view that a single fire had spread accidentally, through the force of the wind.

Mr. Justice Rowlatt did not feel enlightened when the plaintiffs had rested their case. "This is one of the *vaguest* cases I've ever tried," he complained.

"I'm afraid it is very difficult, my lord," Miller conceded.

"If this was a more civilized city," mused the Judge, "one very probable explanation would be that somebody who was looting had got drunk. But as it is a semibarbarous place the question of drink is not mentioned in the case."

The haze began to clear as the defendant's witnesses took the stand. British naval officers offered their logs in evidence that while the wind was pleasantly brisk it was by no means stiff enough to fan the flames from the Collegiate Institute clear to the quay. Nurse Mabel Kalfa, the Reverend Dobson, Major Maxwell of the Royal Marines, Sir Harry Lamb, members of the Smyrna fire department, and others were explicit about the origin and spreading of the flames and about the increase in violence as the days went on. A number of victims described their experiences. Among these was a lady who had been raped, whose daughter had been assaulted, and whose father had been slain by Turkish soldiers. In a dramatic cross-examination Mr. Wright, representing the plaintiff, implied that she was masquerading under a false name, but was unable to prove his allegation. He had no better luck in trying to shake the firemen's stories. "It must have struck you as a remarkable thing that the Turks were saying they were allowed to burn down Smyrna," he told fireman Katzaros.

"Why should it appear remarkable when I saw it myself?"

"Did you mention it to your fellow workmen at the fire brigade afterwards?"

"If I mentioned that," said Katzaros, "they would have hanged me by the tongue."

During his summation Wright noted severely, "This is a charge against a nation," but he drew signs of amusement in the courtroom when he insisted that the Turks had "made every attempt to maintain order." By now thoroughly frustrated, the counsel for the plaintiff asked the Judge to admonish the opposition: "With great respect, my lord, the case here is serious, the evidence is flimsy, and it is not made the less flimsy by my learned friend ridiculing what I am saying!"

"No, no," said the Judge. "But I do not know that the other side, who will not be able to reply, are called upon not to laugh at what you said."

On Friday, December 19, Mr. Justice Rowlatt delivered a considered judgment in favor of the defendant insurance company. The Judge, according to the *London Times,* entertained no doubt about the occurrences.

Neither the trial nor the verdict made much of an impact on the historical record, even in England. Not long afterward a British publisher informed George Horton that *The Blight of Asia* could not be published there because "the British public was now so interested in the Mosul oil interests that they did not wish anything circulated that might offend the Turks." In a letter to Horton, Venizelos confirmed this opposition as "decisive."

In England, as in the United States, Bristol's estimate of the fire has been accepted as the historical verdict to date. In a final report to the Secretary of the Navy in March 1924, the Admiral displayed his characteristic verbal dexterity, declaring in one and the same summation, "The situation at Smyrna turned out to be one of the most remarkable the world has ever known in every sense of the word" and "The stories generally that have been printed regarding the incident in Smyrna have been grossly exaggerated."

Among the missionaries, President MacLachlan of the International College agreed with the diagnosis that the Greeks and Armenians had burned Smyrna; he thought they had probably disguised themselves in Turkish uniforms and fezzes while doing so. Many of his colleagues refrained from discussing the matter. In his history, *Story of Near East Relief (1915–1930),* James Barton managed to avoid the question of responsibility for the fire; and in the official history of the YMCA—*World Service,* published in 1957—the author solved the problem by simply skipping the touchy years 1914–1923.

Despite such graceful gestures the Board of Missions found itself increasingly unwelcome in Turkey, and within a decade of the Smyrna debacle all but a handful of the mission schools had to be abandoned after all. In 1936 the administration of the International College at Paradise turned over MacLachlan's hard-earned campus to the local authorities and moved to Beirut, where it opened a secondary school. The Near East Relief expired in 1930 when the last of its orphans became self-sufficient. Revived as the Near East Foundation, it has since been providing agricultural and technical assistance to Near Eastern countries in the face of growing Moslem antipathy and suspicion of American philanthropic motives.

The stand taken by men of God, now dedicated to spreading democracy or the Word through service and example, has provided an excellent example to the Turks, who have had no reason to acknowledge the nature of their recent past. The most distinguished Turkish spokesmen exhibit a marked reluctance to discuss either Armenians or the Smyrna fire, but when driven to do so they maintain that the Armenians were conducting a rebellion in 1915, and that the Greeks destroyed Smyrna in 1922. Distaste for these subjects—or perhaps a lack of evidence—prevents their offering details. Suggestions to the contrary provoke a defensiveness that was especially noticeable in 1965, during observances of the fiftieth anniversary of the Armenian genocide. Ceremonies in the United States and Lebanon inspired editorial warnings in Turkish newspapers and letters to newspapers in the offending countries, pointing out that nations permitting public commemorations of "so-called," "alleged," "supposed," massacres were straining Turkey's NATO alliance. Plans to erect a commemorative monument in Montebello, California, eventually came to fruition, although a leading Turkish newspaper—*Yeni Gazette*—was in this instance driven to comment editorially that the erection of such a monument in California would threaten the safety of "the sympathetic, harmless, and diligent" Armenian minority in Istanbul. "Do not subject them to the fate of the Istanbul Greeks," the editorial warned, referring to the anti-Greek riots of 1955, at the height of the Cyprus crisis.

After 1923 Western specialists in Near Eastern studies revised the historical record for the years 1915–1922. Among those influential in precipitating the conversion were the missionaries who had discredited their own eyewitness testimonies, and Halide Edib, a Turkish woman with undeniable gifts of imagination and intellect—a novelist, journalist, social worker, and statesman, and a source of wonder to the West as the first emancipated woman of her country. After breaking with Kemal over his dictatorial methods, Madame Edib was invited to teach at Barnard College. She wrote extensively, in excellent English, and became one of the most popular lecturers in the United States. In her writings Halide Hanum, as she called herself, has very little to say of the Smyrna tragedy, although she was on hand as Kemal's chief propagandist. "We moved to headquarters on the quay," she recalls. "There was disturbance in the air. Apparently order was not established yet. The number of queer suspicious-looking individuals increased on the streets. The inhabitants were mostly keeping to their houses. I heard that there was a lot of looting going on. I believe that it was possible to prevent it. It may not have been, however." The fire rates one short paragraph in which she implies that the Greeks prepared the conflagration. By way of contrast, she devotes innumerable pages to the Greek occupation of Smyrna in 1919, in descriptions which are vivid indeed, even though she was in Constantinople at the time. Envisaging the scene, she is aware of "the tortured and martyred on the quay of Smyrna, with horrible clearness, while those civilized and educated people in uniform looked on, callous as the Romans of old gloating over the spectacle of men tearing each other to pieces." Madame Edib thought the Armenians were "continually petted, encouraged, helped, subsidized, and armed against Turkey," until their deportation in 1915, which she professes to have at first deplored, then come to realize was justified. Talaat remained for her "an idealist." She remembers him as "modest, charming, a true democrat. . . . However one may criticize him, one is obliged to admit that he was the truest of patriots."

At a four-day Institute of Politics at Williams College, in the summer of 1928, Madame Edib conducted a round-table discussion and—according to the *New York Times*—won the hearts and minds of two hundred experts. The dean of Near Eastern experts, Arnold Toynbee, had already recorded the change of heart he had undergone after his traumatic exposure to wounded Turks during the Greco-Turkish war led him to atone for his earlier writings, as he later admitted, "by leaning over backwards" in their favor. Reviews of his book, *The Western Question in Greece and Turkey*, were hot off the presses in England and the United States during September 1922. While Smyrna was in flames, *The New Statesman*, on September 16, 1922, was praising Toynbee for his unbiased account of Turkish history and drawing from it the moral that the minorities deserved scant sympathy.

With such illustrious sources to guide them, more recent experts could not fail to follow suit. The latest issue of the *Encyclopaedia Britannica* has expunged all reference to the fire, without failing to point out that the Greek occupation of the city, in 1919, was "marked by atrocities against the Turkish population." Most American and British specialists in Modern Turkish history have continued to overlook the shortcomings and to extol the virtues of Turkey's emergent nationalism under the Young Turks and

—Mustafa Kemal, whose title *Ataturk,* "Father of the Turks," was bestowed by his countrymen in recognition of his services. The fate of the minorities, when mentioned at all, is weighed as a fundamental advance toward homogeneity.

Not everyone is equally concerned about the historical record, but at least one student of history compared the parade of events in Turkey with their subsequent dismissal and acted on a cynical conclusion. "Who, after all, speaks today of the annihilation of the Armenians," Hitler declared as he announced his own plans for genocide to his Supreme Commanders on August 22, 1939. "The world believes in success alone."

After resolving her minority question with such felicitous dispatch, Turkey did not entirely escape making reparation. She lost Palestine to Great Britain, Syria to France, and Mosul to Iraq. She was left with her geopolitical position—an amorphous asset in this nuclear age but one that has apparently been worth five and a half billion dollars in U.S. aid since 1945. Still, neither massive economic aid nor political forbearance have paid off exactly as had been reckoned. Turkey's democracy remains precarious and her economic condition declines. Those Anatolian plains that had once been Turkey's breadbasket now specialize in opium–the nation's most lucrative export to date. Eighty per cent of the heroin currently plaguing American cities originates in Turkey's poppy fields.

The brand of diplomacy that triumphed at Smyrna and Lausanne led to end products no less bizarre and even more costly in areas beyond Turkey. Yet the policy-makers of the 1920's, their agents, and their successors saw no portents of disaster in the discrepancy between what they had to gain and others to lose. They were perhaps insulated by their vacuous rhetoric. In 1927 Admiral Bristol was acclaimed for his "masterful diplomacy" by President Gates of Robert College, the United States Chamber of Commerce, and President Coolidge, and rewarded with the command of the Pacific fleet. He moved to China where he found "a terrible mess, with conditions analogous to those in Turkey, though very different." Until his retirement in 1932 the Admiral continued to offer his friends the benefit of his characteristic insights: "The Chinese people," he perceived, "are lacking in individual character and patriotic feeling." He asserted that "America has her work cut out for her in the Far East," and felt certain that American influence would prevail because "she stands for a square deal for everyone concerned."

The survivors of the Smyrna fire have the advantage of clearer insights into the nature of reality. Those interviewed did not fail to emphasize that in the midst of a holocaust provoked by hatred and abetted by greed, each owed his or her life to an act of compassion and courage. In so doing they acknowledged the ambiguities which so many reject in an age that at once tempts and defies easy solutions. The course of history in recent years suggests that the ultimate victims may be those who delude themselves.

BIBLIOGRAPHY

In addition to sources cited in the Notes, the following list includes only those materials which contributed substantially to my understanding of the events and attitudes described in this account. Contemporary periodicals, notably *The Literary Digest, Current History,* and *The Quarterly Review,* offer many relevant articles beyond those cited. A perusal of the newspaper accounts of this period—especially in the *Christian Science Monitor,* the *New York Times,* and the *Chicago Tribune*—has yielded valuable insights into the events described.

Two published sources deserve special mention: George Horton's *The Blight of Asia* and Esther P. Lovejoy's *Certain Samaritans.* Because both authors were practiced writers as well as principals in this story, their books provide vivid firsthand descriptions which are often impossible to paraphrase with justice. I am obliged to Bobbs-Merrill and to the American Women's Hospitals Service for permission to quote extensively from these works.

Among my most valuable sources have been the following eyewitnesses whose testimony I have taken either on tape or in shorthand, or —in one instance—through correspondence:

Mr. Stepan Ashjian
Mr. Karekin Bizdikian
Mrs. Rose Berberian Cachoian
Mr. Marco Capsuto
Mr. Lester Deffenbaugh
Miss Aznive Dolmadjian
Mrs. Satenig Navassart Gregory
Dr. S. Ralph Harlow
Mr. Melvin Johnson
Mrs. Takouhie Dabanian Kalebdjian

Mr. Charles Kassabian
Dr. Stanley Kerr
Mrs. Anita Chakerian Khachadourian
Mr. Stepan Nalbantian
Mr. Nishan Nercessian
Mr. Ralph Pattee
Mrs. Marika Tsakirides Saddler
Bishop Elisha Simonian
Mr. Victor Tarry
Mr. James Webster

For reasons of tact, the above list does not include the name of the retired sailor whose wife inhibited his testimony.

PUBLISHED SOURCES

OFFICIAL

Bulletin Périodique de la Presse Grècque, 1920–36. France, Ministère des Affairs Etrangères. Paris, Imprimerie Nationale.

Bulletin Périodique de la Presse Turque, 1920–36. France, Ministère des Affairs Etrangères. Paris, Imprimerie Nationale.

Documents on British Foreign Policy 1919–39, First Series, Vol. XIII. Woodward, W. L., and Rohan, Butler (eds.). Her Majesty's Stationery Office, London, 1963.

Mission d'Enquête en Anatolie (12–22 Mai 1921). Rapport de Maurice Gehri, Délégué du Comité, Internationale de la Croix-Rouge.

Papers Relating to the Foreign Relations of the United States, 1915 Supplement, 1922 Vol. II, and 1923 Vol. II. U.S. Department of State. Washington, D.C. Cited as FRUS.

Report of the International Commission of Inquiry to Investigate the Treatment of Greek Prisoners in Turkey. Anglo-Hellenic League, London, 1923.

The Treatment of Armenians in the Ottoman Empire, 1915–1916. Bryce, Viscount (ed.). Documents presented to Viscount Grey of Fallodon, Secretary of State for Foreign Affairs. Blue Book Miscellaneous No. 13. London, 1916. Cited in Notes as Blue Book.

Three publications by the Turks give their view of Greek atrocities in Turkey, and of the fire. Copies in National Archives 767.68 116/36.

Greek Atrocities in Asia Minor. Constantinople, 1922.

Greek Atrocities in the [sic] *Central Asiatic Turkey.* Constantinople, 1922.

Report of Mr. Grescovich, Commender [sic] *of the Smyrne Insurance Fire Brigade on the Great Fire in Smyrna.* Constantinople, 1922. Mr. Grescovich alleges that he saw two Greek soldiers light a box of matches on September 8 and throw the lighted box in the house of an Englishman. Further, that the Greeks said they would burn Smyrna when they left, and that the British signalmen on their ships were signaling to each other as follows: "The British Hospital is to be burned." On the 11th and 12th, Mr. Grescovich saw through his field glasses, "the activities of the Armenians on the Armenian cathedral and on the roofs of their other high buildings." A number of firemen "saw from the steeple of the Armenian cathedral signaling in code known to be previously prearranged."

From here on Mr. Grescovich describes how houses exploded and burned all over the Armenian quarter. He complained to Kiazim Pasha and suggested the area be blockaded. He was fired on while at work, and bullets made holes in his hose.

UNOFFICIAL—BOOKS

Abbott, G. F. *Greece and the Allies*. London, 1922.

Abernathy, R. W. "The Great Rescue," in *The Spirt of the Game, A Quest by* Basil Mathews *and Some Stories by* A. E. Southon *and* R. W. Abernathy. London, 1926.

Albrecht-Carrié, René. *Italy at the Peace Conference*. New York, 1938.

American Committee Opposed to the Lausanne Treaty. *The Lausanne Treaty, Turkey and Armenia*. New York, 1926.

Armenian Historical Research Association. *The Memoirs of Naim Bey*. Newton Square, Pa., 1964.

Ataturk, Kemal. *A Speech Delivered by Ghazi Mustapha Kemal, October 1927*. Leipzig, 1929.

Baker, Ray Stannard. *Woodrow Wilson: Life and Letters*. Vol. VIII. New York, 1935.

Barker, Thomas M. *Double Eagle and Crescent: Vienna's Second Turkish Siege and Its Historical Setting*. Albany, 1967.

Barton, James. *Story of Near East Relief* (1915–1930). New York, 1930.

Beaverbrook, Lord. *The Decline and Fall of Lloyd George*. London, 1963.

Bemis, S. F. *Diplomatic History of the United States*. New York, 1936.

Benjamin, S. G. *The Turk and the Greek*. New York, 1867.

Bent, J. T. (ed.). *Early Voyages and Travels in the Levant*. London, 1892.

Bierstadt, Edward Hale. *The Great Betrayal*. New York, 1924.

Bisbee, Eleanor. *The New Turks*. Philadelphia, 1951.

Boissonas, Edmond. *Smyrne: Photographies de Edmond Boissonas*. Introduction de E. Chapuisat. Geneva, 1919.

Bryce, James. *Essays and Reviews in Wartime*. New York, 1919.

Cadoux, C. J. *Ancient Smyrna*. Oxford, 1938.

Chirol, Sir Valentine. *The Occident and the Orient*. Chicago, 1924.

Churchill, Winston. *The World Crisis*. Vol. V. New York, 1929.

Creasy, Sir Edward. *History of the Ottoman Turks*. Beirut, 1961.

Cumming, Henry Harford. *Franco-British Rivalry in the Post-War Near East*. Oxford, 1938.

Daniel, Robert L. *American Philanthropy in the Near East 1820–1960*. Athens, Ohio, 1970.

Davenport, E. H., and Cooke, S. R. *The Oil Trusts and Anglo-American Relations*. New York, 1924.

Davis, William Stearns. *A Short History of the Near East*. New York, 1922.

Davison, Roderic. *Reform in the Ottoman Empire 1856–1876*. Princeton, 1963.

——— "Turkish Diplomacy from Mudros to Lausanne," in *The Diplomats*. Gordon Craig and Felix Gilbert (eds.). Princeton, 1953.

Delaisi, Francis. *Oil, Its Influence on Politics*. London, 1922.

DeNovo, John A. *American Interests and Policies in the Middle East, 1900–1939*. Minneapolis, 1963.

Derekson, David. *The Crescent and the Cross: The Fall of Byzantium, May, 1453*. New York, 1964.

Djemal Pasha. *Memoires of a Turkish Statesman 1913–1919*. London, [1922].

Driault, Edouard. *La Question d'Orient depuis ses Origines jusqu'à Nos Jours*. Paris, 1912.

Du Veou, Paul. *La Passion de la Cilicie: 1919–22*. Paris, 1954.

Earle, Edward Mead. *The Great Powers and the Bagdad Railway*. New York, 1923.

Edib, Halide. *La Fille de Smyrne*. Algiers, 1948.

——— *Memoirs of Halide Edib*. New York, 1926.

——— *The Turkish Ordeal*. New York, 1928.

——— *Turkey Faces West*. New Haven, 1930.

Eliot, Sir Charles. *Turkey in Europe*. London, 1908.

Elliott, Mabel E. *Beginning Again at Ararat*. New York, 1924.

Emin, Ahmed. *Turkey in the World War*. New Haven, 1930.

Evans, Laurence. *U.S. Policy and the Partition of Turkey 1914–1924*. Baltimore, 1965.

Eversley, Lord. *The Turkish Empire, its Growth and Decay*. London, 1917.

Fisher, H. A. L. *James Bryce*. New York, 1927.

Fisher, Louis. *Oil Imperialism*. New York, 1926.

Forster, Edward S. *A Short History of Modern Greece, 1821–1940*. London, 1941.

Frangulis, A. F. *La Grèce et la Crise Mondiale*. Vol. II. Paris, 1926.

Frischauer, Willi. *Onassis*. New York, 1968.

General Committee of Institutions and Associations in Favor of the Treaty with Turkey. *The Treaty with Turkey*. New York, 1926.

Gibb, George S., and Knowlton, Evelyn H. *History of the Standard Oil Company (New Jersey): The Resurgent Years 1911–1927*. Vol. II. New York, 1956.

Gibb, H. A. R. *Mohammedanism: An Historical Survey*. London, 1949.

Gibbons, Herbert Adams. *The Blackest Page of Modern Turkish History*. New York, 1916.

——— *Europe Since 1918*. New York, 1923.

Gidney, James. *A Mandate for Armenia*. Kent, Ohio, 1967.

Goodell, William. *The Old and the New or Changes of Thirty Years in the East*. New York, 1853.

Grey, Viscount. *Twenty-Five Years*. Vol. II. New York, 1925.

Hamlin, Cyrus. *Among the Turks*. New York, 1878.

Hartunian, Abraham H. *Neither to Laugh Nor to Weep. A Memoir of the Armenian Genocide*. Boston, 1968. Page numbers cited in my

Notes refer to the manuscript of this book which the Reverend Vartan Hartunian was kind enough to offer me before publication.

Hemingway, Ernest. *In Our Time.* New York, 1930.

──── *The Wild Years*, Gene Z. Hanrahan (ed.). New York, 1962.

Hervé, Francis. *A Residence in Greece and Turkey.* Vols. I, II. London, 1837.

Hill, Aaron. *A Full and Just Account of the Present State of the Otto-man Empire.* London, 1709.

Hills, Enis Cecil. *My Travels in Turkey.* London, 1864.

Horton, George. *The Blight of Asia.* New York, 1926.

──── *Recollections Grave and Gay.* New York, 1927.

Hovannisian, Richard G. *Armenia on the Road to Independence, 1918.* Berkeley and Los Angeles, 1967.

Howard, Harry N. *The King-Crane Commission, An American Inquiry in the Middle East.* Beirut, 1963.

──── *The Partition of Turkey.* Oklahoma City, 1931.

Hurewitz, J. C. *Middle East Dilemmas.* New York, 1953.

Joesten, Joachim. *Onassis: A Biography.* New York, 1963.

Karpat, Kemal H. *Turkey's Politics.* Princeton, 1959.

Kazemzadeh, Firuz. *The Struggle for Transcaucasia (1917–21).* New York, 1951.

Kedourie, Elie. *England and the Middle East.* London, 1956.

Keynes, John Maynard. *The Economic Consequences of the Peace.* London, 1920.

Kinross, Lord. *Ataturk.* New York, 1965.

Kurkjian, Vahan M. *A History of Armenia.* New York, 1958.

Ladas, Stephen P. *The Exchange of Minorities, Bulgaria, Greece and Turkey.* New York, 1932.

Lane-Poole, Stanley. *Turkey.* London, 1908.

Lansing, Robert. *The Peace Negotiations.* Boston, 1921.

Lepsius, Johannes. *Le Rapport Secret sur les Massacres d'Arménie.* Paris, 1918.

Lewis, Bernard. *The Emergence of Modern Turkey.* Oxford, 1961.

Lewis, Geoffrey. *Turkey.* New York, 1960.

Lochner, Louis. *What About Germany?* New York, 1942.

Lovejoy, Esther P. *Certain Samaritans.* New York, 1927.

Luke, Sir Harry. *The Old Turkey and the New.* London, 1955.

Lybyer, Albert Howe. *The Government of the Ottoman Empire in the Time of Suleiman the Magnificent.* Cambridge, Mass., 1913.

MacDonald, Duncan. *Development of Muslim Theology and Constitu-tional Theory.* London, 1903.

Mackenzie, Compton. *Greek Memories.* London, 1939.

Mandelstam, André. *Le Sort de l'Empire Ottoman.* Lausanne, 1917.

Mears, Eliot Grinnell. *Modern Turkey.* New York, 1924.

Miller, William. *The Ottoman Empire and Its Successors 1801–1927.* London, 1966.

Mohr, Anton. *The Oil War.* New York, 1925.

Morgenthau, Henry. *Ambassador Morgenthau's Story.* New York, 1918.

———— *I Was Sent to Athens.* New York, 1929.

Nalbandian, Louise. *The Armenian Revolutionary Movement.* Berkeley and Los Angeles, 1963.

Nansen, Fridtjof, *Armenia and the Near East.* New York, 1928.

Nicolson, Harold. *Curzon, The Last Phase, 1919–1925.* Boston, 1934.

Oeconomos, Lysimachos (ed.). *The Martyrdom of Smyrna and Eastern Christendom.* London, 1922.

Ostrorog, Count Leon. *The Angora Reform.* London, 1927.

Pallis, A. A. *Greece's Anatolian Venture—and After.* London, 1937.

Pears, Sir Edwin. *The Destruction of the Greek Empire and the Capture of Constantinople by the Turks.* New York, 1968.

———— *Turkey and Its People.* New York, 1911.

Pococke, Richard. *A Description of the East and Some Other Countries.* Vol. II. London, 1745.

Price, Clair. *The Rebirth of Turkey.* New York, 1923.

Psomiades, Harry J. *The Eastern Question: The Last Phase.* Institute for Balkan Studies, Salonika, Greece, 1968.

Ramsey, W. M. *Impressions of Turkey.* New York, 1897.

Rees, Goronwy. *The Multimillionaires.* New York, 1961.

Richter, Julius. *A History of Protestant Missions in the Near East.* London, 1910.

Robinson, Richard D. *The First Turkish Republic: A Case Study in National Development.* Cambridge, Mass., 1963.

Roskill, S. W. *Naval Policy Between the Wars.* London, 1968.

Ross, F. A., and others. *The Near East and American Philanthropy.* New York, 1929.

Sachar, Howard M. *The Emergence of the Middle East 1914–1924.* New York, 1969.

Sarkissian, A. O. *History of the Armenian Question to 1885.* Urbana, Illinois, 1938.

———— "A Sketch of Early Armenian History," in *Martyrdom and Rebirth.* New York, 1965.

Sforza, Count Carlo. *Makers of Modern Europe.* London, 1930.

Taylor, A. J. P. *Politics in Wartime.* New York, 1965.

Thomas, Lewis V., and Frye, Richard N. *The United States and Turkey and Iran.* Cambridge, 1952.

Tournefort, Joseph Pitton de. *A Voyage into the Levant.* Vol. III. London, 1741.

Toynbee, Arnold and Philip. *Comparing Notes: A Dialogue Across a Generation.* London, 1963.

Toynbee, Arnold. *The Western Question in Greece and Turkey.* Boston, 1922.

Trumpener, Ulrich. *Germany and the Ottoman Empire 1914–1918.* Princeton, 1968.

Tuchman, Barbara. *The Guns of August.* New York, 1962.

Ubicini, Abdolonyme. *Lettres sur la Turquie.* Vol. II. Paris, 1854.

Ussher, Clarence D., and Knapp, Grace. *An American Physician in Turkey.* Boston, 1917.

Walder, David. *The Chanak Affair*. New York, 1969.
Webster, Donald. *The Turkey of Ataturk*. Philadelphia, 1939.

PAMPHLETS

Andreades, A. *La Déstruction de Smyrne et les Dernières Atrocités Turques en Asie Mineure Sept.–Nov. 1922*. Ligue Hellénique pour la Société des Nations, Athens, 1923.
Korganoff, General G. *La Participation des Arméniens à la Guerre Mondiale sur le Front du Caucase (1914–1918)*. Paris, 1927.
Oeconomos, Lysimachos (ed.). *The Tragedy of the Christian Near East*. Anglo-Hellenic League, London, 1923.
Puaux, René. *Les Derniers Jours de Smyrne*. Société Générale d'Imprimerie, Paris, 1923.
Ward, Dr. Mark H. *The Deportations in Asia Minor, 1921–1922*. Anglo-Hellenic League, London, 1922.

ARTICLES

Barker, J. Ellis. Review of *Deutschland und Armenien, 1914–1918*, ed. by Dr. Johannes Lepsius, *Quarterly Review*, April 1920, pp. 385–400.
Buzanski, Peter M. "The Interallied Investigation of the Greek Invasion of Smyrna, 1919," *The Historian*, May 1963, pp. 325–343.
Chester, Arthur Tremaine. "Angora and the Turks," *Current History*, February 1923, pp. 749–764.
Chester, Rear Admiral Colby M. "Turkey Reinterpreted," *Current History*, September 1922, pp. 939–947.
Digoy, Charles. "Izmir," *La Révue de Paris*, Mars–Avril 1924.
Einstein, Lewis. "The Armenian Massacres," *The Contemporary Review*, April 1917, pp. 486–494.
Ellis, William T. "Jennings of Smyrna," *Scribner's*, August 1928, pp. 230–235.
Etmekjian, Lillian. "The Armenian Question in the Nineteenth Century: A Study in Historical Distortion," *Ararat*, Summer 1967, pp. 14–20.
Galib, Colonel Rachid. "Smyrna During the Greek Occupation," *Current History*, May 1923, pp. 318 ff.
Glasgow, George. "The Greeks in Smyrna," *The New Europe*, March 25, 1920, pp. 253–256.
Hamdi, Abdullah. "The Burning of Smyrna," *Current History*, November 1922, p. 317.
Harbord, Major General James G. "Mustapha Kemal Pasha and His Party," *World's Work*, June 1920, pp. 176–192.
Hough, Richard. "Annals of the Sea: The Biggest Battleship in the World," *The New Yorker*, August 20, 1966, pp. 41ff.
Kraft, Joseph. "School for Statesmen," *Harpers*, July 1958, pp. 1–5.
Mackenzie, Albert. "Crimes of Turkish Misrule," *Current History*, October 1922, pp. 28–31.
Marshall, Annie C. "Impressions of Smyrna in Wartime," *The Contemporary Review*, March 1919, pp. 328–336.
Montgomery, George. "Why Talaat's Assassin was Acquitted," *Current History*, July 1921, pp. 551–555.

Pears, Sir Edwin. "Rise, Decline and Fall of Young Turkey," *The Contemporary Review*, March 1919, pp. 264–272.

Pinson, Mark. "Turkish Revolution and Reform in Soviet Historiography," *The Middle East Journal*, Autumn 1963, Vol. 17, 1963, pp. 466–478.

Raber, Oran. "New Light on the Destruction of Smyrna," *Current History*, May 1923, pp. 312–318.

Root, Elihu. "A Requisite for the Success of Popular Diplomacy," *Foreign Affairs*, September 15, 1922, pp. 3–10.

Sproule, James A. "Who Burned Smyrna?" *Islamic Review*, August 1923, pp. 280–284.

Tachau, Paul. "Language and Politics: Turkish Language Reform," *The Review of Politics*, April 1964, pp. 191–200.

Toynbee, Arnold. "The East After Lausanne," *Foreign Affairs*, Sept. 15, 1923, pp. 84–96.

―――― "The Truth About Near East Atrocities," *Current History*, July 1923, pp. 544–551.

Williams, Aneurin, and Bryce, Lord. "Our Obligations to Armenia," *The New Europe*, July 29, 1920, pp. 51–55.

Woodhouse, Henry. "American Oil Claims in Turkey," *Current History*, March 1922, pp. 953–959.

UNPUBLISHED SOURCES

PERSONAL PAPERS

The Papers of the American Board of Commissioners for Foreign Missions. Deposited in the Houghton Library, Harvard University.

The Papers of Mark L. Bristol. The Library of Congress.

The Personal Papers of Clara Van Etten, Director of the Armenian Central Orphanage, Smyrna.

The Personal Papers of George Horton.

The Personal Papers of Onnig Ihsan. An Armenian and a member of the Turkish Parliament, Ihsan was spared in 1915 undoubtedly because he represented a Turkish constituency.

The Diaries of O. E. Jacob, Director of the Smyrna YMCA, and of Mrs. Sarah Jacob. The Historical Reference Library of the YMCA, 291 Broadway, New York, New York.

The Diary of Chief Petty Officer James Webster.

OFFICIAL DOCUMENTS

National Archives of the United States. Files of the Department of State. File numbers 763.72, 767.68, 867.00, 868.48. Cited as NA.

National Archives of the United States. Naval Records Collection. Subject File WT. Record Group #45. Cited as NR.

Transcript of trial held at the Royal Courts of Justice, King's Bench Division, Commercial List, London, on December 2, 1924. Case of the American Tobacco Company, Inc., Versus the Guardian Assurance Co., Ltd., before Mr. Justice Rowlatt. Copy in the Bristol Papers. Cited as Trial.

MANUSCRIPTS *(Unpublished)*

Buzanski, Peter M. "Admiral Mark L. Bristol and Turkish-American Relations, 1919–1922," Ph.D. dissertation, University of California, 1960.

DeNovo, John A. "Petroleum Diplomacy in the Near East 1908–1928." Ph.D dissertation, Yale University, 1948. (See general bibliography for De Novo book which is an expansion of this study.)

Harlow, Elizabeth. "These Are My Sons," courtesy of Dr. S. Ralph Harlow.

NOTES

CHAPTER I

"Powerful kings in Asia": Joseph Pitton de Tournefort, *A Voyage Into the Levant*, vol. III, p. 342.

"So as to preserve to themselves the finest port": *Ibid.*, p. 344.

"The finest city in Asia": Strabo, quoted in Tournefort, p. 344.

"Emperors were more feared . . . than goddesses": *Ibid.*, p. 342.

Crown of Ionia: S. G. Benjamin, *The Turk and the Greek*, p. 131.

"What is this noise?": Lord Eversley, *The Turkish Empire, Its Growth and Decay*, p. 57.

Footnote on Mohammed's wife A'isha: Duncan MacDonald, *Development of Muslim Theology and Constitutional Theory*, p. 10.

"When ye encounter infidels": The Koran, quoted in William Stearns Davis, *A Short History of the Near East*, p. 122.

Mohammed II as protector of the Greek Church: In this action Mohammed II was continuing a practice initiated by Justinian the Great in the sixth century. A. O. Sarkissian, "A Sketch of Early Armenian History," in *Martyrdom and Rebirth*, p. 9.

Regulations controlling behavior of infidels: Julius Richter, *A History of Protestant Missions in the Near East*, pp. 59–60. Also Abdolonyme Ubicini, *Lettres sur la Turquie*, vol. II, p. 6; Sarkissian, p. 8. Up to the seventeenth century, the term *rayah* designated not only Christians but also Moslems who had no part in the administration of the Empire—distinguishing both groups from the ruling Ottomans. After the seventeenth century, *rayah* came to refer only to the Empire's non-Moslem subjects.

"So that they may not be confused with true believers": quoted by Sarkissian, p. 8.

"More skilled in judging boys . . . than colts": Albert Howe Lyber, *The Government of the Ottoman Empire in the Time of Suleiman the Magnificent*, p. 52.

"Beat down the cross": Lyber, p. 46.

"Selim the sot": Eversley, p. 136.

Corruption seeped down: There were, of course, exceptions in the form of honest and conscientious officials, as well as able viziers and sultans, but the exceptions were so rare and their attempts at reform so unavailing that their existence merely supports the rule. (See R. Davison, *Reform in the Ottoman Empire*.)

Unemployed army feeds on own domains: See Thomas M. Barker, *Double Eagle and Crescent*, p. 62n.

The Moslems grew to despise the Janizary system because it gave to the Christian boys opportunities denied to themselves. Moslems were finally admitted, but soon afterward the Corps became so corrupt and unmanageable that it constituted a danger to the Sultan himself, and in 1826 Mahmoud II exterminated it in a bloodbath. Although a relatively able administrator, this Mahmoud was practiced in mass murder—at his father's death he wiped out his nineteen brothers and all the pregnant women of his father's harem (Eversley, p. 152).

Tongue torn out: Sir Edwin Pears, *Turkey and Its People*, p. 271.

Capitulations: For excellent source on their origins see J. T. Bent (ed.), *Early Voyages and Travels in the Levant*.

"On the whole I know of no part of the world": Francis Hervé, *A Residence in Greece and Turkey*, vol. II, p. 155.

"One which every philanthropist": *Ibid.*, p. 136.

American missionary invasion: American missionary institutions far outnumbered the French (Jesuit) and German (Lutheran) missions, which also played a role in the westernization of the Armenians.

"They would be the best . . . missionaries": Richter, p. 72.

"We have on our hands a sick man": quoted in Eversley, p. 297. J. C. Hurewitz, in *Middle East Dilemmas*, p. 159, claims that the famous quotation "the sick man is dying" was coined by the British Foreign Office in a Blue Book published during the Crimean War, and that the Czar actually said to Sir Seymour: "The bear is dying . . . you may give him his musk but even musk will not long keep him alive."

"The Great Elchi": Eversley, p. 293.

"Emanating spontaneously": Edict quoted in Eversley, p. 306.

"The only perfectly useless modern war": Sir Robert Morier, quoted in Davis, p. 319.

"The Porte will never of its own accord": Eversley, p. 301, quoting from Stanley Lane-Poole, *Life of Lord Stratford*, vol. II.

"If you could have seen": Eversley, p. 307.

History repeated itself: Herbert Adams Gibbons, *Europe Since 1918*, p. 148.

"Coffeehouse babble": Disraeli, quoted in A. O. Sarkissian, *History of the Armenian Question to 1885*, p. 47; also Eversley, p. 320.

"To the blessings of Ottoman administration": Davis, p. 341.

"Britain will spare no diplomatic exertion": quoted by Sarkissian in *History of the Armenian Question to 1885*, p. 105.

"To the amazement of the members": Eversley, p. 333.

Midhat's head delivered in a box: Lillian Etmekjian, "The Armenian Question in the Nineteenth Century . . . ," in *Ararat*, Summer 1967, p. 17.

"The only way to get rid of the Armenians": *Ibid.*, p. 19.

Self-defense as excuse; "revolts" in Sassoun, etc.: Richter, pp. 139–140.

"The slaughter of the Armenians was a joy to the Turks": *Ibid.*

Few educated Turks disapproved: Sir Charles Eliot, *Turkey in Europe*, pp. 153, 173.

"Suppression of everything original": Ahmed Emin, *Turkey in the World War*, p. 32.

"The only efficient organization . . . was the huge spy system": *Ibid.*

"Onward, Christian Soldiers" seditious: Edward Mead Earle, *The Great Powers and the Bagdad Railway*, p. 400.

"The *Padishah* dreaded dynamite bombs": Davis, p. 357n.

H_2O treasonable slogan: Davis, p. 357n.

"A . . . flabby . . . witless countenance": George Horton, *The Blight of Asia*, p. 39.

Crush resistance with terror: For background on this compulsion, see Count Leon Ostrorog, *The Angora Reform*, p. 62.

George Horton quotation: *Blight*, pp. 30–31.

Incidents not published: *Ibid.*, p. 32.

It outraged them: See Halide Edib, *Memoirs*, p. 322.

Young Turk leaders resolved to do away with Armenians: Henry Morgenthau, *Ambassador Morgenthau's Story*, p. 333.

Scheme methodically planned: Lewis Einstein, "The Armenian Massacres," in *The Contemporary Review*, April 1917, p. 488; also Ulrich Trumpener, *Germany and the Ottoman Empire 1914–1918*, p. 205.

CHAPTER II

"Allied fleet had failed": Einstein, p. 488.

"The Armenian clergy . . . went among the people cautioning": Morgenthau, p. 296. See also Trumpener, pp. 202–203.

"Not one so high!": Clarence D. Ussher and Grace Knapp, *An American Physician in Turkey*, p. 234.

"Fall from his horse": Einstein, p. 494.

Genocide procedure: Lord Bryce, quoted in Blue Book, p. 640.

"It depended on the whim of the moment": *Ibid.*, p. 643.

"They even delved into the records of the . . . Inquisition": Morgenthau, p. 307.

Talaat documents: First published in London *Daily Telegraph*, May 29, 1922. Reproduced in Mark Ward pamphlet, "The Deportations in Asia Minor, 1921–1922"; also in George Montgomery, "Why Talaat's Assassin Was Acquitted," in *Current History*, July 1921, and in *The Memoirs of Naim Bey*.

Over one million Armenians died: Howard M. Sachar, in *The Emergence of the Middle East 1914–1924*, p. 106, quotes Lepsius figure ("most thoroughly documented") as 1,396,000. Bryce, in Blue Book (p. 651), estimated conservatively 600,000 before the genocide had run its course. See also Trumpener, p. 204, n.12.

Pretext of military considerations exposed: Trumpener, p. 213; Bryce, Blue Book, pp. 639–640; Sachar, pp. 112–114.

Deportations "the result of prolonged . . . consideration": Morgenthau, p. 333.

Wangenheim's attitude: See Trumpener, pp. 205–216. Wangenheim initially presented several mild appeals to the Porte, all of which were ignored. He then washed his hands of the matter.

Wangenheim, "It is obvious": J. Ellis Barker, quoting German documents in review of Lepsius's book, *Quarterly Review*, April 1920; Trumpener, p. 212.

Zionist leaders and Palestine Jews forswore provoking Turks: Sachar, pp. 203, 207.

Von Sanders measures in Smyrna: Trumpener, p. 244.

"The threat suited the *vali*": Personal papers of Onnig Ihsan. (Ihsan, an Armenian, was one of the *vali*'s close friends.)

Campaign against Greeks: Horton, *Blight*, pp. 41–51.

Horton, "There is no doubt": Report to State Department, June 7, 1919, NA 763.72/13197.

Later protests ineffective: Trumpener, p. 239.

"In order to have success": Count Wolff-Metternich, quoted in Barker review, p. 397.

Deportations as such did not trouble them: Trumpener, p. 242, quoting Bethmann Hollweg, German Chancellor, writes: "The relocation of Armenians . . . as such was probably necessary."

Germans suggested deportations: Morgenthau, pp. 365–367.

Julius Kaliski response to appeals: Trumpener, p. 244.

"The worst of the matter is": Barker review, p. 391.

World opinion aroused: Trumpener, pp. 24–41, 250–251.

Lord Bryce undertook task "in the interests of historic truth": H. A. L. Fisher, *James Bryce*, vol. II, p. 143.

Talaat wants Armenian life insurance: Morgenthau, p. 339.

Morgenthau cable: James Barton, *Story of Near East Relief (1915–1930)*, p. 4.

Cleveland Dodge pressure on President: Robert L. Daniel, *American Philanthropy in the Near East 1820–1960*, p. 154. See also Ray Stannard Baker, *Woodrow Wilson: Life and Letters*, vol. VIII, pp. 103, 117–118; and FRUS 1918, Supplement I, vol. I, Letter of U.S. Ambassador Walter Hines Page to Secretary of State, p. 232.

Sermons laden with cant: Daniel, p. 161.

353 American mission schools and 8 colleges: 1908 figures, Richter, p. 419.

Missionary lobby prevented war against Turkey: Daniel, pp. 154–155.

Help admittedly minimal: Barton, pp. 11, 67, 73.

Schools, properties, important consideration: See Daniel, p. 155; Laurence Evans, *U.S. Policy and the Partition of Turkey 1914–1924*, p. 39.

CHAPTER III

"Most of the cooks": Gibbons, p. 37.

Clemenceau "had one illusion": John Maynard Keynes, *The Economic Consequences of the Peace*, p. 26.

Orlando "white, weak, flabby": Harold Nicolson, *Curzon, The Last Phase, 1919–1925*, p. 106.

Wilson "had no plan": Keynes, p. 39.

Lansing disclosed objections: Robert Lansing, *The Peace Negotiations*, p. 41.

Wilson a "blind and deaf Don Quixote": Keynes, p. 38.

Lloyd George judgment clouded: Gibbons, p. 20; also Nicolson, p. 55.

"All the land eastward . . . including . . . Mosul": Anton Mohr, *The Oil War*, p. 166.

Council on Foreign Relations: See Joseph Kraft, "School for Statesmen," in *Harper's*, July 1958, pp. 64–67.

Point Twelve: "an undoubted security": James Gidney, *A Mandate for Armenia*, p. 65.

"Large concessions on the coast of Asia Minor": A. A. Pallis, *Greece's Anatolian Venture—and After*, p. 8.

Clemenceau dangled hints: Pallis, p. 32. (Viscount Grey denied rumors of such an offer by the Allied Powers; see Viscount Grey, *Twenty-Five Years*, p. 194.)

Germans more scrupulous of Greek neutrality: Pallis, p. 78.

"That's when this business was really amusing": Compton Mackenzie, *Greek Memories*, p. 324.

British higher echelons counseled restraint: Pallis, pp. 341–342.

Venizelos political platform: Pallis, pp. 34, 67.

Universal agreement on Armenian question: Sacher, p. 347.

In ensuing confusion he was never recalled: Gidney, pp. 138–139.

A second group had similar experience: Gidney, p. 144.

Zionists opposed an investigation: Harry N. Howard, *The King-Crane Commission*, p. 86.

King and Crane well suited because ignorant: Elie Kedourie, *England and the Middle East*, p. 140.

"Crane had no intention": William Yale, quoted by Gidney, pp. 149–150.

Crane "contributed the geniality": Howard, *King-Crane*, p. 217.

"A roving progress": Winston Churchill, *The World Crisis*, p. 385.

"In January, 1919": Churchill, p. 392.

Turks preparing to fight: Halide Edib, *The Turkish Ordeal*, p. 14.

Tehlirian acquittal: Montgomery article.

Conditions of Armistice of Mudros: quoted in Eliot Grinnell Mears, *Modern Turkey*, pp. 624–626.

On condition that Turkey provide the militia: Vahan M. Kurkjian, *A History of Armenia*, p. 477.

Famine in Armenia wiped out 180,000: Barton, pp. 120 ff. (See also Mabel E. Elliott, *Beginning Again at Ararat*; Esther P. Lovejoy, *Certain Samaritans*.)

Near East Relief aid in Caucasus: Barton, p. 120; Daniel, pp. 159–160.

500,000 men had deserted: Emin, p. 262.

Outlaw bands not new: Tournefort, p. 349; Richard Pococke, *A Description of the East and Some Other Countries*, p. 39; Hervé, pp. 133–134.

Kemal spent winter plotting: Lord Kinross, *Ataturk*, pp. 166–173.

Intercession of G. Ward Price: Kinross, p. 167.

"What a pleasantly diverting place it was!": Clair Price, in *New York Times* feature article on Admiral Bristol, Aug. 28, 1927.

"Their belted grey wool": U.S. Naval Intelligence Report (unsigned) from U.S. flagship *Scorpion*, April 26, 1919, Naval Records.

Sforza connives with Kemal: Kinross, p. 167.

"You may be sure": Kinross, p. 167.

"They have been intriguing everywhere": *Documents on British Foreign Policy,* No. 176, p. 175.

Kiazim to "prepare the ground": Kinross, p. 172.

Kemal "biting his lips": Kinross, p. 177.

Kemal's pass issued at Sforza's request: Pallis, p. 135.

Lloyd George "with charming evasiveness": Nicolson, p. 106.

"In America there is disgust": Wilson, quoted by René Albrecht-Carrié, in *Italy at the Peace Conference,* p. 464.

Unauthorized Italian maneuvers: A. F. Frangulis, *La Grèce et la Crise Mondiale,* vol. II, pp. 61–62.

The American President politely refused: Albrecht-Carrié, p. 218.

Odessa precedent: Toynbee, pp. 66–67; Frangulis, p. 86.

"Mr. Lloyd George asked": Churchill, p. 387.

Venizelos letter of protest: Frangulis, p. 59.

"The occupation is activated because": Venizelos, quoted by Frangulis, p. 63.

"Kindly inform very confidentially": Frangulis, p. 62.

Experts skeptical of Greek landing: Evans, p. 173.

Captain Dayton nervous: Horton to State Department, June 7, 1919; NA 763.72/13197.

The English for "letting the Greeks run the whole show alone": Horton, *Blight,* p. 73.

CHAPTER IV

Eyewitness accounts of the Greek landing were supplied to me by Mr. Nishan Nercessian, Mr. Victor Tarry, and Mr. Stepan Ashjian. For a reconstruction of the events described in this chapter I have also relied on written depositions from Ahmed Vizi, J. D. Langdon, F. Blackler, Fred V. Green, Jr., Cass Arthur Reed, Dr. A. C. Pratt, and the reports of Ali Nadir Pasha, Commander of the 17th Army Corps (Turkish), Captain Dayton, commanding officer of the U.S.S. *Arizona,* the commanding officer of H.M.S. *Adventure,* and Lieutenant George Perry U.S.N. Quotations in my text, unless otherwise cited, are taken from these written reports, all to be found in the Naval Records Collection of the National Archives.

Needlessly tactless gesture: Toynbee, *The Western Question,* p. 271; and Peter M. Buzanski, "The Interallied Investigation of the Greek Invasion of Smyrna, 1919," in *The Historian,* May 1963, pp. 331–332.

Reached point near Turkish boats: Toynbee, p. 397.

Figures on Turkish and Greek fatalities: Toynbee, pp. 392–395; Horton, *Blight,* pp. 72–78; Frangulis, p. 64.

"What is very evident to me": Report of Consul Horton to State Department, June 7, 1919, NA 763.72/13197.

Joining in praise for Greek leaders: Horton, *Blight,* p. 78; Toynbee, pp. 401–402.

Greeks implicated the Italians; senior Italian naval officer exulting: Horton to State Department, June 7, 1919.

Prisoners allowed to escape: Buzanski article, p. 337; Edib, *Ordeal,* p. 61; Frangulis, pp. 64–67.

Greeks offered payment of one thousand Turkish pounds: Report of Captain Dayton, May 18, 1919, NR.

Punishment to fifty-four persons: Toynbee, p. 401.

Inter-Allied investigation: Conclusions published in Frangulis, pp. 64–67.

Sterghiades leaned toward the Turk: Horton, *Blight*, p. 79; Toynbee, p. 165.

Sterghiades slapped Greek priest: Horton, *Blight*, pp. 80–81.

Sterghiades reforms: Horton, *Blight*, pp. 82–92. (Toynbee's account of Sterghiades' administration in *The Western Question* clearly refutes his conclusion that the ledger balanced against the Greek occupation. See pp. 153–207 and appendix, pp. 387–389.

"We *wanted* them to come": Testimony of Mr. Stepan Ashjian.

"If we must be punished": Churchill, p. 388.

"By God what an impertinence!": Kinross, p. 181.

Number of Turks massacred swelled: Bristol wrote to Secretary of State, Nov. 7, 1919: "Daily many dispatches continuing to come protesting against Greek occupation and claiming 30,000 victims and 50 million pounds Turkish loss from Greeks." NA 867.00/1039.

President confesses he forgot: Evans, p. 167.

200,000 swore vengeance: Wallace to State Dept., May 24, 1919, NA 867.00/878.

"A Frenchman by birth": Edib, *Ordeal*, p. 33.

"My nation, my poor nation": *Ibid.*

"The Smyrna affair . . . worked to the limit": Intelligence Report (unsigned), Dec. 18, 1919, NA 867.00/1085.

"First ignored, then insulted": Churchill, pp. 388–389.

"Strong and well armed": Horton to American Mission, Paris, June 23, 1919, NA 736.72/13152.

Greek zone not yet defined: Toynbee, p. 226.

Venizelos pleas to Supreme Council: quoted in Frangulis, p. 70, pp. 73–86.

Turkish attacks encouraged by Italians: Kinross, p. 174; Horton dispatches of June 23, 24, and July 9, 1919, NA 736.72/13199.

Conclusions distorted in Turkish press: Buzanski, p. 341n.

Evidence of Venizelos charges: Evans, p. 171. See also Annie C. Marshall, "Impressions of Smyrna in Wartime," in *The Contemporary Review*, March 1919, p. 335.

Inter-Allied report and conclusions carefully worded: Buzanski's dissertation concedes that the bias is obvious. Bristol and his "pro-Turk" intelligence officer, Lt. Robert Dunn, permitted the minutes "to have a one-sided view." (P. 74; and see also *Ibid.* pp. 71–75.)

Publicity "to insure accurate information": Bristol to Secretary of State, Jan. 28, 1920, NA 867.00/1096.

Actions of Greeks "no surprise": Bristol diary, May 18; Report of Operations, week ending May 25, 1919, Papers of Mark L. Bristol.

"To me it is a calamity": Bristol letter to Admiral W. S. Sims, May 18, 1919, Bristol Papers.

Snidely rumored in certain navy circles: Notably in the Aeronautical Division, where he served from 1913–16. (Bristol did not think there was much of a future for naval aviation; this attitude did not make him especially popular in the Aeronautical Division. Several of the men interviewed who had served under Bristol's command between 1919 and 1922 expressed reservations about his naval talents.)

Two faces to the American position: See Earle, pp. 346–348.

"For years American businessmen": George S. Gibb and Evelyn H. Knowlton, *History of the Standard Oil Company*, vol. II, p. 272.

Opportunities for expansion "unlimited": quoted by Earle, p. 339.

"After 1919 the issue of imperialism": Nicolson, p. 164.

Unprecedented numbers of Turkish widows: Sacher, p. 248.

Bristol suggested they bone up on their bibles: Personal Papers of Clara Van Etten.

"Not a newspaper in the country will print your story": Charles E. Vickrey, Executive Director, Near East Relief, quoted in Van Etten Papers.

Their "interests depend . . . upon American business": Bristol letter to L. I. Thomas, July 24, 1922, Bristol Papers.

Europeans "are going to try to get a division of the spoils": Bristol letter to Adm. W. S. Benson, June 3, 1919, Bristol Papers.

"It is a task worthy of America": Bristol letter to Dr. C. F. Gates, Pres. of Robert College, Dec. 13, 1919, Bristol Papers.

"It is practically a virgin field": Bristol letter of May 15, 1922, to Edgar B. Howard, exporter-importer of Philadelphia, Bristol Papers.

Statement of C. F. Gates at a meeting of students at Robert College, 1919. Copy in Bristol Papers.

Bristol gave himself credit for change of view: Letter to Admiral Benson, June 3, 1919, Bristol Papers.

"As time goes on . . . idea is becoming . . . universal": *Ibid.*

Believer in "pitiless publicity": Bristol letter to Frank Polk, U.S. Embassy, Paris ("You know I am a pitiless publicity man, and I believe it pays. . . . "), Dec. 4, 1919, NR.

"I have tried": Bristol letter to L. I. Thomas, July 24, 1922, Bristol Papers.

"The Turks do not understand": Bristol letter to Edgar B. Howard, April 3, 1922, Bristol Papers.

"A constant fight . . . not to link up with foreigners": Bristol letter to Rear Admiral W. S. Benson, July 25, 1922, Bristol Papers.

"One hundred per cent American personnel": *Ibid.*

Greek influence not "fair and square"; "policy in a nutshell": Bristol letter to Adm. Benson, June 3, 1919, Bristol Papers.

"Moments . . . subjects . . . made him reserved": Clair Price, *New York Times*, Aug. 28, 1927.

"We fought to destroy the Prussian power": Bristol letter to C. F. Gates, Dec. 13, 1919, Bristol Papers.

No attempt to get along: Evans, pp. 324–329.

"Armenians . . . deserve small consideration": Bristol letter to Adm. Benson, July 12, 1919, NR.

"Armenians are a race like the Jews": Bristol letter to Adm. W. S. Sims, May 5, 1920, NR.

"I am holding no brief for any race in the Near East": Bristol letter to Adm. Sims, May 18, 1919, Bristol Papers.

The "Armenians and Greeks have many flaws and deficiencies of character. . . . ": Diary, May 25, 1919, Bristol Papers.

Bristol's conversation with Suad Bey: Diary, Oct. 29, 1922, Bristol Papers.

Department of State forced to ask him to restrain himself: Memo from Acting Secretary of State Davis, July 2, 1920, Bristol Papers.

Bristol discounted and minimized reports: "Now—as regards the information obtained from Azerbaijan, Armenia or from Turkey, I never put much stock in its face value. . . . ": Letter to Colonel Wm. Haskell regarding intelligence reports from Tiflis derogatory to behavior of the Turks. Bristol Papers. (Also Diary, Feb. 9, 1922, NA 867.00/1507: "I had not yet read the article but knowing the author was a native, a Greek of Constantinople, would make me suspicious of the truth of the information contained in the article.")

At times his reports bore little resemblance to reports received: Evidence in Chapters VI, XVII, XIX, to follow.

Rebuked for tone of reports: Letter of June 4, 1919, to Bristol from Admiral H. S. Knapp, Commander, U.S. Forces in European Waters, Bristol Papers.

He could count more on French: Letter of H. V. Bryan, May 4, 1922, to Bristol: "I really believe the French in Paris will unconsciously do more for your policy than the Americans who I further believe are rather influenced by British politics here." Bristol Papers.

Bristol congratulated Toynbee: Letter to Toynbee, July 26, 1923, Bristol Papers.

Footnote—Toynbee's traumatic reversal: See Arnold and Philip Toynbee, *Comparing Notes: A Dialogue Across a Generation*. Toynbee repudiated his earlier writing in *The Western Question*, p. 382.

"The Navy not only assists . . . commercial firms": Navy source, quoted in Earle, pp. 346–347.

The oil war: See Mohr, p. 37.

Fisher the "oil maniac": E. H. Davenport and S. R. Cooke, *The Oil Trusts and Anglo-American Relations*, p. 4.

Fisher quotations: *Ibid.*

Churchill's plan for Admiralty to "become owners": Churchill, quoted in Davenport and Cooke, pp. 18–19.

Chester aware that these "unimportant" claims, etc: Henry Woodhouse, "American Oil Claims in Turkey," in *Current History*; Davenport and Cooke, p. 24.

For details on amalgamation of British oil interests see Davenport and Cooke, pp. 24–25; Gibb and Knowlton, pp. 280–282.

"The Allies floated to victory": Lord Curzon, quoted in Davenport and Cooke, p. 29; also Mohr, p. 156.

British directed strategy with oil in mind: Louis Fisher, *Oil Imperialism*, p. 9.

"All phases of the Company's foreign activities": Gibb and Knowlton, p. 277.

"In the settlement of the division of Turkey": Gibb and Knowlton, pp. 284–285.

"A greater menace . . . than a German victory": Gibb and Knowlton, p. 286.

Standard Oil prospectors denied entry: John A. DeNovo, "Petroleum Diplomacy in the Near East 1908–1928," p. 159.

Shell later acknowledged possession of charts, etc.: Gibb and Knowlton, p. 287.

British would no longer guarantee to fuel Bristol's ships: DeNovo dissertation, pp. 104–105.

"Where his Annapolis background stood him in good stead": Gibb and Knowlton, p. 287.

"Until the situation is entirely clear": Sadler, quoted in Gibb and Knowlton, p. 288.

"An impossible step backward": Daniels, quoted in DeNovo dissertation, p. 103.

San Remo Agreement: See Evans, pp. 297–298 for summary of agreement and U.S. reaction.

U.S. not opening doors, say British: DeNovo dissertation, p. 184.

CHAPTER VI

Smyrna businessmen downcast: Horton to Secretary of State, letter of June 4, 1919, NA 763.72/13120. See also Buzanski article, p. 335.

"In Greece proper you see few foreign companies": Horton to Secretary of State, Aug. 23, 1919, NA 867.00/925.

French financiers held sixty per cent Turkish debt, opposed Greek occupation: Earle, p. 321–322; also Gibbons, p. 424.

French investors ploughed money into foreign works: Francis Delaisi, *Oil, Its Influence on Politics*, p. 69.

Conservative opposition to Lloyd George policy: Henry Harford Cumming, *Franco-British Rivalry in the Post-War Near East*, p. 132.

"Lord Curzon, mounted upon the Foreign Office": Churchill, p. 395.

Moslems of India aroused: David Walder, *The Chanak Affair*, p. 160.

"The pro-Turkish inclinations of British military": Churchill, p. 388.

Inordinate number of "accidents": Kinross, p. 203.

"Do you know how many dreadnoughts": Kemal, quoted in Kinross, p. 204.

Rawlinson tried "to awaken the British": Kinross, p. 210.

Louis Browne emissary (not to be confused with Constantine Brown, Louis Browne's successor as *Chicago Daily News* correspondent): Kinross, p. 218.

"The least harmful solution": Quoted in Kinross, p. 218.

Harbord-Kemal meeting, Turkish view: Quoted in Kinross, p. 219.

Harbord's version: Major General James G. Harbord, "Mustapha Kemal Pasha and his Party," in *World's Work*, June 1920, pp. 176–192.

Turkey's crimes "make the conscience . . . shudder": Quoted in Kinross, p. 211.

"Into the hands of men . . . who could not even command success": Quoted in Kinross, p. 211.

Kemal's reply to Georges Picot: Kinross, p. 234.

Marash: Dr. Stanley Kerr, today a professor emeritus of the American University of Beirut, was in Marash as an official of the Near East Relief during this time. He fled to Beirut and was from there evacuated to Jaffa. "Commander Sharpe, of the U. S. torpedo boat that took me to Jaffa, asked me to write for Admiral Bristol a detailed report of what had happened at Marash," he wrote recently. "This I did. It is obvious that the Admiral must have ignored it." A full account which Dr. Kerr prepared at the behest of the magazine *Asia* was not published. He recently found the ms. in the Houghton Library, Harvard University. Dr. Kerr is now at work on a book about the Marash affair, to be titled *The Lions of Marash*.

French agents pressing negotiations with Kemal: See Paul Du Veou, *La Passion de la Cilicie*, for details of secret terms.

French arms assisting Kemal: Nicolson, p. 260; Kinross, p. 235; Gibbons, p. 452.

British withdrew their few remaining troops: Kinross, p. 225.

Treaty of Sèvres provisions turn Russia to Kemal: Harry N. Howard, *The Partition of Turkey*, p. 248.

French financiers disconsolate: Earle, p. 321; Gibbons, p. 424.

"At last, peace with Turkey": Churchill, p. 399.

Stop shilly-shallying, or "the worst for them": *Bulletin Périodique*, No. 14, 12 Avril–24 Mai, 1926, p. 4.

"If he were permitted . . . he could guarantee": Nicolson, p. 250.

"Greece had saved the Allied positions": *Ibid.*

"They are beaten and fleeing": Quoted in Kinross, p. 268.

"At the eleventh hour Kemal . . . rescued": Nicolson, p. 251.

Nationalist cause people's fight against capitalists: Mark Pinson, "Turkish Revolution and Reform in Soviet Historiography," in *The Middle East Journal*, vol. 17, 1963, p. 466.

"We are the only possible obstacle to . . . Bolshevism": Edib, *Ordeal*, p. 6.

"Never for one moment do we forget": I am embarrassed to report that I cannot for the life of me find my source for this quotation. Since I am reasonably certain that it is not a figment of my imagination, I am letting it stand.

"They presumably have no credentials": Bristol to Secretary of State, Dec. 2, 1921, NA 867.00/1455.

"The Turks will be thrown into the arms of the Bolsheviks": Churchill, p. 419.

"For the sake of Venizelos much had to be endured": Churchill, p. 388.

Lloyd George not only stood fast but gave an astonishing speech to the House of Commons on August 4, 1922, which was interpreted by the

Greek Command as an exhortation to keep fighting. Text in Cumming, pp. 170–171.

"The governments of Britain, France, and Italy": British Foreign Office note quoted by Frangulis, p. 175.

Britain, France, and Italy agreed no financial support to Greece: French Minister to Athens, letter to Greek Cabinet, Dec. 8, 1920, quoted by Frangulis, *Ibid.*

For various viewpoints on Venizelos-Constantine policy, see: Pallis, p. 67; Churchill, p. 416; Frangulis, p. 180; Gibbons, pp. 430, 432.

Confidential hints to Constantine from British minister at Berne: Frangulis, p. 186.

"The great man is with us": Churchill, p. 417.

"Two disconsolate suppliants": Nicolson, p. 263.

"Not a gun, not a shell": H. A. L. Fisher, p. 81.

CHAPTER VII

Supreme Council declaration: Mears, p. 601.

Greeks prevented from applying blockade rules: Gibbons, p. 432; Horton, p. 190.

U.S. discouraging private loans to Greece: Secretary of State to Mssrs. Marvin and Pleasants, January 30, 1922, FRUS 1922, vol. II, p. 456.

"For upwards of nine months . . . the Turks waited": Churchill, p. 434.

Turkish authorities in certain towns permitted help: Report of Miss Emily Wade, Director of Near East Relief, Diyarbakir, to Bristol (undated); report of Miss Mary Holmes, Director of NER, Urfa, to Bristol (undated). Both in NA 867.4016/464.

Near East Relief extracted signed statements: "Mr. Applegate with other members of the NER had been forced under orders to sign an agreement according to which they would say nothing of the deportations until they were out of the service of the organization": Clayton Report, NA 867.4016/618.

Reluctance of American press to publish stories of deportations: Interviews with Dr. S. Ralph Harlow and Dr. Stanley Kerr, both of whom had articles suppressed. See Edward Hale Bierstadt, *The Great Betrayal*, p. 87; Gibbons, p. 456.

Clayton "borrows" Applegate's diary: Clayton Report.

Yowell Report: Extracts of report to Secretary of State published in *The Martyrdom of Smyrna*, by Lysimachos Oeconomos, pp. 33–35.

State Department concerned lest Clayton article be published: Allen Dulles to Phillips, Aug. 25, 1922, NA 767.68116/40.

Bristol warned Yowell "against giving these facts to the public": Diary, May 12, 1922, NA 867.00/1525.

Bristol absolved Nationalists of responsibility: "I told him [Youssouf] that I received the impression from the experiences of Americans in the interior that local officials often failed to carry out the wishes of the Angora government and that the oppressive and shortsighted measures of these officials, acting on their own initiative, had furnished responsibility for a great many of the abuses which had arisen." Diary, February 6, 1922, NA 867.00/1493.

"Yowell's yowl": *Chicago Daily Tribune*, May 19, 1922, quoting NER agent in Constantinople, and Bristol, both of whom insisted Yowell Report was exaggerated propaganda calculated to enhance British political aims. Also: Letter, Bristol to Allen Dulles, May 24, 1922, Bristol Papers.

"It was a fine thing to have Dulles go to the Department": Bristol letter of Aug. 31, 1922, to Capt. Lyman Cotten, Bristol Papers.

If the reports could be declared untrue: Allen Dulles to Bristol, July 25, 1922, Bristol Papers.

Evidence of Turkish atrocities irrefutable: Disclosures of Nurse Edith Wood, Dr. Mark H. Ward, and Miss Ethel Thompson appeared in the *Christian Science Monitor*, May 31, June 21, and July 13, 1922; also in the *Manchester Guardian*, August 17, 1922. Extracts published in Oeconomos compilation, pp. 28–45.

The Secretary of State wanted to avoid giving impression: Allen Dulles to Bristol, April 21, 1922, Bristol Papers.

Murders of Americans: Harlow interview in *New York Times*, Sept. 7, 1922; my interviews with Dr. Stanley Kerr and Dr. S. Ralph Harlow; *Association Men* (YMCA publication), Jan. 1923, p. 240; *British Foreign Office Document* No. 269, March 12, 1920 (Woodward and Rohan); U.S. Consul Jackson, Aleppo, to Department of State, Nov. 21, 1921, NA 867.00/1463.

Dulles disturbed about mandates, busy trying to ward off: Letter, Dulles to Bristol, April 21, 1922, Bristol Papers.

President Harding, "I am wondering": Harding to Hughes, May 20, 1922, FRUS 1922, vol. II, p. 922.

"But I suggest that the real difficulty": Hughes to Harding, May 20, 1922, *Ibid.*

Turkish press notices at Talaat's death: *Bulletin Périodique*, No. 14, 12 Avril–24 Mai 1921, p. 9.

"Beware! We have no intention": *Ibid.* No. 22, 6 Avril–6 Juin 1922, p. 7.

"A shrewd stroke": Churchill, p. 442.

"You of course have read": Bristol to Cotten, Aug. 31, 1922. Bristol Papers; "Harington on own hook" confirmed in Kinross, p. 349.

"They even had to publish in the papers": Kemal Ataturk, *A Speech*, p. 565.

"Soldiers, your goal is the Mediterranean!": Edib, *Ordeal*, p. 383.

Greek headquarters troops had no chance to fire: Report of Lt. Perry, Oct. 24, 1922, Bristol Papers.

This was untrue; two Greek regiments knew it: Churchill, p. 444.

"If it is the will of God that we are defeated": Kemal, quoted by Kinross, p. 198.

For extent of Greek atrocities during retreat, American view, see report of Lt. Perry, Oct. 24, 1922, Bristol Papers. Also NA 867.00/1573. For Turkish view see NA 767.68116/36.

CHAPTER VIII

"Never . . . so struck with any village": Hervé, vol. I, p. 312.

"Most strangers . . . can testify": Hervé, vol. II, p. 35.

"Inhabitants speak nothing but": Tournefort, p. 336.

"A regular Levanter is supposed to speak": Hervé, vol. I, p. 344.

"Richest magazine in the world": Tournefort, p. 333.

"Better enlightened, better paved": Tournefort, p. 334.

Aaron Hill anecdote: Aaron Hill, *A Full and Just Account of the Present State of the Ottoman Empire*, p. 17.

"The same young ladies then change their dress . . . dance all night": Hervé, vol. II, p. 2.

"What! Admit a man": Hervé, vol. I, p. 344.

Smyrna newspapers: According to U.S. Intelligence Report (unsigned), Feb. 4, 1921, NR, there were three Armenian; one anti-Greek published in French by French interests; one anti-Greek published in French by Italian interests; nine Greek (two royalist, five antiroyalist, 2 independent); two Jewish; and seven Turkish.

"Neither to the right nor": Horton, *Blight*, p. 119.

"Silent procession": Hemingway describing exodus from Thrace. See *The Wild Years*.

Formal assurances to Armenians and Greeks: Abraham H. Hartunian, *Neither to Laugh Nor to Weep*, p. 191.

"Therefore, I could not assure": Horton, *Blight*, p. 123.

CHAPTER IX

In this and subsequent chapters the observations of U.S. Naval Officers Merrill, Knauss, and Powell, unless otherwise cited, are taken from their diaries, found in the files of the Department of State, National Archives (NA 767.68/407). Bristol's daily observations, unless otherwise specified, are taken from his diaries, found in the Bristol Papers and also in NA 867.00/1542–81. I have cited these whenever it is not absolutely clear that I am quoting or paraphrasing from the daily record that these men kept.

References to the Reverend Dobson's testimony, unless otherwise cited, are taken from the Oeconomos pamphlet, *The Tragedy of the Christian Near East*. Excerpts may be found in René Puaux, *Les Derniers Jours de Smyrne*, and in Bierstadt.

Hadjianestis mental instability: Horton, *Blight*, p. 121; Walder, p. 169.

"They went through like beaten dogs": Partial transcript of testimony given by Horton at congressional hearings of Immigration and Naturalization Committee, (undated), Horton Papers.

Greek threats to burn Smyrna: "When demoralized Greek army reaches Smyrna serious trouble more than possible and threats to burn the town are freely heard": Horton to Bristol, Sept. 5, 1922, Bristol Papers.

"In the interests of humanity": Horton to Bristol, Sept. 4, 1922, FRUS 1922, vol. II, p. 415.

Department "not inclined": Acting Secretary of State Phillips to Bristol, Sept. 5, 1922, NA 767.68/318.

"I will not land one sailor": Merrill diary, Sept. 6, 1922, NA. Dumesnil had no intention of sitting still: *Ibid.*

It was "infinitely better not to send . . . special instructions": Phillips to Secretary of State, September 5, 1922, NA 767.68/275.

Lieut. Cdr. Rhodes briefed: Bristol to Secretary of the Navy, letter of March 18, 1924, NR.

"I am sending this in code": Bristol to Acting Secretary of the Navy, Sept. 6, 1922, NA 868.48/83.

A number of businessmen criticized British: Hepburn to Bristol, Sept. 10, 1922, Bristol Papers.

Admiral Brock now promised "to give . . . protection . . . to all": Dobson testimony.

Kemal proclamation: Hepburn diary, September 9, 1922, NR.

"The Greek High Commissioner did not grant this request": Horton, *Blight*, p. 122.

"The interregnum . . . began, *but nothing happened"*: Horton, *Blight*, p. 123.

Rumbold and Bristol—no love lost: Walder, p. 133; Evans, pp. 325–326.

Bristol's conversation with Beaverbrook and his observations thereon are recorded in detail in his diary of Sept. 8, 1922.

Beaverbrook had gone to Turkey in the hope of prevailing on Kemal to name peace terms satisfactory to the British Cabinet. When he discovered that the Turks were on the verge of total victory, he returned to London without completing his mission: Lord Beaverbrook, *The Decline and Fall of Lloyd George,* p. 158.

Mark Prentiss background: See articles in *System,* Sept., March, 1920.

Mark Prentiss joined NER out of compassion: *New York Times,* Sept. 18, 1922.

Ward Price hitched ride: Walder, p. 182.

"I told them that . . . going on my permission and on one of our own destroyers . . . they were not free to report": Bristol diary, Sept. 5, 1922.

"I did lose my temper": Merrill diary, Sept. 9, 1922, NA.

Two years later, under oath, Cherefeddin gave different version: Transcript of Trial, Bristol Papers.

"I had a feeling of relief": Dobson testimony.

CHAPTER X

Civilian Turks armed to the teeth: Cross-examination of Col. Mouharren Bey, Transcript of Trial.

Italians protecting Jewish quarters organized Jewish militia: Interview with Mr. Marco Capsuto, who as a boy of fourteen was a member of this militia.

Italy not averse to inflating number of its citizens: Interview with Mr. Victor Tarry.

To Captain Hepburn's dismay: "The worst problem is the refugees. They are just rushing all the American institutions": Diary, Sept. 11, 1922, NR.

Hepburn's instructions are outlined in detail in final report from Hepburn to Bristol, Sept. 25, 1922, and in letter from Bristol to Secretary of the Navy, March 18, 1924, NR.

"The most effective measure that can be taken": Hepburn to Bristol, Sept. 9, 1922, Bristol Papers.

Dilboy incident was published in the *New York Times* on April 8, Nov. 1, and Nov. 5, 1923. References in Bristol Papers—Bristol to Treat, March 13, 1923.

Horton "plainly fair and square": Bristol to Secretary of the Navy, March 18, 1924, NR. Also in NA 767.68/624.

"I saw no connection": Horton, *Recollections Grave and Gay*, p. 1.

"I cultivated Rahmi Bey": *Ibid.*, pp. 220–221.

"My position here . . . extremely difficult": Horton, Report to Secretary of State, Sept. 12, 1922, NA 767.68/449.

"No reason to impute bad faith": Bristol to Department of State, Oct. 28, 1922, FRUS 1922, vol. II, p. 946.

"Carathima was undoubtedly killed": Bristol to Secretary of State, March 18, 1924, NR.

The conviction that many would be killed: Horton to Secretary of State, Sept. 12, 1922, NA.

Least of all could he understand: See introduction, Horton, *Blight*.

Some businessmen more interested in moving tobacco: Powell diary, Sept. 20, 1922, NA.

"A matter of considerable importance" that *Hog Island* be at dock: Hepburn diary, Sept. 9, 1922, NR.

Horton had saved hundreds of lives: Letters in Horton Papers—from Dana Getchell, Oct. 12, 1922; Alekos Karaghiogiades, March 9, 1962— testify to this fact.

Horton composed memoranda urging U.S. to offer asylum: Letters of Sept. 12 and Sept. 18, 1922 to Secretary of State, NA 767.68/449–50.

"As he sat there in the consular office": Horton, *Blight*, p. 135.

"It would be interesting to know": Report, Lt. Perry, Oct. 24, 1922, Bristol Papers.

Knowledgeable foreigners discounted distinction: Testimony of Sir Harry Lamb, Trial; Intelligence Report, Dec. 18, 1919, NA 867.00/- 1085; Edib, "The Last of the Irregulars and the New Army," in *Ordeal*, pp. 231–260.

Discipline "excellent": Intelligence report (unsigned), June 13, 1923, NR.

"They proceed without interruption or qualms": French officer, quoted in Charles Digoy, "Izmir," *La Révue de Paris*, Mars–Avril 1924.

"At this hour . . . everything is quiet": Hepburn, letter to Bristol, Sept. 9, 1922, Bristol Papers.

CHAPTER XI

Kemal's entry into Smyrna: Edib, *Ordeal*, p. 381.

Noureddin reputation: "Noureddin Pasha is . . . noted for his narrow-minded and antiforeign feelings": Bristol to Secretary of the Navy, March 18, 1924, NR.

French ready to hedge: See Evans, pp. 378–381.

Motto "Turkey for the Turks": Merrill diary, Sept. 16, 1922, NA.

Campaign to purify the language: See Paul Tachau, "Language and

Politics: Turkish Language Reform," in *The Review of Politics*, April 1964, pp. 191–200.

Discriminatory taxation and cultural pressures on Jews: See Geoffrey Lewis, *Turkey*, pp. 118–119.

Kemal to rid land of unassimilable elements: Horton, *Blight*, p. 148.

Turks turned on Armenians first: "The fury of the Turks burst first upon their usual victims"—Horton, *Blight*, p. 128. "There seemed to be a definite plan to clean out the Armenians—loot and kill them—and carry off the Greeks to deal with them at their leisure"—Horton testimony at hearings; transcript in Horton Papers.

"No Armenian can be our friend": Morgenthau, *Story*, p. 339.

Kemal and aides decide fate of Armenians: "On the previous day I had been told by Count Senni, the Italian Consul General who was far more in the confidence of the Turks than ourselves, that an important meeting was to be held that evening at the *Konak* to decide on the disposition of the Armenians." Report of (British) Vice-Consul Hole, dated Sept. 25, 1922. Copy in NA 767.68/517.

A new proclamation appeared: Horton, *Blight*, p. 141.

Evidence that Turkish quarter being roused: Horton testimony, in Horton Papers.

Armenian bands alleged to have preyed on Turks: Bristol to Secretary of the Navy, March 18, 1924, NR.

Not safe to enter Armenian quarter: Oran Raber, "New Light on the Destruction of Smyrna," *Current History*, May 1923, pp. 312–318.

Testimony of Sergeant-Major Fripp: Trial.

"All the looting was most orderly": Knauss diary, Sept. 10, 1922.

Murder of Archbishop Chrysostomos described in Puaux, extracts in Bierstadt, pp. 24–25.

"He got what was coming to him": Dumesnil quoted by Horton, letter to Secretary of State, Sept. 18, 1922, NA. ("When the massacre of Chrysostomos was reported to Admiral Dumesnil of the French Navy, he replied, sardonically, with a French idiom which means exactly 'He got what was coming to him.'")

Murder of Dr. Murphy described in Dobson testimony; Oeconomos pamphlet; also Horton, *Blight*, p. 134.

Boudja, Dutch couple murdered: Horton, *Blight*, pp. 133–134; Oeconomos pamphlet.

Bombs raining on Armenian Cathedral: Testimony, Father Choren Boutchakjian, Trial.

Jacquith estimated destitute at three hundred thousand: FRUS 1922, vol. II, p. 423.

"Entire population of seven hundred thousand faces starvation": FRUS 1922, vol. II, p. 418.

Systematic flushing out of Armenian population: Horton, *Blight*, pp. 128, 141.

Men led away to edge of city and killed: Vice-Consul Barnes, Report, Sept. 18, 1922. NA 767.68/463.

One hundred at a time murdered: Roy Treloar, *Daily Telegraph* (London), Sept. 20, 1922, in Oeconomos compilation, p. 8.

CHAPTER XII

"The evacuation would soon be interrupted": Hepburn to Bristol, Sept. 11, 1922, NR.

Interview with Noureddin Pasha described in Merrill diary, Sept. 11, 1922, NA, and Hepburn diary, Sept. 11, 1922, NR.

Noureddin expressed resentment: Letter, Peet to Briggs, Sept. 20, 1922. ABCFM Papers, Houghton Library.

"Refugees must leave country or be taken away": Telegram, Davis to Bristol, Sept. 11, 1922. Bristol Papers.

"She did not say what had happened to her boy": Horton, *Blight*, p. 137.

American officers assuring Turks of concern for citizens only: Horton, *Blight*, p. 154.

Newsmen's conversation and Horton's reactions recorded in his report to Secretary of State, Sept. 18, 1922, NA; also *Blight*, pp. 205–206.

News dispatches from Smyrna before the fire: See Oeconomos compilation; by special arrangement with *Chicago Tribune*, Clayton's dispatches were appearing simultaneously in *Daily Telegraph* (London). Ward Price in *Daily Mail* reported, "The discipline of the Turkish troops is excellent." See also A.P. reports, *New York Times*, Sept. 10–13, 1922. News reports to the contrary were evidently being supplied by eyewitnesses arriving at foreign ports, not by newsmen in Smyrna.

CHAPTER XIII

Bristol wanted exact body count: Bristol diary, Sept. 25, 1922; Knauss diary, Sept. 17, 1922. See also Bristol letter to Secretary of the Navy, March 18, 1924, NR.

Attack on Chief Crocker and President MacLachlan described in Hepburn diary, Sept. 12, 1922, NR; also Horton, *Blight*, pp. 138–139, quoting Mrs. Cass Arthur Reed, wife of College dean and daughter of President MacLachlan.

Turkish guards tried to get inside buildings; showed loot: Personal diary of Chief Petty Officer James Webster.

"The Armenian quarter is a charnel house": Digoy article.

"As you have seen, there have been no massacres": Oeconomos compilation.

Report in *New York Times* datelined Italy: Sept. 13, 1922.

Barnes estimated seven of ten Armenian houses raided: Report to Department of State, Sept. 18, 1922, NA.

Abdul Hamid's largesse: Text of Chester concessions in *Current History*, June 1923. See also Earle, pp. 339–342.

Chester convinced Turks wanted him: DeNovo dissertation, pp. 244, 254.

Chester thought he had blessing of British: *Ibid.*, p. 252.

Kemalist officials encouraged Chester: *Ibid.*, p. 261.

Bristol considered family indiscreet: Diary, Sept. 15, 1922, Bristol Papers.

Bristol sympathetic to Chester's schemes: DeNovo dissertation, p. 249.

Bristol nudges businessmen, boycotts Guaranty Trust: Diary, Sept. 13, 1922, Bristol Papers.

CHAPTER XIV

Testimony of Mabel Kalfa: Trial.
Miss Mills: "I could plainly see": quoted by Horton, *Blight*, p. 145.
See also *New York Times* interview with Miss Minnie Mills, Sept. 27, 1922.
Testimony of fireman Emmanuel Katsaros: Trial.
James Webster, letter to his family: Published in *Omaha Evening World-Herald*, Oct. 10, 1922.
"It looked to me as though they wanted to burn them up": *Ibid.*
"I have human baggage": Elizabeth Harlow, "These Are My Sons."
"We were about twenty": Haroutune Casparian, one of Mrs. Birge's "sons", described his escape and Mrs. Birge's heroic role in an address delivered at a memorial service for Mrs. Birge at the Bristol Congregational Church, Bristol, Conn., November 27, 1927. A copy of the address was provided me through the courtesy of Dr. S. Ralph Harlow, Mrs. Birge's brother. Dr. Harlow was also on the faculty of the International College but had left Smyrna exactly a week before the fire. See interview with Dr. S. Ralph Harlow, *New York Times*, Sept. 7, 1922.
Travelers on Sea of Marmara: Ward Price in *Daily Mail*, Sept. 18, 1922, writing from Chanak, in Dardanelles.
Clayton dispatches in Oeconomos compilation: also *Chicago Daily News*, Sept. 14, 15, 1922. Constantine Brown dispatches in Oeconomos compilation and *Chicago Tribune* for those dates.
Horton's last view of Smyrna: *Blight*, pp. 152–153.

CHAPTER XV

Vice-Consul Barnes saw Turkish soldiers pouring kerosene: Barnes report, Sept. 18, 1922, NA.
"Half the people arrived without clothes": Testimony of Capt. Allan, Trial.
"They were . . . driving them toward the fire": Testimony of Mr. Vrbkazetanko, son of Czech consul, Trial.
"They invoke martial law": Colonel Giordano, quoted in Andreades pamphlet.
A British businessman on S.S. *Bavarian*: Roy Treloar. See *New York Times* interview, Sept. 21, 1922. Also in Oeconomos compilation.
"The lamentations of the women": Ed Fisher of YMCA, in A.P. interview, *New York Times*, Sept. 19, 1922. Further details about Fisher's experiences may be found in the YMCA Historical Reference Library.
Incident of boys with flag: Told in slightly different version in Barton, p. 153.
"My God! They're trying to burn the refugees!": Major Arthur Maxwell testimony, Trial. See also report of Vice-Consul Hole, NA.
Raft turned into torch: Also in Horton, *Blight*, p. 160.
Italian ships took up everyone: All survivors interviewed agreed on this

point, as they agreed on the fact that the American and British ships refused, and that the French were generous in providing passes to their ships.

Men were threatening to get out of hand: Report of Consul Horton to Secretary of State, Sept. 18, 1922, NA: "The crew of the destroyer was so overcome by this and other sights that it nearly got out of hand."

Brock had to give Noureddin assurances of neutrality: Kinross, p. 368.

The fact that Brock's officers argued with him for several hours is recorded in Hepburn, diary, Sept. 13, 1922, NR, and Merrill diary, Sept. 13, 1922, NA.

Frail woman in rowboat with son: Oran Raber article.

Later . . . a Japanese ship arrived: Consul Horton confirmed actions of the Japanese in his report to Secretary of State, Sept. 18, 1922, NA.

"By the time I get there all . . . will be dead": quoted by Horton in report to Secretary of State, Sept. 18, 1922, NA.

Turkish cavalry chased refugees on the beach all day: Webster, letter in *Omaha Evening World-Herald*, Oct. 10, 1922.

Almost no young women saved: Report of Vice-Consul Hole, NA: see also Horton, *Blight*, p. 163.

Jacob found bakeries destroyed: Jacob diary, Sept. 16, 1922, YMCA Historical Reference Library.

"The proceeding was brutal beyond belief": Barnes report to State Department, Sept. 18, 1922, NA.

CHAPTER XVI

Archbell could be counted on: This was clearly brought out at the trial during cross-examination by counsel for the defendants.

The Turks had been so proud: Hepburn diary, Sept. 15, 1922, NR.

"We have lost the war!" Merrill diary, Sept. 15, 1922, NA.

"A disagreeable incident": Kinross, p. 372.

Robbery of Jacob and Fisher described in Merrill diary, Sept. 15, 1922, NA.

All in attendance agreed: Hepburn diary, Sept. 15, 1922, NR.

"There will be no refugee problem": *Ibid.*

"I have been reluctant to violate our policy": Hepburn diary, Sept. 16, 1922, NR.

CHAPTER XVII

Navy bands and phonograph music: Lovejoy, p. 15; also in interviews with Stepan Nalbantian, Takouhie Dabanian Kalebdjian.

Admiral apologized for being late: Horton, *Blight*, p. 191.

Greeks were willing: Powell report entitled "Smyrna Disaster, Sept. 1922," sent to Bristol Oct. 9, 1922, NR.

"Kemal . . . would not take responsibility": Powell to Bristol, Sept. 19, 1922, FRUS 1922, vol. II, p. 427.

"Prey to both soldiers and civilian rabble": Jacob diary, Sept. 20, 1927, YMCA Historical Reference Library.

"There is almost no water": *Ibid.*

Archbell and Griswold organized partnership as shipping agents: Powell diary, Sept. 17, 1922, NA. Also Trial.

American manager fled on witnessing murder: Powell diary, Sept. 17, 1922; also Horton, *Blight*, p. 132.

Shipping out twelve hundred bales: Powell diary, Sept. 17, 1922, NA.

Barnes "considerably inconvenienced": Bristol diary, Sept. 25, 1922, Bristol Papers.

"Get these people out": *Ibid.*

The whole of Eastern Thrace would have to be cleared: *Ibid.*

Rich Uncle Sam not about to be trapped: "Allies and Greeks seemingly shirking all responsibility and assuming we will handle entire situation": Bristol to Secretary of State, Sept. 13, 1922, Bristol Papers.

Bristol and Dulles determined to discourage notion that Turks burned Smyrna: This fact emerges clearly in the zeal with which both Bristol and the Department hastened to deny on-the-scene reports to the contrary. The subsequent lawsuit (Trial) bears out the motive.

Bristol had not warned against risks: "He [F. W. Bell of the Gary Tobacco Company] stated that his company desired to increase their insurance on the tobacco in Smyrna. I told him that as far as the Turkish occupation was concerned, I did not think that the property of his company could be endangered." Bristol diary, Sept. 7, 1922, Bristol Papers.

Tobacco losses alone in the millions: Incomplete estimates of commercial losses to Americans listed in Powell diary, Sept. 20, 1922, NA: also Bristol diary, Sept. 21, 1922, Bristol Papers. Later figures in *New York Times*, Sunday, Dec. 21, 1924, placed losses at over $100,000,000.

"In accordance with the observations . . . these gentlemen made": Bristol diary, Sept. 17, 1922, Bristol Papers.

Thomas "very decidedly pro-Turk before": Bristol diary, Sept. 21, 1922, Bristol Papers.

"Such loose talk will . . . boomerang": Bristol diary, Sept. 25, 1922, Bristol Papers.

"A little hysterical": Bristol diary, Sept. 25, 1922, Bristol Papers.

"When one's emotions are all calmed": Bristol diary, Sept. 17, 1922, Bristol Papers.

Interview with Hamid Bey: Bristol diary, Sept. 21, 1922, Bristol Papers.

Greasing palms: Jacob diary, Sept. 16, 1922, YMCA Historical Reference Library.

CHAPTER XVIII

"My observation on the discipline": Hepburn report entitled "Policy," following his dated reports, NR.

"I have seen men, women, and children whipped": Asa Jennings, report to Dr. D. A. Davis of YMCA (undated), copy in NA 767.68/605.

Sailors saved girls from Turks: *Ibid.;* also Powell diary, Sept. 17, 1922, NA.

Rescue of girl and brother: William T. Ellis, "Jennings of Smyrna," in *Scribner's*, August 1928, pp. 230–235.

"Everyone was praying for ships": Jennings report, NA.

"Uncontrollable urge": *Ibid.*

Jennings arranges with *Constantinapoli:* R. W. Abernathy, "The Great Rescue," in *The Spirit of the Game.*
"They kissed my hands and my clothing": Jennings report, NA.
The story of Jennings's negotiations with the Greek authorities and of his entry into Smyrna harbor has been derived from the two published accounts (Abernathy and Ellis) and from Jennings's report in the Archives.

CHAPTER XIX

All references to Dr. Lovejoy's experiences and details about the evacuation not otherwise cited are from her book, *Certain Samaritans.*
Numbers rescued: Powell report, "Smyrna disaster," NR; Jacob diary, YMCA Historical Reference Library.
New Greek rulers sanctioned enterprise "without hesitation": Jennings report, NA.
"We have not, repeat not": Bristol to U.S. Naval Headquarters, Athens, Sept. 25, 1922, Bristol Papers.
Churchmen badgering State Department: FRUS 1922, vol. II, pp. 939 ff.
Hughes asks Bristol to impress on Kemal: *Ibid.*
"Keenly alive to every humanitarian interest": Hughes to Bishop Cannon, Oct. 2, 1922, FRUS 1922, vol. II, p. 940.
"Every Greek is wearing a fez": Henry Wales, *Chicago Tribune,* Oct. 12, 1922, Oeconomos compilation.
"Other considerations . . . cannot be ignored": Hughes, quoted in Evans, p. 390n.
Cabinet could not rely on help from dominions: Sacher, p. 438.
Rumbold conference with High Commissioners described in Bristol diary, Sept. 24, 1922, Bristol Papers.
He had thought Rumbold impertinent: Bristol diary, Sept. 6, 1922, Bristol Papers.
Clayton interview with Kemal reported to Bristol by Powell (who was present), forwarded by Bristol to State Department Oct. 5, 1922, NA 876.00/1555.
Bristol's orders: Bristol to Acting Secretary of State, Sept. 20, 1922, FRUS 1922, vol. II, p. 427.
Statement to offset "exaggerated . . . reports": Bristol to State Department, Sept. 22, 1922, NA 868.48/133.
Numbers lost at Smyrna before, during, and after fire: Horton, in testimony at Immigration Hearings (Horton Papers) referred to Smyrna's "normal" population as 450,000, but indicated that even before the influx of refugees, in September, it had grown to about 500,000 (not counting Greek troops) during the Greek occupation. At least half of this 500,000 consisted of Ottoman Christians. In addition, at least 150,000 Christian refugees poured into Smyrna during the first days of September, according to Davis (Sept. 9, 1922, Bristol Papers). Native Christians thus totaled at least 400,000 at the peak of the crisis. Of these, 30,000 were removed during the fire and 180,000 more were evacuated after Sept. 25, leaving 190,000 unaccounted for. The Greek estimate of the numbers deported into the interior exceeded

100,000 (Greek representative to Allen Dulles, Oct. 10, 1922, FRUS 1922, vol. II, p. 941). I have found no hard figures on the number of deportees, or of how many returned. Survivors estimate that very few were so fortunate. Vice-Consul Barnes reported to Bristol on Oct 18, 1922, that an estimated 45,000 men were being held as prisoners of war and that those sent into the interior were "dying off rapidly." NA 767.68114/40. Bristol (and Barnes, who estimated 1,200 killed before and during the fire in his report of Sept. 18, 1922, NA) evidently based this figure on the number of bodies actually counted on the streets.

Prentiss "high hat": Interview with James Webster.

"Brutality and robbery . . . were . . . the rule": This and subsequent statements by Powell are from his report "Smyrna disaster," NR.

"My confidence in history has been so shaken": Lovejoy letter to Horton, May 28, 1927, Horton Papers.

Strange Levantine craft: Described in Lovejoy, p. 159.

CHAPTER XX

Chicago Tribune consulted a phrenologist: Sept. 20, 1922.

Lloyd George hopeful: Kinross, p. 380.

"Escape without utter shame": Churchill, p. 464.

Kemal's troops friendly: Kinross, p. 381.

Harington interview with Turkish press: Merrill Intelligence Report to Bristol, Sept. 27, 1922, NA 867.00/1550.

"One of the blackest spots in . . . history": Clayton, *Chicago Tribune,* Sept. 25, 1922.

"No Greek can live in Anatolia": *Chicago Tribune,* Sept. 26, 1922.

Fethi Bey offered "to freely exchange": Merrill to Bristol, Sept. 27, 1922, NA.

"Boiling Frankie": Kinross, p. 384.

"Space was limited": *Ibid.*

Franklin-Bouillon "urging the former to resistance": S. W. Roskill, *Naval Policy Between the Wars,* p. 199.

Fall of Lloyd George: See A. J. P. Taylor, *Politics in Wartime,* p. 147. Unlike a great many historians, Taylor does not consider Lloyd George's dogged support of the Greeks and their subsequent defeat the primary cause of his political demise.

"We closed on eight thousand": Walder, p. 316.

Kemal's speech of Oct. 4: *Bulletin Périodique,* No. 25, 16 Sept.–25 Oct. 1922, p. 3.

The Thracian exodus: Unless otherwise specified, my source for details about the exodus and about the attitude of Western officials toward the refugees is the Oeconomos compilation (*The Martyrdom of Smyrna*), pp. 179–230. In this section are gathered vivid and detailed firsthand accounts by reporters on the scene during the exodus. Hemingway's dispatches to the *Toronto Daily Star,* published on Oct. 20 and Nov. 14, 1922, which include some of his finest writing, are collected in *The Wild Years* (ed. by Gene Z. Hanrahan). The Hemingway excerpts in my text have been taken from this volume (pp. 200–203).

Bristol wants "to restore stock": FRUS 1922, vol. II, p. 444. See also *New York Times,* Nov. 4, 1922.

Constantine Brown blames "exaggerated tales": *Chicago Daily News,* Oct. 21, 1922.

Greeks should "handle all relief": Bristol to Acting Secretary of State, Sept. 22, 1922, FRUS 1922, vol. II, p. 431.

Bristol urged relief "for Turks left behind": FRUS 1922, vol. II, p. 444.

"4,000 REFUGEES. NO WATER": Lovejoy, p. 220.

Stop shipments until Greeks can thin out: FRUS 1923, vol. II, p. 449.

U.S. reply to Greek request: *Ibid.*

American Red Cross would not work under League or Nansen: FRUS 1922, vol. II, p. 443. See also FRUS 1923, vol. II, p. 337.

Red Cross and NER aid in Greece: Barton, p. 431; FRUS 1922, vol. II, p. 430.

NER to work only with orphans: Barton, p. 154.

American Women's Hospitals: Esther Lovejoy and Mabel Elliott (see bibliography) provide two lively accounts of the work of this extraordinary group of women between 1918 and 1924.

International Red Cross unable to investigate: FRUS 1922, vol. II, p. 941.

National Geographic failed to mention AWH: Lovejoy, p. 223.

"We have never been rich enough": Lovejoy, p. 6.

England could not give assurances: FRUS 1923, vol. II, p. 377.

"My French colleague is indifferent": Atherton (chargé in Greece) to Secretary of State, May 17, 1923, FRUS 1923, vol. II, p. 338.

French offer to take refugees: FRUS 1923, vol. II, p. 336.

Italian government offering no assistance: FRUS 1923, vol. II, p. 336.

Red Cross notice of withdrawal: FRUS 1923, vol. II, p. 321.

State Department refuses to pass on names: FRUS 1923, vol. II, p. 376.

Morgenthau telegram and reply of "simple acknowledgment": FRUS 1923, vol. II, p. 378.

Refugee loan at 8.71 per cent: Stephen P. Ladas, *The Exchange of Minorities, Bulgaria, Greece and Turkey,* p. 635.

Hemingway on Chateau d'Ouchy: *Wild Years,* p. 212.

Attitudes at Lausanne re Exchange: Ladas, pp. 724–725.

Bristol has confirmed the fact that the Turks deliberately precipitated the "exchange," in his dispatch of Nov. 19, 1922 to Secretary of State Hughes (FRUS 1922, vol. II, p. 961): "Latest information makes me certain that Nationalist Government wishes to get rid of the entire Greek and Armenian population of Anatolia and Constantinople and would like to have this a *fait accompli* or at least well under way before the question of minorities arises at the [Lausanne] Conference."

For examples of Turkish blackmail see Ladas, pp. 347, 429, 498.

No harvest for winter: Lovejoy, p. 281.

Turks violated all terms: Ladas, pp. 415, 429, 486–512.

"Inability of Commission to take courageous stand": Ladas, p. 496.

Turkish defiance encouraged: Ladas, p. 497.

Exchange of population figures: Ladas, p. 724.
"In an orderly manner": Ladas, p. 705.
"Treat them with same consideration": Barton, p. 170.
Greek request for help in returning prisoners; Dulles ignored it: FRUS 1922, vol. II, pp. 940–941, 942.
Men yet to be released in Oct.: Ladas, p. 434.
Although about one in three reached Magnesia, this does not mean that all survived thereafter. Many apparently died from pneumonia, malnutrition, and assorted epidemics during the ensuing 15 months.
Bishop Simonian was kind enough to provide me with copies of his relevant correspondence, including the document here referred to.

CHAPTER XXI

"Oil usurped the center of the stage": Gibb and Knowlton, p. 295.
State Department busy enlisting writers: NA 767.68/114.
Child "typically American": Nicolson, p. 269n.
Child embarrasses diplomats: Ibid., p. 269.
"It was better to give the Americans a share": Gibb and Knowlton, quoting Gulbenkian, p. 291.
Sadler to Teagle, "Keep the list . . . small": Ibid., p. 292.
Venture a violation of antitrust laws: Ibid., p. 293.
Chester: New York Times articles April 11, 12, 1923 give a clue to the consternation in France over Chester's success.
Chester's prospects went downhill: For downturn and nefarious intrigues see DeNovo dissertation and articles in New York Times, April–Nov. 1923.
Gulbenkian says "eyewash": Gibb and Knowlton, p. 297.
References to oil claims deleted from final draft: DeNovo dissertation, p. 302.
"We believe in America for the Americans": This and the quotations which follow are taken from The Treaty with Turkey, listed in bibliography under authorship of General Committee.
"The torch was applied": Horton, Blight, pp. 148, 154.
State Department reaction and correspondence concerning Bierstadt book, including the quotations in my text, are to be found in NA 767.68/600¼–623½.
Sources for Jennings's career after 1922 are pertinent papers in YMCA Historical Reference Library, and Daniel, p. 185.
Jennings's story progressively anti-Greek and pro-Turkish: Abernathy and Ellis articles.
Information concerning the trial is taken entirely from the transcript found in the Bristol Papers.
Mr. Justice Rowlatt's decision published in London Times, Dec. 20, 1924, in New York Times, Dec. 21, 1924.
Verdict to decide $100,000,000 in insurance claims: New York Times, Dec. 21, 1924.
"Mosul oil interests" opposed Horton's Blight: Correspondence with Venizelos (reply by the latter's secretary) in Horton Papers.

Bristol's contradictory evaluation: Letter to Secretary of the Navy, March 18, 1924, NR.

Most missionaries silent on the matter: Horton, pp. 146, 227.

MacLachlan's diagnosis of fire: ABCFM Papers, Houghton Library.

Closing of mission schools: My chief source for this paragraph is Robert Daniel.

For the attitude of Turkish spokesmen on their former minorities, I rely on my conversations in Turkey during the summer of 1956, on my correspondence and conversations with American and European specialists in Near Eastern history, on editorials in Turkish newspapers as translated in the Armenian press, and on the statements of public figures—see, for example, pp. 61–71 of the Provisional Minutes of the United Nations General Assembly for January 25, 1965.

Straining NATO alliance: Myron Goldsmith, Honorary Consul General of Turkey at San Francisco, letter to *San Francisco Chronicle* reprinted in *Armenian Mirror-Spectator,* May 15, 1965, writes that commemorations constitute "a barrage of intolerance directed against the modern Turkish Republic and its people that can only . . . create a breach in the NATO defense wall for the benefit of Soviet Russia." Jehad Baban, a Turkish M.P., says in the Ankara newspaper *Oulous:* "The only result of this kind of behavior will be to strain relations between Turkey and Lebanon which allows the organization of this kind of commemoration on its own territory." (As reprinted in Armenian newspaper *Zartonk,* Beirut, May 7, 1965.)

Yeni Gazette editorial: reprinted in Armenian newspaper *Baikar,* February 12, 1967.

Historical revision: Columbia University historian Edward Mead Earle set the stage for this in his introduction to Halide Edib's *Turkey Faces West.*

Halide Edib on the Smyrna massacre and fire: *Ordeal,* p. 386.

"Armenians continually petted . . . armed": *Turkey Faces West,* p. 144.

Edib came to consider deportations justified: *Memoirs,* p. 388.

Talaat an "idealist": *Ibid.,* p. 387.

"Her Talk Wins 200 Experts": Headline in *New York Times,* Aug. 4, 1928.

Toynbee's reversal: Despite his protest (July 1923, *Current History*) that he still believed in "the truth of the evidence presented in the Blue Book," Toynbee went on to say that "equally dark deeds have been inflicted by Greek soldiers . . . during the War for Greek independence." This was the same man who had written, in 1917: "The Turks will say, after the war, 'We were at war. We were fighting for our existence. The Armenians were traitors at large in a war zone.' But such excuses are entirely contradicted by facts. These Armenians were not inhabitants of a war zone. None of the towns and villages from which they were systematically deported to their death were anywhere near the seat of the hostilities." *Armenian Atrocities, The Murder of a Nation,* London, 1917, p. 69.

Toynbee admits to "leaning over backwards": Arnold and Philip Toynbee, p. 59.

Toynbee thought Armenians provoked the fire: See "The East After Lausanne," in *Foreign Affairs,* Sept. 15, 1923, p. 96.

Encyclopaedia Britannica: 1970 edition, "Izmir."

Most American and British specialists: one recent exception is Howard M. Sachar, *The Emergence of the Middle East 1914–1924.*

Interestingly enough, a select number of historians concerned with American or German foreign policy vis à vis Turkey during the period in question—among them James Gidney and Ulrich Trumpener —have shed more light on this crucial phase of Turkish history than have such experts as Kemal H. Karpat, Bernard Lewis, Geoffrey Lewis, Sir Harry Luke, and Richard Robinson. The nature of the Smyrna fire, however, has until now remained unexplored.

"Who, after all, speaks today": Adolf Hitler, quoted by Louis Lochner in *What About Germany,* pp. 2–4.

Five and a half billion dollars in U.S. aid since 1945: Figure released, Jan. 29, 1971, by Senator Walter F. Mondale.

Eighty per cent of heroin in U.S. from Turkish poppy fields: *New York Times,* Aug. 2, 1970, citing official studies.

Kudos to Bristol: *New York Times,* June 21, Aug. 28, 1927.

"A terrible mess . . . analogous . . . though very different": Bristol to S. Sheldon Crosby, Jan. 11, 1928. Bristol Papers.

"Chinese people lacking in individual character and patriotic feeling": *Ibid.*

"America has her work cut out for her in the Far East": Bristol to A. K. Jennings, Jan. 11, 1928. Bristol Papers.

INDEX

265

175, 181, 187; postwar, 55–58; World War I, 31–32. *See also* Bristol, Adm. Mark L.; Dulles, Allen; Hughes, Charles Evans; Wilson, Woodrow

Venizelos, Eleutherios, 37–39, 46–48, 54, 75–79, 199

Wangenheim, Baron Hans von, 29, 30, 239
Webster, James, 144, 145, 149
Wilson, Woodrow: Fourteen Points, 36–37, 53; at Paris Peace Conference, 33–35, 39, 40, 45–47; World War I, 31–32, 217
World War I: Secret treaties, 35–37, 39; Turkey's allegiances, 22–24. *See also* European influence, intrigue; France, policy or position; Great Britain, policy or position; Greece; Italy, policy or position; United States, policy or position

YMCA, YWCA, 91, 97–98, 103, 107, 217, 219, 223. *See also* Jacob, E. O.; Jennings, Asa
Young Turks, 19, 24–32